European Economic Integration

The Role of Technology

European Economic Integration

The Role of Technology

Edited by

Gerald R. Faulhaber
University of Pennsylvania

Gaultiero Tamburini
University of Bologna

Kluwer Academic Publishers
Boston/London/Dordrecht

Distributors for North America:
Kluwer Academic Publishers
101 Philip Drive
Assinippi Park
Norwell, Massachusetts 02061 USA

Distributors for all other countries:
Kluwer Academic Publishers Group
Distribution Centre
Post Office Box 322
3300 AH Dordrecht, THE NETHERLANDS

Library of Congress Cataloging-in-Publication Data

European economic integration : the role of technology / edited by
    Gerald R. Faulhaber, Gualtiero Tamburini.
        p.   cm.
    Includes bibliographical references and index.
    ISBN 0-7923-9080-6
        1. Technological innovations—Economic aspects—European Economic
    Community countries.   2. Technology—Economic aspects—European
    Economic Community countries.   3. Europe 1992.   I. Faulhaber,
    Gerald R.   II. Tamburini, Gualtiero.
    HC240.9.T4E93   1990
    337.1 '42—dc20   90-42063
                                                                         CIP

Copyright © 1991 by Kluwer Academic Publishers   Second Printing, 1993

Printed on acid-free paper.

Printed in the United States of America.

Contents

v

CONTRIBUTING AUTHORS

Jürgen Müller, DIW, Germany
Alexis Jacquemin, University of Louvain, Belgium
John H. Dunning, University of Reading, England
Henry W. de Jong, University of Amsterdam, The Netherlands
Jacques De Bandt, C.N.R.S., France
Brian Bayliss, University of Bath, England
Charles Baden-Fuller, The London School of Economics and Political
  Science, England
Brian Hindley, The London School of Economics and Political Science,
  England
David J. Teece, University of California, Berkeley, U.S.A.
Almarin Phillips, The Wharton School, University of Pennsylvania,
  U.S.A.
Edmund S. Phelps, Columbia University, U.S.A.
F. Gerard Adams, University of Pennsylvania, U.S.A.

Chapter 1

Introduction

Gerald R. Faulhaber and Gualtiero Tamburini

University of Pennsylvania and
Universita Delgi Studi di Bologna

This book brings together chapters by a group of European and North American economists, all of which focus on a single aspect of the ongoing plan for European economic integration -- the role of technology.

Indeed, the plan for European integration has many aspects -- social, institutional, and political. From a broad standpoint, the program approved by the 12 member states of the European Economic Community (Single European Act) in 1986 addresses these problems. Among other things, the Act provides for the progressive establishment of a single internal market by 1992. At its most basic, this single European market means the unrestricted circulation of goods, people, services, and capital, unhindered by borders, tariffs, or restrictive national practices.

The actual economic integration as planned by the Single Act will have a variety of consequences. On the whole, there will be the consolidation of the benefits already gained over the previous 30 years due to the progressive lowering of tariff barriers within the Common Market. In particular, there has a been a shift away from limited national markets toward the wider market of the Community. In turn, this expansion of the market promises improved economies of scale and scope for many industries and a more efficient geographic allocation of production. Furthermore, the sharper competition among European firms should stimulate the introduction and acceleration of technical innovation, resulting in more competitive European exports as compared with Japanese and North American exports.

According to the European Economic Community Commission's forecasts, by 1992 there should already be an increase in the Community's GDP of about 5 percent. This increase is comprised of various different advantages: (1) reduction of delays in the exchange of goods and in transportation due to the elimination of border formalities; (2) reduction in costs and prices due to increased competition, followed by an increase in the Community's output; (3) reduced inefficiencies in public stock offering, as well as in essential services like transportation, energy, and telecommunications. Public stock offerings will be deprived of protectionism and national restrictions, and opened up to competition from all of Europe.

Significant positive effects should follow from the liberalization of the financial services. This should also yield a reduction in costs, both in interest and transactions, for financing government operations for all member states.

Many analysts see as a principal positive factor of European integration improvements in the economic performance of firm, entrepreneurs, and the labor force, via expanded opportunities for economies of scale and scope as well as more thorough exploitation of the experience curve. These effects should lead to greater productivity and lower unit costs.

In summary, increases in the European Community's (EC's) economic welfare due to integration are anticipated to flow from greater productivity, improved infrastructure, and increased competitiveness of European exports in world markets.

But, as with all change, the anticipated economic benefits are accompanied by anticipated problems and costs. It is the technological dimension of this tradeoff that the chapters of this book address.

Tamburini's chapter describes the stages of the integration process. He analyzes the economic principles underpinning the decision to eliminate the nontariff barriers that still hinder intra-European trade. The roots of these principles run deep: Adam Smith first postulated that the greater the scope of the market, the greater the opportunities for efficiencies from the division of labor. The global economy of the 1990s adds greater competitiveness and a faster rate of innovation to Smith's basic insight.

Profits and losses that derive from the European integration process are examined, with particular reference to information goods and product markets in the chapter by Edmund Phelps. After having highlighted several of the negative effects that may occur as a result of the 1992 program (such as the social costs that derive from a new spatial distribution of work, costs linked to mobility because of the new competition), Phelps concentrates on the effects that 1992 will have on the industries producing information goods.

As the latter are characterized by incremental costs (for the additional information distributed to consumers) which are virtually nil, with the opening of the European market information industries will be exposed to greater competition (lower markups) compared to the companies producing traditional goods. So the countries with the greater share of information goods will gain more benefits (in terms of price reductions) than the ones that can be obtained by less advanced countries. However, the conclusion regarding the effects of 1992 is, on the whole, positive and in harmony with the studies on Europe 1992 carried out by the Cecchini Report.

According to Phelps, the heightened competition should actually lead to lower prices, higher output, and a higher real wage. As a result, the European market expands because Europeans will be bigger earners and thus bigger spenders. In this regard, European economic welfare unambiguously improves. Overseas, welfare may also improve, due to increased savings by Europeans and lower real interest rates. However, the impact of European integration on the rest of the world is less clear than the impact on Europe itself.

The impact of integration on technological innovation would appear, according to Phelps, to favor the more technologically advanced European communities such as France and Italy at the (possible) expense of those less advanced, such as Greece and Spain. He notes, however, that these countries stand to gain from the ability of firms to locate plants within their borders post-integration, thus providing employment for their citizens. On balance, then, integration will not only lead to greater efficiency will also narrow the income gap within the EC.

A changing world economy has strong implications for the outcome of the Europe 1992 program, but the creation of a bigger internal market than the one in the United States of America may in turn have strong repercussions outside of the European Community. The problem of the economic growth of the European countries and the United States in the international arena is, according to Adams, basically linked to the development of many industries that have lost ground in the competition with Japan and the NICs (Newly Industrialized Countries).

On the basis of ample evidence, Adams analyzes the possible alternatives and scenarios of the changing world economy, in which Europe is seen as a player trying to offset the negative effects of economic "maturity" with the integration program to be accomplished by 1992.

For Adams the achieving the objectives of European integration can have positive as well as negative effects on the international scene. One positive effect is that the greater internal efficiency within Europe, mainly due to greater economies of scale, will mean greater worldwide efficiency, thanks to the widening of international trading that an open Europe would involve.

There is also likely to be a negative effect as well, made possible by the same variables as discussed previously. Indeed, a great single market, with large companies producing on a higher scale, may tempt European countries toward protectionist choices that leave out the small countries for whom the costs of market protection are too high.

So protectionism is the imminent danger in the event of a successful integration policy; yet achieving success means that such a policy cannot just rely on the elimination of nontariff barriers. Europe must design its integration policy to permit the benefits to be shared by the entire world economy.

According to de Bandt, the increasing European lag in the leading technologies and the information-intensive services has generated the so-called Europessimism. It has also generated the ambitious program of reducing barriers between various countries.

The elimination of those obstacles must, however, represent a beginning of a more far-reaching process oriented toward removing cultural obstacles that have caused the European delay in information services for production.

The fundamental phenomena that will influence the structural change in the European economy should be sought in the demographic trends (aging of the population), in technological developments (including the growth in services), and last, in trends in international relations (rivalry and competition among businesses).

An industrialist approach has been favored in developing the economic and industrial policies of the European countries. Among its effects is the maintenance of educational systems that are not suited to the needs of the information society. Hence, companies have focused on the rationalization of the production technique rather than on the rationalization of human resources. Investment in human capital, taking account the structural phenomena mentioned above, is the only path for Europe to achieve the "new technical system" that will be the key to future economic growth.

The loss of ground which occurred in the economies of the European countries during the 1970s and in the first half of the 1980s, is the main point of the chapter by de Jong, and it is also the strong point of the program for the completion of the internal European market. De Jong puts the responsibility for the slowing down of the European economy with respect to the Japanese and American economies on the reduced competition (and on the relative increase in controls and regulations).

It follows that the European recovery will only find a partial response in the liberalization of the markets, which can only be completed with a parallel program of deregulation and privatization of large sections of European public enterprise. Professor de Jong makes this point on the basis of detailed comparisons of the structure, conduct and performance of European industries and their American and Japanese counterparts.

The fundamental cause behind the relaunching of the process of economic integration is seen by Professor de Jong as the decline in the European countries' competitive edge beginning in the 1970s. Although the European economy is behind in respect to the United States and Japan, it nonetheless tends to develop into an economy based on a strong tertiary and quaternary sector, whose growth depends on policies tailored to encouraging the growth of information technology.

De Jong distinguishes four types of industry that characterize the European arena: first, industries that produce standardized mass-production goods, characterized by stagnant demand; second, industries whose products can be differentiated but that are nevertheless characterized by large-scale production.

A third type is comprised of systems products industries; they are industries with strong entrance barriers caused by the very nature of the product, which is indeed a system rather than an individual product (as in the case of IBM where there is a combination of hardware, software, services, and equipment in an operating system).

However, these industries tend to develop monopolistic attitudes, given the fact that they are equipped with such entry barriers. They become "natural monopolies," not from any economic rationale but simply because they have been monopolistic for a long time. Often these are public companies that run their monopolies in the "national interest." This is the fourth type of industry which, unlike the previous one, tends to waste resources rather than create new ones; it is this kind of industry that involves the greatest problems for the integration policies being enacted in Europe. In de Jong's view, the success of European integration hinges upon the Community's ability to break down these monopoly-protecting regulations within each country.

If de Jong stresses the importance of the abolition of the regulations that create monopolistic conditions, the contributions by Dunning and Cantwell, Baden Fuller, Dell'Osso and Stopford,

Teece, and Jacquemin see in the rules of business competition the focal point behind the processes of growth and integration.

According to Dunning and Cantwell, the multinational enterprises offer fresh problems for the industrial and technological policies of the European governments. Indeed, they conceive of technology as a resource uniquely produced by the government policies of each country.

These policies may be highly polarized: for example, "sunrise" industries may be encouraged to make new investments while the "sunset" ones may be driven to seek new locations in the less developed countries. An industrial policy that gives special advantages to firms that locate their high-tech activities within a country may enhance that country's economy, according to Dunning and Cantwell. Governments who ignore these aspects may well end up penalizing their own economy. For the European Community as such, this means that the growing linkages between technological developments are likely to entail an increasing interdependence between innovation in different countries.

With reference to two sectors, the motor industry and pharmaceuticals, the authors examine the impact of economic integration from a UK perspective. They conclude that the polarization of innovation activities will be intensified with multinational enterprises playing a more, rather than less, important role in affecting their location. They conclude that a "structuralist" approach, rather than a laissez-faire, comparative advantage approach, is best suited to the world economy of the 1990s.

Baden Fuller, Dell'Osso, and Stopford put forward the hypothesis that some industries evolve in similar patterns over time. Their analysis focuses on the European washing machine industry, but from this point they generalize four typical stages ("boxes") in the evolution of an industry: dominant firm, uncertain imitation, monopolistic competition, and a network of small units. For the mature European industries the problem then is to understand the nature of the changes in competitive patterns, changes that will be made all the more rapid owing to the 1992 initiatives. The lack of understanding or ignorance of the phase (box) and of the competitive patterns may lead to the failure of the industry and thus represent a further problem for the European industrial policy that aims to steer the mature industries along paths that allow resistance to be put up against foreign competition.

Teece examines the problem of the corporations in the present-day economy by looking at the importance played by a network of small units. Indeed, along with the ongoing changes in the composition of international trade, there has been an interesting debate on the role of corporations (American, European, and Japanese), and their relative effectiveness within their cultural milieux.

In Teece's opinion, the striking aspect of the new industrial firm is that corporations find themselves in a network of relations with smaller companies, functioning less as pure competitors and more as (partial) cooperators, especially in markets dominated by high technology and information-intensive services.

This opens the field to the reconceptualization of cooperation and competition, in particular for matters ranging from research and development (R&D) to standardization, as Jacquemin underlines with reference to the European corporation in his chapter.

The European Commission White Paper on "Completing the Internal Market" underscored the role played by cooperation among firms, which is viewed as an important means of improving European competitiveness, especially in high technology.

Starting from that point, Jacquemin analyses the main factors that either facilitate or hinder cooperation in general, and that constitute the basic ingredients of a private firm's cost-benefit analysis: the probability of collusion, tacit or explicit, is greater than what is suggested by conventional wisdom.

Then he discusses the public view of cooperation in the light of the goods and tools of European competition policy and stresses the pragmatic application of Article 85 of the Treaty of Rome.

In particular, Jacquemin analyzes the effects of the cooperative agreements on technology (R&D), showing that from a private point of view benefits from cooperation, although real, are more difficult to identify and capture. He explores the arguments in favor of the socially beneficial effects of cooperative research and shows that cooperation can improve the incentive problem as well as provide a more efficient sharing of information than noncooperative behavior. This gives some support to the permissive European regulation allowing cooperative research, whereby member firms share costs and the results of a research project.

The technological prospects of European integration may have an effect not just in terms of cooperation and competition, but also in new opportunities focused in certain sectors. Among others, the financial services sector and the telecommunications sector seem to present special problems and opportunities, not only in their own right but in their impact upon the rest of the economy.

In fact, the integration of financial services in the European Community is among the objectives contemplated in the White Book of the European Community Commission -- one of the most important and also the most difficult to achieve. The topics range from the creation of a European Central Bank through the harmonizing of prudent and protective regulations to the various schemes for assuring the stability of credit.

Looking at the regulation of banks and other financial deposit intermediaries, Phillips provides insight into the likely effects and outcomes of lessened national regulation for Europe as a whole, in light of the recent experience in the United States in freeing financial services from price, product, and geographic constraints.

The main indication seems to be that in Europe a full harmonization of the banking system is not necessary in order to get the highest benefits from the union. Phillips cautions of the need for a careful "phasing in" of financial reforms. The reasons for this caution range from the political tolerance for radical restructuring of important national institutions to possible excessive rivalry among European firms which may bring about a distortion in the use of resources and in the selection of the most efficient companies and institutions. The tension to be resolved is between institutions that will seek to preserve inefficient national niches in a global financial market, and the need to create sufficiently common institutional rules to reap the benefits of integration among the European financial markets.

Again on the problem of integration in the field of financial services, with an approach that starts from the evaluation of the potential gain in consumer surplus, estimated by the Cecchini Report, Hindley discusses several issues that the Report did not fully consider.

The first aspect regards the pervasive nature of the financial services with the consequent effects on the productivity of each sector in the economic system. It is thus a question of assessing not only the direct benefits for the consumers of financial services but also the more general ones in the whole of the economic system, which the financial services generate indirectly.

The second aspect regards the position of the European Court of Justice which, with the famous Cassis case, had laid down that a product of "one Member State must, in principle, be admitted to the market of any other Member State."

With this famous sentence in 1985 the basic principle which is the foundation of the 1992 program was introduced. Together with this principle, however, a long tradition of decisions by the Court that limited competition "in view of the general interest" goes in the opposite direction, also as a result of the ambiguity of the phrase. On the basis of numerous detailed cases, Hindley reaches the conclusion that the grounds for the Court's caution are weak and that in the future "it will provide more cutting edges in this area."

The importance of telecommunications in the development of financial services and in retail sales, through the expansion of the market that they guarantee, is also analyzed by Faulhaber. As an infrastructure service, telecommunications is an enabling technology that yields benefits through its ability to expand the capabilities of other industries. Two such industries are financial services and retail trade. In the first, the expansion of financial services to a global reach has been permitted by the accurate and instantaneous interconnection and information flows of modern telecommunications. The maintenance of different technical and tariff standards by national PTTs threatens to block further integration of this vital industry.

In retail trade, recent advances in marketing and distribution to the U.S. mass market have been made possible through the provision of "800 Service," a uniform, nationwide "called party pays" telephone service. It has changed retailing from a purely localized service to an increasingly national one. In order for an integrated Europe to take advantage of this new distribution channel, its telecommunications system must appear to be without boundaries as well.

It is from the historically determined conception of telecommunications as a natural monopoly, as was observed by de

Jong, that European PTTs took their present shape. The essay by Müller addresses telecommunications problems of both equipment and services. The current fragmentation in Europe is analyzed along with the various models that characterize the sector.

The main objective of Community policy, as set out in the European Community Green Paper, is to ensure that the Community industry derives the utmost benefit in terms of cost, quality and variety from the full development of the sector, so Muller attempts to quantify the cost of a "non-Europe" in the telecommunications services.

Finally, the essay by Bayliss points out how success in the development of European transportation and communications systems mainly depends on the policies adopted rather than on investment decisions dictated by yields. The infrastructure program adopted by the European Commission has singled out some priorities aimed at the completion of an integrated market in transportation and communications by 1992. Among these, the technological high points are represented by high-speed trains, combined transport telecommunications and by the Channel tunnel (Channel fixed link).

However, the history of the national transport systems in Europe has been very different from one country to another, and today we still have strong differentiations. Although it has been decided to head toward a common market in transportation, several problems still remain in the development of a single market. In Bayliss' view, it follows that the entry into international operations subject to restrictive national legislation will mean that such operations will not be conducted optimally.

In summary, the technological perspective pervades virtually all sectors of the European economy and virtually all decisions of the EC and its member states regarding Europe 1992. It is to these problems and issues that this book is directed.

Chapter 2

European Economic Integration: Technological Prospects

Gualtiero Tamburini

Universita Delgi Studi di Bologna

The European Economic Community (EEC) was founded by the six European countries -- Belgium, Germany, France, Italy, and the Netherlands -- that signed the treaty in Rome in 1957.

The following decade witnessed some important achievements for the EEC as it fulfilled its objectives ahead of time, as regards the first transitory phase. In particular, besides wholly developing the institutional framework, a total customs union was established, a common agricultural policy was launched, and fiscal measures were carried through. The latter allowed the EEC to have its own resources available. So in 1969 the heads of government of the member counties agreed on a gradual program for the enforcement of an economic and monetary union. The Werner Report in 1970 laid down the phases of that schedule which was then adopted in 1971.

However, in the 1970s the drive toward integration was not as fast as it had been in the 1960s. Indeed, although three new members joined in 1973, i.e., Denmark, Ireland, and the United Kingdom, the intra-EEC exchanges, with regard to the total foreign trading of the member states, unlike in the previous period, progressively diminished.

The European Economic Community bases its very existence on the hypothesis that the economic and social development of the member countries benefits from the increase in trade.

In the founding treaties of the EEC, signed in Rome on March 25, 1957, the complete freedom of trade is the backbone principle. However, both among the member countries and with regard to the rest of the world, that principle was subjected to many deferments.

Among the member countries there still are rigid nontariff barriers, while protectionist policies are often enforced with the rest of the world. The most striking of these is the agricultural policy that keeps the prices of European agricultural products artificially high, thus restricting imports from outside in a number of ways. The relaunching of the European integration process, made official on July 1, 1987, with the ratification of the Single European Act, fits into the overall trend toward the revitalizing of international trade sanctioned by the works of the Uruguay Round in the General Agreement on Trade and Tariffs (GATT)[1].

If the hastening of international trade has represented the hallmark of growth ever since the 1970s, it might be argued that even in the 1990s the growth in exchanges could play the same role. Of course, for the 12 EEC members this means heading toward a true and proper unification of the internal market, by means of the unrestricted circulation not only of goods and services but also of people, companies, and capital. This should occur thanks to the abolition of physical, fiscal, and technical barriers that do still exist.

As has been stated, the process of integration for the European economies had been especially fast until the end of the 1960s. However, in the last 15 years, rather than a deepening of the economic union between the member countries, there has been a widening, by way of the enlargement of the EEC. Indeed, in 1972, Great Britain, Denmark, and Ireland decided to join[2], and they became members on January 1, 1973, just as Greece joined on January 1, 1981, and lastly Spain and Portugal on January 1, 1986.

Even if the 1970s and 1980s were marked by significant Community economic policy decisions, especially in the monetary and institutional fields, it was nevertheless a period in which the slowing down of the process of economic integration among the various economies was rather marked[3]. In fact, while intra-Community trading in the period 1958-1973 compared to world trade increased by 53.1%, since 1973 till the present day it has remained somewhat unchanged.

In attempting to revitalize both the economies of the individual member states and European economic integration, the single European Act was passed on July 1, 1987. This treaty required the economies of the 12 member countries to become a large single market by December 31, 1992. This involves transforming what has so far been a common market into an internal market[4] by accomplishing a European union.

In order to bring about this objective, a program has been laid down in a White Book published in 1985 and coordinated by Lord Cockfield as vice-president of the Commission.[5] Since the founding treaties of the EEC had to be modified in order to achieve a unified market, the necessary changes were introduced by the Single European Act, as mentioned before[6]. Besides the White Book, the Commission undertook three studies known after the names of their authors: the Padoa-Schioppa Report, the Cecchini Report, and the Emerson Report.

The Padoa-Schioppa Report was supposed to define the strategic guidelines for the EEC economy in view of the attainment of higher levels of "efficiency, stability and equity." The Cecchini Report was supposed to provide an assessment of the advantages still to be gained from integration -- in other words, the "costs of a non-Europe." The Emerson Report, last of all, was to provide a deepening of the Cecchini Report aiming at evaluating the potential economic impact of the completion of the internal market of "1992: the new European economy[7]."

So the Single European Act, upon which "1992" is based, plans for the free movement of people, goods, services, and capital. These objectives will be achieved by the adoption of about 300 measures[8], half of which have already been put into effect since the start of 1990.

This means abolishing the physical, technical, and fiscal barriers that still heavily limit free trade and in general, the freedom of movement of capital, goods, services, and people. Indeed, even controls on people need to be removed when they cross the borders of the Community states. In such a case cooperation among countries will have to be engendered and individual national laws in many fields will have to be harmonized. Controls on people arriving from third-party countries will also have to be harmonized, while it will be necessary to give legal validity to academic and professional qualifications issued by other member countries so that people may work with equal opportunities and recognition anywhere in the Community. Thus the Europe 1992 program hinges not only on direct economic issues but also on important social problems.

In order to deal with these problems, measures that accompany ongoing European integration have been ratified. They involve such fields as the freedom of movement, economic and social cohesion (professional training and education), and employment. They are measures inspired by the rationale of offsetting the effects that increased competition and the consequent recomposition and restructuring of the economies will have on a societal level.

The Scenario of the Processes of Integration in Europe

The countries belonging to the EEC have thus accepted the "challenge of 1992" because, on the one hand, they have realized that their competitiveness on a world level was diminishing, and, on the other, that European union could not have materialized without an acceleration in the process of integration among the various national economies.

The 1980s represented a period of marked changes in the makeup of international trade. There was a strong dynamic drive in the innovative processes within a scenario of growing globalization. The speed of technological progress and innovation has characterized the pace of development and determined the placing of the countries; apart from the remarkable Japanese growth, other formidable competitors have turned out to be "new" countries like Korea, Taiwan, Singapore, and Hong Kong who presented growth rates even higher than those of Japan. In all of these new countries the growth rate over the last two decades was over 10% per annum, as opposed to 2.4% for the already industrialized countries. In the meantime, even more countries, such as Thailand, Malaysia, and Indonesia, have started to make their voices heard.

The longer-term proposals cannot exclude the rest of Asia and thus an economic power that is even stronger than that of the above-mentioned countries. While these new arrivals were being evaluated, the capacity to respond to the old leaders of the world economy was no longer the same. It was differentiated within Europe, from country to country, but an even more worrisome thing was that it was weak and unfavorable, not only in relation to the South-Eastern Asiatic countries but also with regard to the United States.

Throughout the 1950s and 1980s the European growth rate surpassed the American rate, and again in the four-year period 1968-1972, while the annual growth rate in Europe was 4.8 percent, in the United States it stayed about 4 percent. However, at that point in time there was a U-turn in the trend, and it later proved to be increasingly significant. In the period 1974-1981, compared with a European growth rate of 1.9 percent, the U.S. growth rate was +2.1 percent, and in the 1982-1986 period the comparative rates were +2 percent in Europe and +3 percent in the United States. Even more recent years confirm a greater growth of the United States' economy as compared with the European economy as a whole.

There is hardly a need to mention Japan, whose growth in the 1980s was on average about three times higher than European growth. In the period from 1972 (that preceded the first oil crisis) until the present day, the average increase in Japanese Gross Domestic Product was about 90 percent, while the United States' growth was about 50 percent and European growth about 40 percent.

People thus spoke of "Eurosclerosis" caused by the presence of excessive rigidity in Europe with a negative trend in relative prices as a result.

While these events were taking place within each nation state, there was the growth of the so-called "fly-the-flag companies." Companies tried to respond to the challenge of world competition by the processes of concentration and enhancement. In the second half of the eighties, however, what could have been done within the borders of each country seemed to have already been accomplished in Europe. In order to be leading players on the scene of the ongoing European oligopoly, the large concerns triggered off tremendous mergers that have mainly taken place among companies in the same sector. So with the coming of 1992, Gary Hamel of the London Business School has pointed out that by that time, "all the nice girls will already have chosen their partners, after having looked for them all over the world[9]."

For the large European enterprises, 1992 is turning into a deadline before which time they will have to be ready to compete on the world market by adopting global strategies in research, finance, and production.

However, while new equilibriums are being established in Europe in response to the international oligopolies, and measures for internal integration are being carried forward, we also realize that all of those moves cannot cannot suffice in accomplishing long-term goals. The international changes in the composition of trade are not adequate parameters for a comprehensive view. Indeed, there are at least two geopolitical areas toward which the EEC is especially committed, largely because of geographical proximity.

The first one is represented by the Eastern European countries, from the Soviet Union to countries such as East Germany, for which there has even been talk of a possible "unification" with the 12-country Europe through West Germany or countries like Poland, Czechoslovakia, Hungary, Rumania, Bulgaria, and Yugoslavia. These countries represent the direction in which the EEC's international trade may head as a result of the cultural, historical, and geopolitical affinities linking the two areas.

The other area is that of the "southern banks of the Mediterranean," overlooked by a vast population, still cut off from the roads to development but undergoing a demographic boom (from now until the year 2005, about 2 million extra jobs a year will be needed in those countries), and so the politico-economic prospects are very uncertain indeed.

For the populations of both areas the EEC represents an important point of reference. The EEC's policies will have to give a balanced but decisive answer to their needs.

The need to pursue European integration springs from the awareness that without a supranational coordination in Europe it is no longer possible to draw up an effective industrial policy. Many scholars have, however, observed that in the various European countries in the 1980s, no significant industrial policy was worked out. That not only seems to depend on the failure or the scare efficiency of French-style planning and on the choice to deregulate, like in the recent economic policy decisions of the United States and the United Kingdom, but on the fact that the same EEC measures, oriented at pursuing the 1992 objective, have made the classical measure of supports and subsidies to crisis sectors and firms impracticable.

The EEC's economic policies have definitely moved toward great world projects, on the one hand, and toward the elimination of nontariff barriers, on the other.

The spirit of the Single European Act is thus to make an invisible hand act on the inside, while the large projects (Espirit, Race, Mediterranean) at the same time crested the right conditions for a response to the competition that comes from the outside. This way Europe's presence is felt in the leading sectors of the world economy, thanks to the technological and innovation progress being made.

This is why the Europe 1992 program has been viewed with some trepidation in the United States and in Japan, where the sense of an aggressive program aiming at reorganizing the balance of world trade has been primarily felt. On the other hand, the fact that the program is a collection of measures to restructure and rationalize on the inside has taken a secondary role.

The research on which the Single European Act is based sheds light on the advantages that derive from a single market consisting of 320 million inhabitants. The reason quantifies the costs of the current fragmentation which is seen as the cause for the delays that the EEC has built up as compared with Japan and the United States.

From the macroeconomic perspective, the effect consists mainly in a drive toward trade creation among the member states.

When the exchanges increase this means that the efficiency of the producers has increased. That is, all other things being equal, there has been a shift in the productive factors toward the production which is the object of trade, so that the marginal productivity increases both for the trading sectors and for those sectors that are not subjected to international competition.

The effect of trade creation should, however, be offset by the effect of diversion, i.e., the damages incurred by the non-European companies that may be cut off from European trade because they are substituted by European businesses that have become more efficient following the breaking down of internal barriers[10].

From the microeconomic standpoint, the advantages of integration are connected to the chance to better exploit the economies of scale, both in production and in research as well as in marketing itself.

There are also advantages for the consumers because they may benefit from the lower prices and from the wider range of goods and services of better quality on offer[11]. The Cecchini Report estimates that the advantages that may result from the elimination of nontariff barriers by 1992 will amount to 220 billion European Currency Units (ECUs).

These barriers range from controls at borders, to various rules, norms, and technical regulations in the various countries, to national differences in company laws, to red-tape applied in the field of public tenders.

The costs of a non-Europe have been analyzed in detail in its 13 studies that deal with:

Multisectoral barriers - border formalities, including delays imposed by road transport, red-tape complexities for public tenders; divergences between the national norms and regulations; obstacles to the transnational growth of businesses;

Barriers in the services sector - the services to companies, financial services, telecommunications services;

Barriers in some manufacturing sectors - telecommunications equipment, automobiles, agro-food products, building materials, textiles and clothing, pharmaceutical products.

So it has been possible to estimate the potential earnings of the wealth deriving from the completion of the internal market, subdivided into phases. Phase 1 accounts for the costs of waiting at borders and waiting for customs formalities to be carried out.

In phase 2 the earnings from the abolition of the red-tape complexities of public tenders, the standardization of domestic technical norms, the increase in competition for services and production of goods are worked out.

Phase 3 considers the reductions in costs that can be obtained from the exploitation of economies of scale, while phase 4 evaluates the advantages that derive from the sharper competition.

Table 2-1 EARNINGS FROM INTEGRATION

	ECU(Bil)	% GNP
Phase 1: Earnings from the abolition of trade barriers	8-	0.2-0.3
Phase 2: Earnings from the abolition of production barriers	57-71	2.0-2.4
Phase 3: Earnings from the more thorough exploitation of scale economies	61	2.1
Phase 4: Earnings from reduced inefficiency and monopoly profits attributable to more intense competition	46	2.1[*] 1.6
TOTAL: For 12 member states, 1988 prices	174-258	4.3-6.4
average of estimate	216	5.3

Note: The double figures are the result of estimates made with different methods.

[*]This estimate cannot be subdivided between phases 3 and 4.

Source: EEC Commission, a study by the General Board of Economic and Financial Affairs.

The technique developed by the Cecchini Report is articulated following a macroeconomic approach and a microeconomic one that together provided a definition of the overall size of the advantages gained.

The macroeconomic approach analyzed the effects on Gross National Product (GNP), inflation, employment, the national debt, and the foreign trade balance. The mechanisms that are triggered off by the increased productivity[12] and the reduction in costs bring about a reduction in process, the consequences of which are reflected on the macrovariables. The microeconomic approach starts off with an assessment of the impact of the 1992 program on the individual players in the economy (consumers, businesses, governments) and tries to estimate the advantages that result from the completion of the program. While the advantages for the consumer, measured by the increased purchasing power following the fall in prices, can be directly measured, the result is more complex for businesses. Indeed, the sharpened competition may in the short run reduce the profit levels, but it will eventually increase the net level of well-being on the whole EEC level, thanks to heightened efficiency.

Thus the effects expected from the increased competition generated by the reduction in the barriers involves such aspects as costs, efficiency, competition, and innovation.

However, the report does not provide a measurement of the effects generated by the new entrepreneurial strategies that will be created by the unification of the markets, nor does it measure the effects deriving from the consequent technological innovation; the works in this collection of essays focus particularly on this aspect.

The business strategy will be influenced both by the demand-side (thanks to the widening of the markets), and by the supply-side (from a survey carried out at the companies during the study on the completion of the Single European Market, there is a forecasted reduction of 2 percent and a 5 percent increase in sales).

There will follow an increase in competition and therefore opportunities, but also stress for those who will have to adapt to new market rules after being used to national protection.

The increase in competition should particularly involve the services sector, in which the financial services are at the forefront.

Given the freedom for banks and insurance to establish themselves anywhere in the EEC, and given the consequent increased freedom to trade all over the EEC, a really new market will be created for the financial services sector.

Of course, even the consequences of a social nature will be nature. The greater competition and the reduction in costs may be translated into a growth in profits for the business sector (especially in some oligopolistic sectors), or into higher salaries/profits, even if that tendency seems to be offset by the likely reduction in process that the competition should lead to.

In that case even exports should be encouraged, although the increased domestic demand should have a multiplier effect on imports that benefit from the competitive edge.

This hypothetical scenario depicted in the studies carried out by the 1992 program shows an altogether positive balance for the Community even if worries do remain about the regional disequilibria and some sectoral disequilibria that may occur.

Both kinds of disequilibria might be reabsorbed if the overall European growth is sufficiently sustained, even though, as the Padoa-Schioppa Report argued, it is necessary for a more sustained economic growth to take effect than did in the 1987-1987 period, so as to underpin the program for the completion of the internal market. Indeed, the Report indicates concern that the infraregional disequilibria may grow during the integration phase based on liberalization, so measures are called for to establish structural re-equilibrium in the slow regions of the "two-speed Europe."

The Report also points out the need for concerted economic policies, and especially monetary policies aimed at maintaining the stability of the currencies, given the objective of keeping process and exchange rates stable.

In any case, in the midterm it has been estimated[13] that the GNP increase could range from between +4.5 percent and +7.5 percent (the latter hypothesis is valid if together with the measures for the completion of the internal market, accompanying economic policy measures are also adopted), together with a reduction in process of -6.1 percent and -4.3 percent, respectively, and increases in employment of +1.8 million or +6.7 million jobs, respectively.

The multiplier effects that spring from the liberalization of the market are renowned from a theoretical perspective and are also quantifiable. However, in the preparatory studies prior to the Single European Act, they were not estimated in dynamic terms. It should be noted that the interest that the first estimates arouse was justifiable on the grounds of the modest GNP growth rates that were mentioned before. This might depend on the fact that the observers did not fully realize the further opportunities at hand.

The fact that the initial effect is also accompanied by a more lasting developmental effect is highlighted in an essay by Baldwin, who singles out two growth factors.

The first factor derives from the positive effects on investments that originate from the higher levels of saving. The higher savings in turn are triggered off by the higher level of production expected.

In the second phase it would be necessary to take account of the effect played by the economies of scale that, by expanding the market, would involve a permanent increment in growth.

On the grounds of a formal method that takes the two above points into account, Baldwin concludes that "previous studies of 1992 have seriously underestimated its economic impact[14]."

The assessments of the effects of the 1992 program have been thoroughly discussed even though, on the whole, it may be said that they have been accepted too lightheartedly. On the other hand, the Cecchini Report estimated an incremental growth in output, according to the scenarios sketched out above, based on a very wide field of variation, ranging from +2.5 percent and +6.5 percent. The debate has already examined the presence of one rather than another scenario, but has not particularly looked deeply into the evaluation of the estimated benefits. The exception is the previously cited contribution by Richard

Baldwin[15] who estimated that the effects of 1992 will be greater than what has been forecasted by the Cecchini Report. Indeed, it would be enough to measure the effects deriving from the market liberalization, not in static terms (as in the Cecchini Report), but in dynamic terms, so as to achieve better policy measures. "If 1992 raised Europe's growth rate even half a percentage point, it would chalk up an extra 5 percent real income not just once, but every 10 years[16]."

The medium-run effect, the impact of 1992 on earnings (in the 10 subsequent years), is about double compared to the EEC estimates. Indeed, the strengthened integration might permanently add between 0.28 percent and 0.9 percent to the growth rate of the 12-country Europe.

Of course, along with the dynamic advantage, such as those deriving from the better exploitation of economies of scale, there are others that may be considered. These range from the increases in productivity to the reductions in costs following the increased competition; the increase in the supply of infrastructure, means of transport, and communications system linked to the increase in trade; and the general improvement in the terms of trade with other countries.

Notes

1. The evolution of the world economy is characterized both by the growth of total imports and exports, which is stronger in certain sectors, and by the development of regional commercial areas. Besides the European area, the United States and Canada are developing forms of economic integration that are increasingly intense. Another vast area growing rapidly is represented by the countries of South-East Asia (Japan, Korea Taiwan, Hong Kong, Singapore) and other regions are beginning to get a look in, such

as those of North Africa, those of the Arab Gulf, and the Central American regions as well. A vast region where a major process of recomposition is underway is that of the homogeneous countries belonging to COMECON. They may regroup according to rationales that differ from the ones that have prevailed so far. In particular, the very EEC configuration may change deeply with the unification of Germany and with the general increase in trade exchanges especially with the ex-communist European countries.

2. On January 22, 1972, Norway too had wished to join the EEC, but on November 26 of the same year, Norway decided not to become a member following the negative responses of the popular referendum.

3. The fundamental stages of the EEC can be summed up as follows:

On March 28, 1947, the Economic Commission for Europe was founded on the initiative of the Economic and Social Council of the United Nations. It was the first organization which tried to promote collaboration among the European states.

On January 1, 1948, a customs union was organized involving Belgium, the Low Countries and Luxembourg (Benelux). On April 16 the OECD (Organization for European Economic Development) is set up, with the task of coordinating the aid provided by the ERP plan. On May 5 the Council of Europe was set up; it is an organization for intra-European cooperation.

On November 4, 1950, in Rome the member states of the Council of Europe signed the European Agreement for the safeguarding of human rights and of fundamental freedoms. The European Payments Union (EPU) was set up.

On April 12-18, 1951, Belgium, France, Germany, Italy, Luxembourg, and the Netherlands signed a treaty in Paris for the creation of the European Coal and Steel Community (ECSC).

On May 27, 1952, the ECSC countries signed the treaty for European Community Defense (ECD); this is an alliance aimed at the integration of the European military forces. (The project will later be rejected by France in 1954.) On August 10, the High Court came into being in Luxembourg; it is the executive body of the ECSC.

On June 2-4, 1955, the Messina conference of the foreign ministers of the ECSC took place. They gave a committee the task of analyzing the possible creation of a European Common Market. March 25, 1957 marked the signing of treaties in Rome for the European Economic Community (EEC) and the European Community Atomic Energy Agency (Euratom).

January 1, 1958: the EEC treaties came into effect along with Euratom. The European Parliament was established, was made up of 142 members elected by their respective national parliaments. November 20, 1959: the European Free Trade Association (EFTA) was set up. The members are Austria, Denmark, Finland, Great Britain, Ireland, Iceland, Norway, Portugal, Sweden, and Switzerland.

January 14, 1962: an agreement was made by the Six on the Common Agricultural Policy (CAP); the European Fund for Agricultural Management and Protection was set up.

June 20, 1963: the Yaoundé Accord was signed by the EEC countries and the 18 African states belonging to the community of ex-colonies of the EEC countries. The accord will later be repeatedly renewed and widened to other countries.

April 8, 1965: the treaty was signed for the unification of the three communities: ECSC, EEC, Euratom.

July 1, 1968: the EEC customs union was completed following the removal of the last customs duties.

April 24, 1972, saw the beginning of a monetary agreement called "European Monetary System" (EMS) also known as the "snake." Among other things, it requires the currencies of the member countries to be exchanged according to certain ratios that fluctuate within certain predetermined bands.

January 1, 1973: the United Kingdom, Denmark, and Ireland entered into the Community. February: Italy left the EMS, later followed by France (January 1974), while the United Kingdom and Ireland had left it in June 1972. April: the European Fund for Monetary Cooperation was set up.

December 10, 1974: the European Council of Paris set up the regional development fund with the aim of acting toward the rebalancing of the EEC regions.

March 13, 1979, the European Monetary System came into being and replaced what was left of the snake.

June 7-10: direct election ws held by universal suffrage of the 410 members of the European Parliament.

January 1, 1981: Greece entered into the EEC. The ECU (European Currency Unit) substitutes the EAU (European Account Unit) in the EEC's overall balance.

June 19, 1983: the Council of Europe of the Heads of State and Government in Stuttgart approved the "Declaration on the Union of Europe."

February 14, 1984: the European Parliament approved the Treaty Project that sets up the European Union.

June 29-30, 1985: the Council of Europe decided to call an intergovernmental conference with the task of working out the changes to the treaties. On December 16-17, the Council of Ministers passed the Single Act that modified the existing Treaties.

January 1, 1986: Spain and Portugal joined the EEC.

July 1, 1987: the Single European Act was enforced, so the Project 1992 is definitely underway.

4. In the United States and Japan the plan for Europe 1992 has been criticized as actually being a protectionist plan, because by getting rid of the internal barriers the external ones grow proportionally. The EEC's explicitly protectionist policies toward the outside are another matter altogether.

5. The European Community Commission, *The Completion of the Internal Market*," Brussels, June 14, 1985. (This later became the White Book of the Commission for the European Council of Milan, June 29-29, 1985.)

6. These regard the EEC, Euratom, and ECSC treaties.

7. No Community-level studies have been carried out into the problems and costs incurred by each region from the completion of the internal market; this is probably because there was no desire to arouse further policy difficulties on top of the ones already existing in trying to enforce such a vast plan.

8. In Community law the principle norms either come from treaties or directives and regulations. The 300 measures laid down in the White Book are either directives, i.e., compulsory objectives that each one of the member states must translate into its respective national legislation, or regulations, i.e., real "Community laws."

9. Just in 1987, the transactions involving companies worth more than 25 million dollars amounted to 654, and one-third involved European businesses.

10. Numerous studies have been performed (Robson, 1987; Swann, 1985) to estimate the net balance of the two effects.

According to these studies it would be positive with regard to the phase subsequent to the creation of the EEC. According to Pelkmans (1986), the growth of European trade, induced by economic integration after 1959, totaled a figure fluctuating between 50 and 100 percent of the intra-Community total.

11. For instance Owen (1983) estimated the advantages deriving from the growth of scale brought about by European integration.

12. From the theoretical perspective we can go back to the Kaldor version (1966) of the Veroorn Law which argues that the growth of productivity of manufacturing industry is the function of the rate of growth of demand.

13. Estimates made from the econometric models Hermes (EEC) and Interlink (OECD) reported in the Cecchini Report.

14. Baldwin (1989, p.269).

15. Baldwin (1989)

16. Baldwin (1989, p. 249).

References

Agnelli, G. "The Europe of 1992" in *Foreign Affairs* 4, (Fall 1989).

Baldwin, R. "The Growth Effects of 1992", *Economic Policy*, October, 1989.

Basevi, G. "Liberalization of Capital Movements in the European Community: A Proposal, with Special Reference to the Case of Italy," A Report to the EC Commission, Bologna, (typescript), 1987.

Blanchard, O., Dornbusch, R., and Layard R. (eds.). *Restoring Europe's Prosperity*. Cambridge, Mass.: MIT Press, 1986.

Catherwood, F. *The Institutional Consequences of the Cost of non-Europe*, Committee for Institutional Affairs, European Parliament, February 1988.

Cecchini, P. (ed.). *The European Challenge: 1992*. Aldershot: Gower, 1988.

Davenport, M. "The Economic Impact of the EEC," in A. Boltho (ed.), *The European Economy, Growth and Crisis*. Oxford, England: Oxford University Press, 1982.

EEC Commission. *The Economics of 1992*, February 23, 1988.

EEC Commission. "The Economics of 1992. An Assessment of the Potential Economic Effects of Completing the Internal Market of the European Community," Bruxelles, February 23, 1988, *Economy, 35* March, 1988.

Emerson, M., Anjean, M., Catinat, M., Goybet, P., and Jacquemin, A. "The Economics of 1992," in *European Economy*, 1988.

Giavazzi, F., Micossi, S., and M. Miller. *The European Monetary System*. Oxford: Oxford University Press, 1988.

Guerrieri, P., and Padoan, P.C. *The Political Economy of International Cooperation*. London: Croom Helm, 1988.

Helpman, E., and Krugman, P. *Market Structure and Foreign Trade: Increasing Returns, Imperfect Competition, and the International Economy*. Cambridge, Mass.: MIT Press, 1985.

Hoffman, S. "The European Community and 1992" *Foreign Affairs*, (Fall 1989).

Jacquemin, A., and Sapir, A. "Inter-EC Trade A Sectoral Analysis" Bruxelles: Center for European Policy Studies, 1987.

Kaldor, N. *The Causes of the Slow Rate of Growth of the U.K.* Cambridge, England: Cambridge University Press, 1966.

Owen, N. *Economies of Scale Competitiveness and Trade Patterns within the European Community.* London: Clarendon Press.

Padoa-Schioppa, T. et al. "Efficiency, Stability and Equity" Bruxelles: Rapporto per la Commissione delle Comunita Europee, 1987.

Pelkmans, J. "Completing the Internal Market for Industrial Products" Maastricht: European Institute of Public Administration, 1986.

Pelkmans, J. "The New Approach to Technical Harmonization and Standardization" *Journal of Common Market Studies* (March 1987).

Pelkmans, J., and Winters, A. "Europe's Domestic Market," Royal Institute of International Affairs. London: Routledge, 1988.

Pelkmans, J. *Market Integration in the EC.* Boston/The Hague: M. Nijhoff, 1984.

Pelkmans, J. "The Institutional Economics of European Integration," in M. Cappelletti, M. Seccombe, and J. Weiler (eds.), *Integration through Law, Europe and the American Federal Experience*, vol. 1. Berlin/New York: Walther de Gruyter, 1986.

Prodi, R. "La Poltica del Industriale," in *Incontro del Credito Italiano*. Milano: Libri Scheiviller, 1988.

Robson, P. *The Economics of International Integration*. London: Allen & Unwin, 1987.

Secchi, C. "Il Completamento del Mercato Interno della CEE entro il 1992: Problemi   e prospettive," *Economia e Banca* 2 1988.

Smith, A., and Venables, A. "The Cost of Non-Europe: An Assessment Based on a Formal Model of Imperfect Competition and Economics of Scale." EEC, Economic Commission, Bruxelles, 1988.

Swann, D. *The Economics of the Common Market*. Harmondsworths: Penguin Books, 1985.

Wyatt, D. and Dashwood, A. *The Substantive Law of the EEC* (2nd ed.). London: Sweet & Maxwell, 1987.

Chapter 3

1992 Europe as a Unified Customer Market

Edmund S Phelps

Columbia University

My objective is to try to isolate some gains and losses from the unification of markets that the European Community is planning for 1992, paying some special attention to what may be called information goods. To narrow the focus somewhat I will confine this essay to the unification of the product markets. If there is a common theme running through these notes it is my view of these markets as <u>customer</u> <u>markets</u> in the sense of a now-rather-old paper by Sidney Winter and me.

Let me get down to business by describing the particular customer-market model to be applied here. The hallmark of any customer market model is that commerce -- or marketing -- to be more precise takes place in the face of informational frictions which act as impediments to a firm's capturing additional market share from the other firms. A consequence of these frictions is that two firms whose products would command exactly the same price in a setting of perfect information may nevertheless maintain a certain inequality in their prices for a long time. The law of one price does not hold as a static, continuously applicable relationship. Yet it will be convenient to suppose that there is a single industry in the world and to suppose further that there is a long-run tendency for competition to drive out a firm that insisted on a price "above the market"; no firm has any natural, sustainable advantage over any other firm -- a firm will be different from the others but not inferior, the inferior ones having long ago been driven out -- so the law of one price does hold in the post-shock steady state toward which the system is always gravitating.

A further consequence of the informational friction is that, except in the unlikely case of a zero (or negative) real rate of interest, the competition of firms does not go so far as to drive their price all the way down to their marginal cost of production; even in the steady state there is a positive markup of price over marginal cost. The frictions confer on every firm only a transient (or one might say momentary) monopoly power that lasts until the last customer has escaped, but with all firms simultaneously exercising the (optimal fraction of their) monopoly power, the customers cannot make a collective escape and so the exploitation of the transient power continues indefinitely. The size of the equilibrium markup is somewhere between zero, which is the familiar competitive-equilibrium case, and the textbook monopoly-equilibrium case (in which marginal cost equals marginal revenue, as Amoroso showed). The markup will be higher, thus closer to the latter case, the higher the real rate of interest and the greater the frictions, which would slow the response to a firm's temporary price cut intended to gain more customers.

I will suppose that initially the firms in every one of the European Community countries together number as their customers all the consumers in their home country -- their aggregate market share at home is 100 percent -- and they may in addition have some customers overseas, that is, in non-EC countries; but these firms have no customers in the other European countries as a result of hindrance to foreign penetration of their markets -- hindrances put by the European governments that the 1992 liberalization will reduce or remove. With only one product, it follows that the European countries do not spend on imports, disbursing their overseas revenues either by the payment of net interest and dividends to overseas owners of financial instruments or by net foreign lendings and other capital outflows. If, at the moment liberalization is introduced, 1992 finds Europe initially in a steady state, it is implied that the European nations are in a net debtor position, the interest on which counterbalances exports.

THE 'MACRO' PERSPECTIVE ON LIBERALIZATION

This is not the right place to put flesh on the above bare-bones outline of the model and to study it with any rigor, so I prefer to proceed somewhat intuitively in considering what the customer-market model (and other versions of it) has to say about the effects of 1992 trade liberalization.

First, however, I would like to examine for a moment the determination of the steady state. Does national wealth accumulation determine the extent of net indebtedness (to foreigners) and thereby ultimately dictate the export surplus and and thus the customer base overseas? Or do a country's firms, through the profitability of their drive for overseas market share, determine national wealth and net foreign indebtedness? Causation works in both directions in the following sense. If wealth initially exceeds its steady-state value, demand for the product by national consumers will be correspondingly swollen, the price level in relation to the world price level will be inflated accordingly, and hence market share will be eroding so that profits and wealth will be declining. If the stock of overseas customers initially exceeds its steady-state level, the price level will be correspondingly swollen (as before) and hence market share and wealth will be declining. It should be noted that if the European countries take policy steps intended to increase the competitiveness of European firms (vis-a-vis overseas firms) the result will indeed be a rise of exports if and only if the policy actions somehow induce national consumers to contract their consumption and/or to augment their labor supply, either gradually or abruptly, so that national firms will have the output capacity to supply a larger share of the overseas market. If the new steady-state indeed displays increased overseas customers and thus increased exports, a corollary effect must be a lower level of national consumption and wealth or a higher level of national labor input or both, accompanied by an increased net foreign indebtedness.

Tariff Reduction

What are the effects if trade liberalization amounts to reducing the uniform tariff rate of each European country because the hindrances to import competition in the European countries consist simply of straightforward tariff rates? Then national customers will drift away to overseas firms unless and until national firms have dropped their money prices in proportion to the drop in the world price including tariff, which is the price that potential new entrants from abroad could offer. It follows from every known way of modeling the labor market that, if there exists a unique equilibrium, the new post-tariff-reduction equilibrium must exhibit an equiproportionate drop in the money price level and money wage level that equals the proportionate drop in the price of potential imports inclusive of the tariff, hence an unchanged real wage and product wage, and, as a corollary, no change in the level of employment and output. This neutrality result via pure deflation could also be arrived at via a currency devaluation. Actually this result holds exactly only if initially the firms in the home country had zero customers overseas. If there is a positive market share abroad and hence positive net indebtedness, the domestic real value -- the value in terms of purchasing power over domestically purchased home-firm output -- of the home firm's export revenues is increased; it does not matter whether the tariff reduction brings pure deflation or devaluation. On the same "if," there is also an increase in real net foreign indebtedness in the event of deflation (rather than devaluation) if that indebtedness takes the form of foreign-currency-denominated or unindexed-home-currency-denominated interest obligations. In that case, the initial real interest burden must have been equal to the initial real export revenue, so the increase in the former would equal the increase in the latter. But if the indebtedness takes the form of foreign holdings of shares in home firms, the foreigners merely obtain their pro rata share along with national shareholders of the rise in the real value of the firms' equity resulting from the increase in real export revenues; so there is a clear gain left for national shareholders from the increase in the real value of export revenue. It could be argued, however, that this benefit is not a genuine collective, or social, gain for home citizens; it seems more like an improvement in the accounting, but that, too, may be worth something.

Let me acknowledge in the next breath that the above analysis certainly adopts an unusual and perhaps strange perspective on tariffs. My excuse, however adequate, is that the subject is already quite complicated without bringing in the familiar microeconomic baggage of two or more goods with comparative advantage, intermediate and capital goods, and so on.

Reducing Informational Hindrance to Import Competition

We have been assuming that before the 1992 trade liberalization in the EC countries a temporary price reduction by an EC firm with the objective of gaining customers in other EC markets would not have elicited a sufficiently rapid growth of market share to make such a strategy profitable in view of the hindrances that the various EC governments have placed in the way of foreign firms attempting to do business there. These hindrances in some cases take the form of licensing requirements which, although they would impose only a trivial cost in a world of frictionless markets, loom as a significant cost when the revenues from import penetration would begin to develop only a year or further in the future. If import competition is hindered at least as much by overseas governments, a result of the European hindrances is that European firms stop short of producing up to the point where marginal cost equals price by even a greater distance than would have been the case without these governmental hindrances in Europe -- with only the natural impediments raised by the costs of transmitting and acquiring information in markets.

The point I want to make here is that much of the 1992 trade liberalization will consist of reducing or eliminating these hindrances to import competition. As a consequence, a price reduction by a European firm will then hold out the hope of capturing customers in the other European markets at a faster rate than previously. This increased responsiveness to a below-the-market price policy will, according to customer-market theory, have an impact on the individual firm's optimal price: the optimal price drops because the present and future costs of a temporary price reduction are not greater than before -- they are the same -- while the (future) benefits of the price reduction in the form of greater future market share are magnified. Of course, as all the European firms proceed to cut prices in anticipation of making inroads into one another's market territory, they will find that, collectively and on the average, they are making no progress in that objective. But they will also realize that, as a result of this stimulus to competition, each firm must now offer a lower price than before (in relation to costs) just to preserve its pre-existing market share in the market of its own home country; there is no way, short of collusion on an industrywide and countrywide scale, by which the firms can go back to the old price policy -- to the old, high markup. The results of this new price policy are a higher real wage rate, a consequent increase in the amount of labor supplied and the volume of employment and real income earned, and hence also an increase in the amount of output that each firm sells to its European customers -- the same customers it had before, but now bigger earners in real terms and hence bigger spenders. In those models of the natural rate of unemployment that focus upon the problem of quitting or the problem of shirking facing the firms, a further result is a fall, although perhaps not an important fall, in the natural rate of unemployment.

There is considerable interest in the consequences of 1992 trade liberalization for the rest of the world. It does not seem to me that there are any unambiguous implications of the process I have described above for the prosperity of countries overseas. There is some presumption that, with increased real incomes, the European countries will also increase their saving, and this effect will tend to reduce the net foreign indebtedness that Europe exports to service: in the long run, then, European exports will be reduced, so that overseas firms will have their home-country markets more to themselves. A further effect of increased real income and saving in Europe is a reduction of the world real interest rate, which would also tend to increase economic welfare, or potential welfare, overseas, at least in the long run. Much of the cogitation on the effects of 1992 on the rest of the world has been inspired by the thought that the European firms may exhibit increasing returns to scale, also known as decreasing costs. The pitfalls in this way of looking at the question of overseas effects are a tendency to forget that European labor will doubtless remain a scarce factor of production and that European consumers will doubtless remain interested in spending on European output all or most of the increased real income that 1992 brings.

LIBERALIZATION AND INNOVATION

Trade liberalization in 1992 will provide an impetus for increased research and development (R&D) expenditure. The reason is that liberalization will confer on each firm a much wider market than before -- all of Europe instead of just the national market -- if it is lucky enough to hit upon a new technique of production or marketing that gives it a cost advantage over the other firms. The incentive to take gambles in winner-take-all sweepstakes is clearly greater the larger the "all" amounts to.

The consequences of this effect of trade liberalization are not wholly benign. We generally take for granted that an optimum world would allocate to R&D more of the actual aggregate investment in the various kinds of "capital" -- tangible capital, human capital, and knowledge-- than occurs in the actual world. But it may also be true at the same time that there is too much bunching of R&D expenditures on certain high-payoff gambles in which much of the reward comes from being first to win it rather than from what the price is. You can become as rich as Croesus if you can discover an epsilon-improvement in mousetraps or in the method of producing mousetraps before the others since you can use the advantage to take market share away from the others; once the others have finally mastered the new trick they will be starting from a lessened customer base. The social gain from this sort of innovation is less than the private gain, some of which consists of gains to the innovator at the expense of the others. Hence it can be argued that there is too much of this kind of research going on and not enough of the other kind. My point about 1992 in this connection is that removing the hindrances to competition across European borders will to some degree intensify the reward to the first kind of research while doing nothing to increase the reward to the second kind.

Another point I would make in this context concerns the social losses from disturbances and the uncertainty surrounding them. In the United States, when a defense contractor in, say, Long Island succeeds in winning a contract for some military product at the expense of some heretofore successful contractor in California, the workers made unemployed in California can cross the country to take similar jobs in Long Island -- though there may be some loss of time waiting to be hired, some loss of seniority, and various other risks of a decline in satisfaction in the new place. In contrast, there are not so many Germans, say, who would be quick to relocate in, say, France, and few French who would readily move to Germany. People become accustomed to their native language, culture, and even climate, and evidently find it costly or unpleasant to adapt to another language, culture, or climate. In Europe, as a result, labor is notoriously immobile, not only across borders but even, to a degree, within borders.

INFORMATION GOODS -- A 'MICRO' PERSPECTIVE

We are concentrating here on the tertiary sector of the economy and its emphasis on the "information goods" which make up so much of that sector's production. So it is a pleasant coincidence to note that, once we take a disaggregated view of the output of the economy, the industries producing information goods will tend to show the largest effects of 1992 liberalization, along with other strongly decreasing-cost industries.

A feature of the production of information goods, I suppose, is that it does not cost very much more to produce and make available an information good to more people, although profit-maximizing firms will naturally insist on charging the additional buyers for their use. That suggests to me that opening up the national markets of the EC will greatly intensify competition among producers of information goods, resulting in a reduction of markups and an increase of output. In contrast, the producers of mineral waters and capital-city hotel services will show comparatively little effect of the liberalization.

In this respect one would expect the more technologically progressive countries of the European Community, such as France and Italy, to obtain a disproportionate share of the benefits from 1992 trade liberalization, and to expect the more traditional economies, such as Greece and Portugal, to obtain proportionately little benefit. But it must be added quickly that the less developed countries of the European Community may gain quite a lot from 1992 if it encourages firms elsewhere in the EC to locate additional plants in these countries to take advantage of lower wages. This observation brings us to a point about customer market theory that concludes this chapter. We think of a country as struggling for increased market share in the world economy, its national firms being the spear carriers in the front line of this battle.   But plants and workers do not have customers in the ordinary sense of that term; firms have customers.   Overnight, workers in one country can become the work force of a firm, producing the output for its customers, if the firm decides to move its plant or set up a new plant in that country.   It follows that the consequences of 1992 will be not only a welcome tendency to higher real and employment wages but also a welcome tendency to higher relative wages at the bottom of the European range.   Thus the prediction of the analysis here, its narrowness being constantly borne in mind, is that there will be an improvement not only in intra-national efficiency -- prices closer to marginal cost -- but also in international efficiency and justice.

Chapter 4

Implications of 'Europe 1992' in a Changing World Economy

F. Gerard Adams

University of Pennsylvania

The imbalances in the world economy reflect long-run problems of competitiveness linked closely to the maturity of the industrial countries. The extension of the European Common Market into a grand barrier-free economic zone in 1992 may serve to deal with the maturity problem. It will create a market bigger than that of North America, containing both high technology industries and low cost labor. It will greatly stimulate competitive entrepreneurship and innovation in Europe. Whether the new Europe will participate in the world economy or whether it will build protective walls greatly affects economic welfare in the rest of the world.

The world economy has avoided the swings of the business cycle during the 1980s. While growth has slowed, and Europe has suffered from high levels of unemployment, the principal concern from a world perspective is not so much the present as the future.

The imbalances of the international economy between the United States and other industrial and "newly industrializing countries" reflect long-run problems of competitiveness, a significant change in the ability of the mature industrial countries to compete. The imbalances cannot and will not continue. At worst, they may lead to international economic crisis or crash, an event many thought was occurring last October. At best, they cause natural economic reactions and policy responses that will significantly alter the economy of the 1990s.

Europe is beginning to deal with some of the underlying issues by extending the Common Market into a barrier-free economic zone in 1992. As a result, Europe stands at a special crossroads. On one hand, the maturity phenomenon has engulfed Europe almost as much as it has the United States. On the other hand, Europe stands at the threshold of a new economic structure, the frontierless expanse of Europe in 1992. What are the potential implications of the world economic setting for the changing structures of the European economy, and for its future role in the world economy?

This chapter considers the nature of the competitiveness problem and evaluates its implications for the world economy. In particular, we appraise these developments in connection with their implications for the United States and Japan and for the new Europe after 1992.

THE CHANGING WORLD ECONOMIC ENVIRONMENT

Looking back at the 1980s, economic historians will describe them as a period of economic transition. The changes in the economic environment have been building for many years. The United States and, to a lesser extent, Europe have lost their supremacy as industrial producers, and the locus of production for many products is shifting. From the perspective of the industrial countries, particularly Europe and the United States, one may speak of a period of economic maturity, characterized by slow growth, lower inflation, and in the United States, by balance of payments deficits, and, in Europe, by high rates of unemployment. The details of these developments are summarized below in Figures 4-1 through 4-3.

The United States economy (figure 4-1) has had slow growth during the second half of the 1980s. Further slow growth is being projected with gradual increases in the rate of inflation. The unemployment rate in the United States between 5 and 6 percent is relatively modest, but the balance on current account represents a serious imbalance. This reflects the failure of the U.S. economy to adjust its trade balance, and consequently the need for continued massive capital inflows, despite the drastic depreciation of the U.S. dollar. And this, in turn, reflects the changes in international specialization that have affected the competitiveness of the United States in world markets.

In Europe (figure 4-2), the phenomenon of slow growth is equally apparent and, here, with very high unemployment rates. While Europe has been successful with its trade balance and is keeping down inflation, like the United States it is a mature economy.

Japan (figure 4-3) has been more successful, both in growth and unemployment performance. And Japan has run enormous trade surpluses. This is a case of an economy that is not as far along on the path to maturity as the United States and Europe. This is also a surprisingly adaptable economy that has been able to advance in high technology manufacturing as a response to the shift of mass production and export industries to other new producers in South East Asia. Japan is seeking an outlet for its excess saving, in part, by building new industries in South East Asia.

Figure 4-1.   UNITED STATES -- INDICATORS OF ECONOMIC ACTIVITY

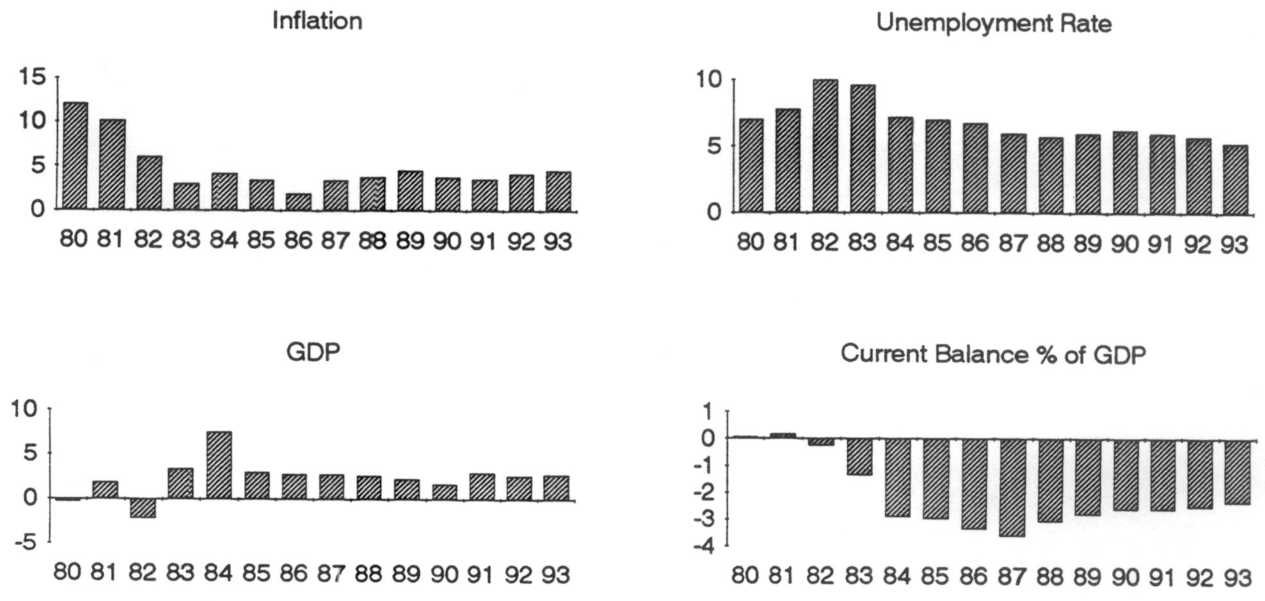

Inflation

Unemployment Rate

GDP

Current Balance % of GDP

Source: WEFA

Figure 4-2.   EUROPE -- INDICATORS OF ECONOMIC ACTIVITY

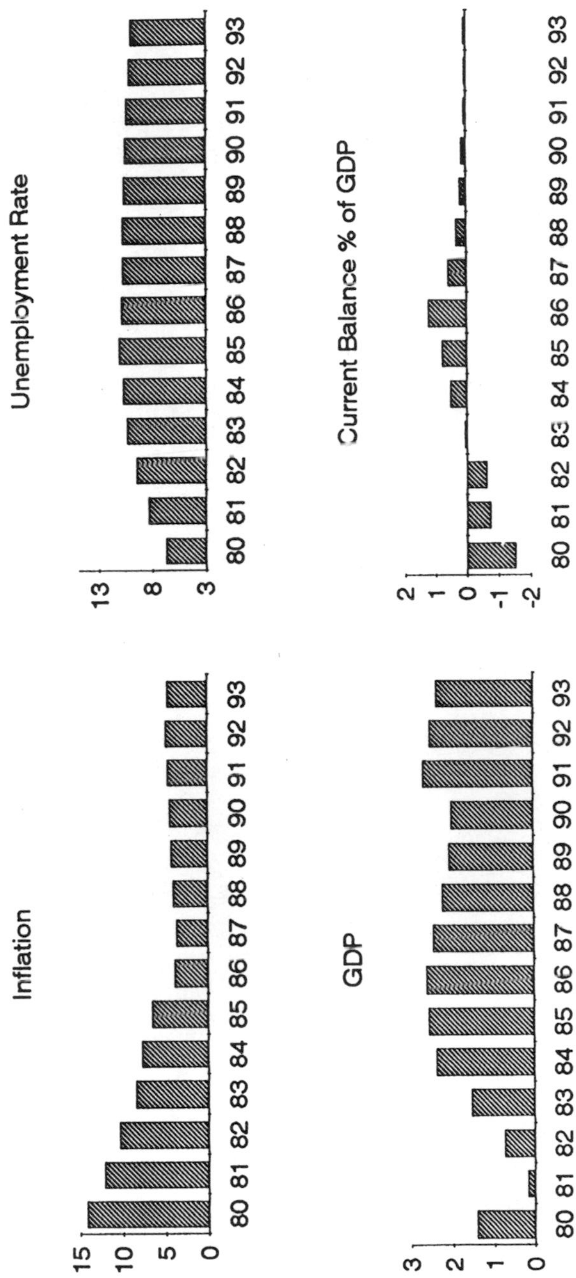

Source: WEFA

Figure 4-3.   JAPAN -- INDICATORS OF ECONOMIC ACTIVITY

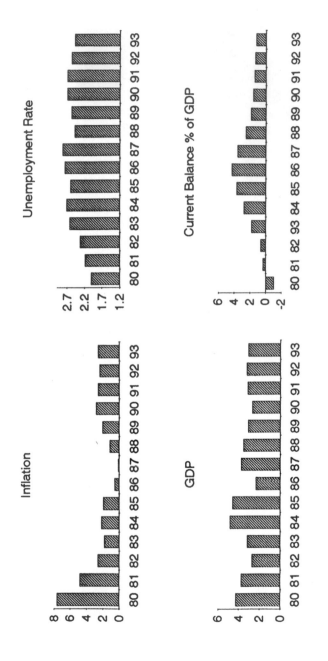

Source: WEFA

Finally, (figure 4-4) shows the various parts of the less developed world. The striking success is the high and maintained rate of growth in the Pacific Basin and, to a lesser extent, in Latin America. These countries have become effective mass producers of autos and consumer electronics. The differences between these countries and the mature industrial countries lies at the heart of the European-American problem.

If we were to look more closely we would find massive differences in productivity growth with the United States very much at the low end of the scale. We would find low rates of investment, lagging technology, and aging industrial plants. That, along with high wages, has made many industries in the industrial countries (in Western Europe as well as the U.S.) noncompetitive except at extraordinary exchange rates. The causes of these lags in the high industrial countries are still being debated, but it does not take deep theory or econometrics to infer that the problem is one related to maturity.

Behind these developments lie longer term trends of industrial maturity, a gradual shift out of basic industrial products into services, and a slowing of the long-term productivity trend. The longer term perspective is unclear, but we can visualize some scenarios, some desirable if they can be achieved, and some not so favorable and hopefully avoidable. For example, we can visualize a high technology scenario where high technology industries set a high pace of progress and productivity. Alternatively, we can visualize a low productivity scenario where we simply "take in each other's washing" using old-fashioned technologies. It is important to stress that the service sector may include high technologies as well as traditional methods. The desired post-industrial society will focus on high technology and service activities.

Figure 4-4.   REGIONAL GDP GROWTH

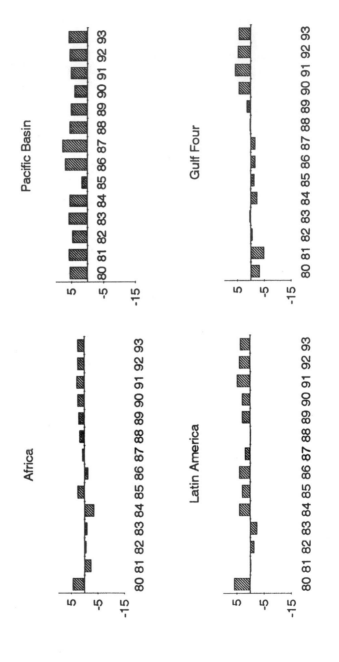

Source: WEFA

CHANGING PATTERNS OF TRADE

Perhaps the best way to characterize the changing role of the country blocks in the world economy is to look at the bilateral trade pattern between the United States and other areas over the period 1980 to 1988 and projected into the future to 1993. These developments have become clear, particularly with regard to the United States.

Figure 4-5 shows the balance in primary commodity trade. Note that except with Canada, the balance is positive. Indeed, it becomes more so with Europe and Japan. The balance for primary commodities is positive even with the Pacific Basin Newly Industrialized conunties (NICs). Figure 4-6 shows the balances with respect to trade in manufactures. Here there has been an enormous change. The balance was close to even in 1980. A deficit with Japan was offset by a large surplus to the rest of the world. But by 1980 the deficit with respect to Japan has increased four times, and trade with the Pacific Basin and Europe is also in deficit. This picture will change only to a limited extent as we look forward to the 1990s. It is noteworthy that the deficit with respect to Europe will be sharply reduced (i.e., Europe's advantage will shrink) but the deficits with Japan and the Pacific Basin will remain enormous. Figure 4-7 shows the energy trade balances. In this respect, the United States is clearly a deficit country, with the Middle East and Latin America, but in the future the situation is not quite as bad as it was in 1980.

The figures show clearly the change in the pattern of trade for the United States. This represents the pattern one would anticipate in the new international economic order. The United States has fallen behind, a victim of its maturity. Some have argued a similar position with regard to Europe, calling it Eurosclerosis. The phenomenon has another important dimension in that some of the developing countries have caught up and now have the potential to compete with high quality industrial goods, something they could not do 20 or 30 years ago.

Figure 4-5.

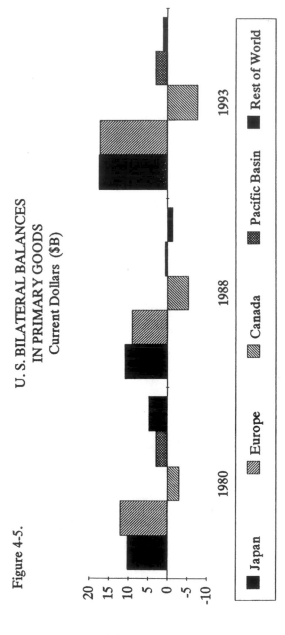

U. S. BILATERAL BALANCES
IN PRIMARY GOODS
Current Dollars ($B)

Source: WEFA

Figure 4-6.

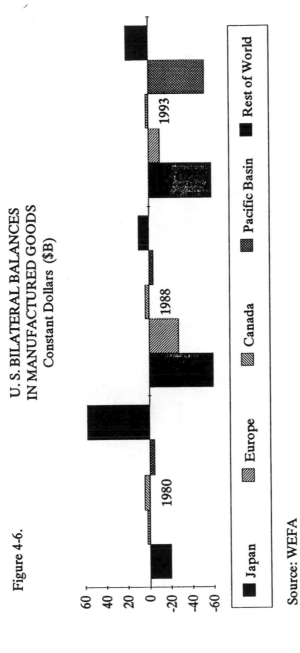

U.S. BILATERAL BALANCES
IN MANUFACTURED GOODS
Constant Dollars ($B)

Source: WEFA

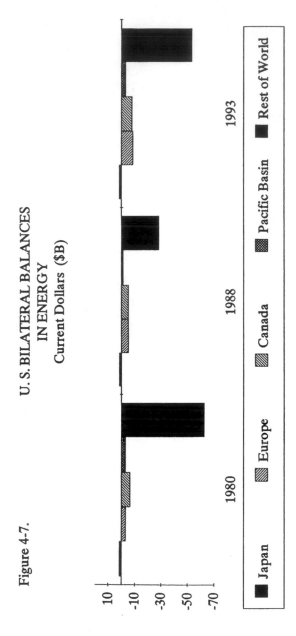

Figure 4-7.

U. S. BILATERAL BALANCES
IN ENERGY
Current Dollars ($B)

Source: WEFA

Two points must be made with regard to this development. From the perspective of the developing countries, if not always from the point of view of their industrial competitors, this is a positive development. It is moreover, one that did not "just happen." In fact, it is in large part attributable to the transfer of technology and investment by firms in the industrial world which sought production locations where products could be produced more cheaply on a worldwide scale. Some industries like textiles exemplify the process of internationalization.

The ability of the NICs to produce quality products competitive in the industrial world represents a new product cycle. The problem is that the changed competitive position is not likely to be easily reversible. Once the requisite technological transfer has taken place it will remain difficult for the industrial countries to compete successfully. Clearly, they cannot compete on the basis of wages. Possibly they can compete on the basis of labor costs, recognizing that labor is more efficient in the industrial countries and therefore can maintain its competitiveness even at higher wage levels. But for many products that are fairly standardized and where the NICs have acquired the technology, competitive production in the industrial countries may no longer be possible. An example is the small car which has been left by the American automobile industry largely to the producers in the developing countries like Korea, Mexico, and Brazil.

Much of the future development in the industrial world will focus on the service industries rather than traditional industry. Many service activities are closely linked to industry, and these fields, too, are increasingly becoming internationalized. The recent turmoil in international investment banking is evidence of the rapid internationalization of this field. Other aspects of financial services, telecommunications, insurance, management and engineering consulting, construction, and even transportation are not far behind.

The new product cycle represents a difficult challenge for the industrial world. The mature industrial countries must find ways to adapt. We see the process of creating a unified Europe as part of this process.

EUROPE 1992 IN THE WORLD ECONOMIC ENVIRONMENT

How does the new Europe to be developed in 1992 fit into the world economy? In many ways the new Europe is going to be a very different trading area. In place of a number of industrial countries, "Europe without barriers" will be a broad economic expanse. It will be a very large trading area, with a Gross Domestic Product (GDP) bigger than that of the United States. A principal objective of Europe 1992 is to break down the barriers remaining in the service fields: in transportation, finance, communications, capital movement and professional activities, and so on. If the common economic territory can be worked out effectively, and that remains to be seen, Europe 1992 has the potential for revitalization into the world's premier trading country. Internally in Europe there will be a market big enough to gain economies of scale, competitive enough to break past cartel barriers and to stimulate innovation, and yet, with low labor costs and greatly more resources. Externally, the new Europe has great potential in the world economy.

My focus here is on the position of the unified market in the world economy. Will the unified market be able to meet the competition of the NICs? What kind of an industrial structure will it present to the world economy? Will it develop international service industries? Will it interact successfully with the other industrial countries of the world economy?

There are reasons to be optimistic:

o   The unified market will be large and diverse, possessing
      economies of scale in many industries equal to those of
      North America.

o   The unified market will have high technology.   The
      world's most advanced technologies will be available not
      only   at   the   universities   but   also   in   the   large
      technologically advanced firms in electronics, chemistry,
      and the service activities like finance.

o   Yet the unified market will also contain some low wage
      areas   which   can   compete   with   the   NICs   in   mass
      production industry.   The diversity of the countries that
      make   up   the   unified   market   will   give   it   distinct
      advantages on a world market.

o   Hopefully the unified market will have more competition,
      reducing the power of traditional oligopolies and rising
      pressures for efficiency and innovation.

o   The unified market will have financial power.   It will
      contain   the   large-scale   financial   and,   one   might   add,
      organizational   resources   needed   to   operate   modern
      industry.

We can visualize a major power in a competitive world.   A
revitalized Europe could take its place in the world economy and
could pose massive competition to the United States, Japan, and
the NICs.   Such competition could be in high technology industry,
in mass production, and in high quality service sectors, although
clearly there remain activities like primary industry where other
parts   of   the   world   will   have   and   probably   should   have
comparative   advantage.   Optimistically,   Europe   1992   could
represent the shot in the arm that Europe needs to overcome the
problem of maturity.   Some of the maneuvering of business firms
which are already looking forward to 1992 points to large,
emerging changes.

On the other hand, one must be realistic.   It will be difficult
to break down the innumerable barriers in local institutions, laws,
fiscal rules, and so on, that still separate Europe.   The complex

and diverse rules of transport and telecommunication systems in various countries will be difficult to harmonize, for example. And Europe is not the only part of the world striving for a place in the world market. The Japanese have been very effective in designing for themselves an advanced place in a changing world market. The NICs, particularly in South East Asia, have demonstrated what can be accomplished in 20 years, and the United States is also in transition, responding to the need for change in ways that are only gradually being recognized.

From the perspective of the world economy, and particularly of the newly industrializing economies, a great deal depends on the posture of the new Europe with respect to trade barriers. Europe is wiping out internal trade barriers, but what about external barriers, with respect to the rest of the world? A Europe without internal barriers represents a market big enough to achieve scale economies. This means that the new Europe could, if it so desired, protect its industries from world competition without incurring the large costs related to protecting small markets. On the other hand, Europe will be more competitive so there will be less need for protectionism. And, surely there is no intent, at present, to build up a protectionist block. We hope that the new Europe will take its place as a free competitor in world trade, allowing some of the gains from European integration to benefit the entire world economy.

Chapter 5

European Perspectives: The Role of Services in the New Technical System

Jacques De Bandt

Directeur de Recherches, CNRS

By way of introduction, the scope of this Chapter must be clarified: this is part of an exercise aiming at identifying future prospects for Western Europe (hereafter called Europe), not only (or even not mainly) in terms of growth and employment, but in terms of the various -- economic, socio-political, cultural, organizational, institutional, and so on -- dimensions of the future of Europe.

The basic idea is that, beyond the difficult adjustment problems of the last 15 to 20 years, the period ahead -- let us say, the 10 to 15 years to come -- will still be characterized by deep transformations in the context of seemingly very strong constraints.[1]

Depending upon whether the economic agents (or systems) are just undergoing such transformations or are more or less mastering and managing them, the content as well as the ways and means of these structural transformations are likely to be different. This is why an assessment of future prospects is so important.

I would like to suggest -- without justifying it here -- that three types of phenomena are likely to be decisive:

o   demographic trends : Europe is heading toward a situation in which the age structure of the population is becoming older and older, and thus toward a reduction of the proportion of active versus nonactive population,

o   the emergence of the new technical system, i.e., of new production, consumption, financial, organizational, and similar modes, and the role of services within these evolutions.

o   the international relations, made of the very intense rivalries that characterize the technological race.

Of course, this selection of three major types of phenomena -- which are likely to interact with each other -- doesn't mean that other phenomena will not play an important role. For example, it does seem evident that both individual and collective value systems are changing in some significant ways. This and other types of evolutions will, of course, condition the future. But the hypothesis here is that these evolutions are only of second order of importance as compared with the three types of phenomena as selected.

I will be rather brief concerning demographic trends. But it is necessary, even if brief, to stress these trends so that we keep them in our mind. They are indeed most likely to affect deeply, and probably negatively, the future prospects.

The problem is generally -- as above -- presented in terms of the diminishing proportion of the active population as compared with the nonactive one. The problem is also presented in terms of the changing modes of consumption, due to the ways of life of the aged population. The main problem, however, as I see it, is likely to be conservatism imposed by the increasing numbers and powers of the older people and generational conflicts within European societies. These evolutions mean less creative imagination and a greater emphasis on distribution problems. In other words, more attention will be paid to the distribution than to the production of the cake. And the resulting social tensions are likely to be aggravated by the migration movements from the South.

I share the opinion of those who think that, for several reasons, migrations will play a still larger role in the future than in the past, particularly in the case of Europe. This will result not only because of the demographic evolutions in the South (supply factors) but because of the quantitative and qualitative scarcity of available workers in the North (demand factors).

The second type of phenomena, mentioned above, is linked with the transition from the "old" technical system to the "new" system, which we suppose to be actually emerging. The questions to be discussed here do concern on the one hand, the position of Europe within this transition process and, on the other hand, the role of services in the emerging technical system.

Several aspects of the problem have to be clarified.

Without going into the details -- even while general definitions are not quite satisfactory -- the notion of technical system refers to the compatible coexistence of various ways of doing or norms: technological, production, consumption, organizational, financial norms. The technological norms or the technical ways of doing certain things, which essentially satisfy human needs, are in a certain sense more visible, and are anyway very important and to a large extent decisive, because they define the space of constraints and degrees of freedom. But these technological norms are themselves social products, and the other norms are equally part of the definition of the technical system. These norms do correspond concretely to production techniques and capacities but also to specific relations and rules. However, more than by these objects and realities, the technical system is defined by the way these various elements or norms are adapted to each other, so that relatively high degrees of cohesion and consistency exist among them, allowing the actors to explore and exploit the thus existing potentialities. As such the system can only be defined in a rather abstract way, by a number of norms and dominant rules: the actual states of the system are only approximations, differentiated through time and space, the dynamics of the system being characterized by continuous processes of adaptation and improvement, but also by maturity and entropy phenomena, while the repeated interferences of external factors make the picture less clear.

The former technical system was the one which, revivified, so to speak, by the second world war, was incarnated by the U.S. economy, which thus held in the 1950s a (nearly) undisputed dominant position. The system was characterized

1. by production sectors and structures, such as automotive, chemical, electric construction industries;

2. by modes of production, such as the assembly line;

3. by consumption modes, such as standardized mass consumption;

4. by organizational norms, such as big plants and firms;

5. by specific rules, such as the distribution of productivity gains.

The diffusion of this system -- partly through direct investments and technology transfers made by the United States -- made it possible for the other industrialized countries to grow very rapidly in the 1950s and 1960s and as a matter of fact to catch up with the United States

This catching up process was well advanced in the course of the 1960s, both because the United States, having exploited the system close to its limits, were more and more facing decreasing returns phenomena, and because the other countries, having not yet attained those limits, had still at their disposal some margins left for further progress within the framework of the existing technical system.

The limits of the technical system were being made apparent by various phenomena showing characteristically that progress within the industrial was getting out of steam: the significant reduction of substitution elasticities, and thus of the possibilities to adapt factor proportions; the slowdown, down to zero, of total productivity growth; the reduction of profitability, inducing the strong reduction of capacity investments, of growth, and of (direct) employment.

This must be rightly understood. Those limits don't mean that these production techniques are not efficient anymore or even that their efficiency cannot be improved still further. What this means is that relative to the prevailing economic requirements -- in terms of competitiveness (compared with countries having different price systems), in terms of costs (increasing organizational costs) -- the possible efficiency improvements or technical progresses are insufficient and more so too expensive. Increasing the rotation speed of an engine ends up with costs -- capital costs -- increasing more than returns.

In the course of the 1960s, more and more countries other than the United States, in particular the European Countries and

Japan, have reached the same limits of the technical system. This process came to an end in the final third of the 1960s. It must be added that during the same period, in other countries the diffusion of the same technical system -- or at least of some of its components -- was producing productivity and production growth. As a consequence, during the 1970s, industrial growth was strong in some countries (e.g., the Eastern Countries), has been accelerating in others (e.g., the newly industrialized countries (NICs)), or has even started in a number of countries (the "intermediate" countries).

To a certain extent, the crisis in the developed countries was opening opportunities for these countries, whose industrial performances were, as a feedback, aggravating, at least in several traditional sectors, the difficulties of the developed countries.

The crisis, i.e., the using up of the (former) technical system, is making obsolete particularly the production modes, but also the organizational and financial norms.

The solution to the crisis is linked -- this is at least the hypothesis -- with the emergence of a new technical system, which means of a new set of "ways of doing things." This set has to be characterized by sufficient degrees of cohesion and consistency so that new accumulation processes might become feasible, and that something like a new efficient industrial model might appear to be workable.

If so, the transition crisis -- from the former obsolete system to a new one, which has still to be build up -- implies naturally two quite distinct but, to a large extent, complementary processes, which are conditioning each other.

The first one is a *de-structuring* process: due to the exhaustion of the former technical system, a whole set of elements -- production capacities and structures, techniques and capital goods, organizational forms, rules, and so on -- are obsolete and appear to be irrelevant and out of the mark.

The actors have to face this situation, which means that they have to eliminate a number of these elements. This is the Schumpeterian "creative destruction" aspect of the problem. But this is likely to happen, spontaneously, in a disorderly manner, everybody seeking to get out of the venture without loss.

In these de-structuring processes, the performances (of countries, regions, enterprises, workers, and so forth) are very differentiated. This is due to the fact that the adjustment capabilities of the various actors appear (suddenly) to be very different, while some actors are benefitting from the weaknesses and lack of capabilities of others.

For this reason, the management of the de-structuring processes is a major stake for the actors. The propensity to adopt purely defensive behaviors but also the existence of more or less important rigidities lead, in a number of cases, to the wasting of resources and time.

The other kind of processes consists of *restructuring* processes, through which, on the one hand, series of new elements -- production techniques, organizations, rules, and so on -- are being built up, and, on the other hand, consistency relations and adjustments are worked out between these elements.

Of course, the new technical system -- which remains an hypothesis, as long as it is not built up -- is not predetermined. Even if a number of its likely elements can be more or less clearly identified -- as the importance of information technologies all over the place -- it is not possible actually to identify it as such. It will eventually come out of multiple decisions and actions, aiming in most cases at solving, by trial and error, partial and localized problems, without consideration for the technical system to come as such. These actions are, to a large extent, independent, even while various conditioning forces and restructuring processes may be at work, partly due to the actions of the state or of big enterprises.

Here also, already because of the difficulties encountered in the management of the de-structuring processes, the differentiation effects are very important. In this phase, in which technological progress and innovations are likely to be crucial, advances are benefitting from cumulative processes. This is so because the one (country) which has succeeded in taking the lead, reaps the innovation margins, which are increasing its resources available for further progress. This is so also because this leading country defines the path to be followed, imposes his norms, and fixes to a certain extent the rules of the game.

To what extent is the growth of service activities linked either to the transition itself or to the emergence of the technical system?

There is probably no unique answer to that question. Service activities are quite heterogeneous, and the explanations of the growth of these various service activities are likely to be diverse. We have to abandon the Fisher-Clark model or every other model referring to the progressive substitution of services for goods at the level of consumers or to the slow productivity growth in service activities. None of these explanations results from any clear necessity stemming from the characteristics of service activities.

Schematically speaking, the various explanations which can be put forward are of three different types, according to their relation with the transition crisis.

We have first to refer to the long-term tendencies of services to grow. While it doesn't seem possible to assert that the consumer will necessarily increase his direct consumption of services[2] -- because goods can equally be substituted for services, because self-service activities can develop, because new goods may appear attractive to the consumer, and so forth -- we are obliged to see that, because of their development, their internationalization, their use of more sophisticated technologies, and so on, the economic systems have become more and more complex. The development of service activities -- or at least of a number of them -- must be viewed as corresponding to decreasing returns and thus to increasing organizational costs.

I am referring here to the complexity of urban, transport, communication, health, and training systems, taking account, in some of those cases, of the increasing internationalization. In particular cases, this complexity has been compensated, in terms of costs, by significant technical progress (e.g., air transport). For the rest, these increasing organizational costs were easily absorbed because of the productivity surpluses obtained elsewhere.

Over time, however, some of these organizational costs have become excessive, either because the crisis simply couldn't absorb them anymore, or because the costs were becoming out of proportion with the given service.

Two types of reactions have been and are still looked for: it would seem possible, at least for some systems, to try reducing the complexity, by substituting for excessively centralized systems, sets of decentralized subsystems; it would also seem possible to try introducing technical progress so as to increase organizational returns. This is akin to what will be described below as the "new ways of doing things".

It would seem to be a fair guess that this tendency toward a higher degree of complexity of the systems will continue, implying the necessary growth of services in order to face this increasing complexity. It seems also fair to predict that the attempts which will be made in order to compensate for the consequences of this increasing complexity will only be partially successful.

Second, we must take account of those aspects of the growth of service which are linked with the transition itself. We have to consider here -- although the increases here are mainly in terms of employment -- the fact that a certain proportion of those who have lost their status of wage-earners in the industrial sector have been looking for jobs and incomes in activities with low barriers to entry and, as a matter of fact, in many low skilled service activities. We also consider the development of activities in the "circulation sphere," linked either with the intensification of competition and the resulting emphasis on marketing (particularly in advertising) activities, or with the speculative activities surrounding the management of productive assets in the de-structuring and restructuring processes brought about by the crisis. Finally, we must consider service activities whose development corresponds to the transformation of production modes, i.e., of the ways of doing things in the field of production of goods and services. These are mainly information-intensive service activities.

One can rightly suppose that their development, made possible by the information technologies, do constitute -- like those technologies -- basic components of the new technical system.

The nonmaterial investments -- aiming essentially at increasing the production capabilities and capacities on the basis of the treatment of large and increasing volumes of information -- constitute the typical "production detour" characterizing the new technical system (corresponding to the "information society").

Evidently, one of these key activities within the informational tertiary sector -- namely, the R&D activities -- becomes particularly important in the restructuring phase leading to the new technical system. But it is a fair guess to suppose that the development of R&D activities is not only a transitional phenomenon, but that these R&D activities will permanently constitute a key feature of the new technical system.

One of the reasons of this increase of R&D expenditures and activities is of, course, referring to the increasing intensity of rivalries in the international technological race.

This technological race and the resulting rivalries at the international level constitute the third type of phenomena which are here considered as decisive for the future of Europe.

The technological race means very simply that the attempts to get out of the crisis take place in a context of exacerbated competition between the various actors, and particularly so at the international level. The de-structuring phase had already led to such intensification of competition -- everybody looking out for himself, for better or worse, to save his own interests, eventually by trying to transfer the burden of adjustments on some other actors placed in a less favorable position.

The restructuring phase, which is to lead to the new technical system, is adding a new dose of competitive pressures. The stakes are this time enormous. The problem is, of course, as already indicated, to find a way out of the crisis, but the objective is also to be among first to occupy the good places, where it will be possible to reap the cumulative benefits linked with the new technical system. In order to get there -- taking account of the relatively high indeterminacy of the new technical system -- important efforts have to be made on broad fronts. As a consequence, the resources to be affected are very important.

In other words, if the expected benefits are likely to be quite important, the required resources and the risks involved are equally important. It is thus necessary to try to increase the chances for being in a good position and for reaping the largest share of the expected cake.

Several lines of rivalries are interfering with each other: rivalries between countries, between firms, between capitals, and so on; but, within those complex games, the rivalries between countries do appear to be the most decisive ones and may remain so.

Of course, conflict-cooperation relations are eventually substituted for pure conflict relations, while the actors (enterprises or countries) may be trying to reduce the risks or to increase their chances.

We cannot enter here into the analysis of those complex games.

Let me only say that, at the international level, the technological race can be characterized as follows :

o   Japan is obviously ahead along the path likely to lead to a new technical system. Its position at the front line is based on a higher degree of control of information technologies and services. Accumulation processes are under way, which can get Japan effectively out of the crisis, unless the counteroffensives of the United States succeed in blocking this process. But this doesn't appear to be very likely.

o   The situation of the United States looks paradoxical. They have undoubtedly the largest scientific and technological potential. But they don't succeed in transforming this potential in decisive technical and productive advances and are beaten by the Japanese on their way to the emergence of a new technical system. This paradox -- which some observers are qualifying with the term of *deindustrialization* -- refers to a whole services of reasons (the excessive importance of military expenditures, the possibility to live above the real standard of living, speculation, and so on). Of course, the United States are attempting by all means to take the lead again and to regain their dominant position. The reduction of the value of the United States dollar is likely, while reducing the competitiveness of Japan and blocking Europe, to assure the effective takeoff of high tech activities. This may be possible, to the extent that the technological potential is supported by information-intensive service activities whose restructuring is already well advanced in the United States.[3]

o   Europe is rather significantly behind in the field of information technologies as well as in the restructuring of information-intensive service activities. In other words, in the course of the transition, Europe has, in a few years, been outpaced.

o   A limited number of NICs, still taking benefit of productivity surpluses through the exploitation of the "former" technical system, seem able to keep pace. But the road is narrow, because both the technological potential and the development of information-intensive service activities are quite limited. But these countries are rapidly developing both.

o   The large majority of developing countries -- which have already lost during the 1980s a large part of their earlier industrial achievements -- are likely to be left behind in the technological race. They have neither the required potential nor the necessary resources for developing such potential. As a consequence, they are, for most of them, unable to reach the new emerging technical system. The distance between the most advanced industrial countries and the developing countries has, as a matter of fact, never been so big.

In this context, it can be said that Europe (more or less according to the different countries) is lagging behind, in technological evolution as well as in the field of services.

Taking account of this, Europe is engaged in an ambitious catching-up process.

Two important conditions are met. The first is general mobilization: the actual acceleration of the integration process has put an end to "Europessimism" and is in the process of eliminating series of barriers; the second is the availability of the required resources: Europe is allocating rapidly increasing resources in order to develop cooperation.

I have, however, many doubts as to the feasibility of such a catching-up process. The position of the follower is necessarily uncomfortable. The leading country is reaping the profits, is taking benefit of cumulative processes, and is defining the norms. For that reason, it is always difficult, or even impossible, for the followers to make profitable the resources and efforts they have to engage in these catching-up attempts.

I would like finally to insist on the stakes which the development of service activities actually represent. As already indicated, what is at stake is not the development of services in general, but -- taking account of what has been said above about the various possible explanations of the growth of services -- the information-intensive activities, which represent, within the various production processes, new ways of doing things in the production sphere.

The main hypothesis here -- to a large extent confirmed by the observations made regarding both the lead taken by Japan and the advances seen in the United States -- is that the restructuring of the new technical system rests not only on a number of new technologies but on the complementarity of these technologies and of the information-intensive service activities.

It would be completely wrong to consider those service activities as something which, some way or another, is superimposed on the efficient impact of the new technologies. They have to be seen not only as a basic component of the new technical system, but as part of the essence of the system through which fundamental consistency requirements can be satisfied.

The idea here -- based, of course, on observations relative to the productivity of services which appears to be "indirect" in the case of the information-intensive activities (see De Bandt, 1989) -- is that those service activities are playing, within the trial and error processes which are to lead to the new technical system, a decisive role in facing the increasing complexity of production systems, in mastering the large volumes of information which have to be integrated, and thus in restructuring the production processes.

It is from this angle that the fact that Europe is lagging behind must be seen. While Europe has been rather unsuccessful in entering the electronics and information age -- probably because Europe has been sticking too long to the "old" technical system -- maybe more important is the fact that Europe, on the way toward the new technical system, has not yet really succeeded in entering the "nonmaterial" or information age.

The technological gaps, which are significant, can be defined in terms of years and/or resources. In these fields, it would seem possible -- this is at least what the decision makers, both at the level of government and in the big enterprises are thinking -- not necessarily to catch up completely, but to reach significant performances, on the condition that the required resources be allocated.

On the opposite, the gap in the field of services or non-material services is structural and important. Too attached to a technician view of production, most actors have difficulties imagining that information can be transformed into goods and services.

This means that there is something like a cultural gap.[4]

Two final remarks have to be added.

First, giving priority to the techniques, Europe has not (re)oriented the training systems as a function of the requirements of the information society. The training systems -- heritage as they are of the past -- have not been moving together with the technical and production systems. The discrepancies are today very large between supplies and demands, but the decision makers don't seem to perceive the transformations underway.

At the same time, the European enterprises have continued to rationalize production technically -- and thus to try reducing costs and to eliminate jobs -- instead of investing in human resources and "gray matter." Second, when the actors will have taken due notice of this gap and of the stakes at hand, it will appear difficult to make the necessary nonmaterial investments. This is because of the fact that, placed in relatively unfavorable competitive conditions compared to the other developed countries, the European countries are likely to be obliged to be continuously looking for price competitiveness through rationalization, having thus no possibility to mobilize the resources required for strategies aiming at developing the required services and human resources.

Notes

1. This is only a very general presentation; it is not possible, within the framework of this short Chapter, to go into the methodological questions raised by this prospective analysis.

2. We consider here the final consumption of services directly by the consumer, independently of the consumption of goods. We do not consider either the indirect consumption of services "included" in the goods or the consumption of services tied with that of goods.

3. The integration of a service component in the Uruguay Round discussions can be seen as an attempt to build on the superiority of the United States in this field.

4. It is something of a paradox to think that Europe, considered as the birthplace of culture and civilization, may have difficulties in entering the information age, for cultural reasons.

References

De Bandt, J. "Can we measure productivity in services activities?" In A. Bressand and K. Nicolaïdis, *Strategic Trends in Services* New York: Harper & Row, 1989.

Chapter 6

Stagnation and Competition in the European Economy

H.w. de Jong

University of Amsterdam

In this Chapter, it is argued that European economic
performance, which was on a high level in the fifties and sixties,
has given way in the seventies and early eighties. However
measured, the European economy showed a deteriorating absolute
performance and, in comparison with its major competitors, the
United States and Japan, exhibited *relative stagnation*. The
growth of output declined to a level below the average of the past
hundred or so years, investment stagnated, unemployment rose,
profitability fell, and new opportunities were missed or picked up
rather late. The main explanation for this disappointing
performance of the past 15 years has been the shift from free to
controlled competition. Under free competition, entrepreneurs,
who are the prime movers of the market process, get the
opportunities to create added-value, while established firms have
to imitate and emulate them and ultimately to rearrange their
processes or to disappear from the market. By means of a
restructuring of their activities, they would be equipped to renew
the economic process and to improve economic performance. This

sequence of events is shown schematically in the concept of the competitive cycle (Figure 6-1). However, in Europe, controlled competition blockaded a sufficiently fast restructuring and resulted in relative stagnation. Under controlled competition, the effects of the free entrepreneurial moves are prevented from working out or those moves themselves are suppressed and restrained. The main elements here have been public regulation in its myriad forms, private combinations in maturing markets, supported by subsidies and protection, and inflexible labor market institutionalism. Thus, the competitive cycle was blocked, restrained, or prevented from smoothly running, depending on the relevant market. Of recent years, it has dawned upon European opinion that controlled competition offers no solution to the problems of the future. European competitiveness was threatened, both in advanced and in low-demand sectors. The key to the prevention of relative stagnation degenerating into absolute stagnation has to be sought in a restructuring of the economy so that free, entrepreneurial competition is restored. Important steps were already taken to effectuate this goal, but more has to be done. Restructuring means not only the creation of a unified European market but also instituting an enterprise culture.

THE EC ECONOMY: SOME COMPARATIVE DATA

Figures 6-2,6-3 and 6-4 show that the indicators for the main *macroeconomic aggregates* were not favorable during the eighties for the European economy. The real gross domestic product grew at a slower rate in Europe than in the United States or Japan. Also, between 1973 and 1987, the average real rate of growth of the gross domestic product of the EC countries was barely 2 percent, below the long-term average of 2.28 percent (1870-1979); industrial output has scarcely risen, as against some 20 percent growth in both the other economies, and the unemployment rate has stuck in Europe at over 10 percent, in comparison with less than 6 percent in the United States and some 3 percent in Japan. Gross fixed capital formation in Europe was level between 1972 and 1986, as against a 65 percent increase in the United States and a 55 percent rise in Japan (E.C. 1987, 45 Annex 8). Figure 6-5 compares the profitability of investment by business in the United States and the EC. The period is 1960-1984, and though the trend in both economies is similar, the positions have been reversed since 1974. In the sixties and early seventies, EC profitability of investments was, on average, higher than in the United States; since 1974 the United States leads. These figures derive from a study made by J. Mortensen of the EC Commission, making use of some national and international studies undertaken in the main member states. These shifts in relative profitability coincide with, and make plausible, the reversed direction of foreign direct investments and acquisitions: in the sixties, the trend was toward Europe; since 1975, toward the United States.

Figure 6-1.   THE COMPETITION-CYCLE

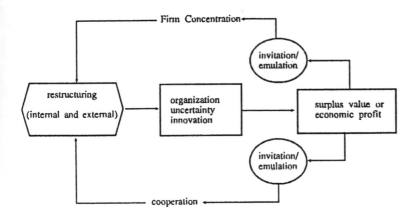

Table 6-1. BREAKDOWN OF BIG INDUSTRIAL COMPANIES BY SECTOR OF ACTIVITY

SECTOR	EUROPE						JAPAN AND ASIA						AMERICA					
	No	Persons employed '000	%	Turnover US bn $	%	R	Nb	Persons employed '000	%	Turnover US bn $	%	R	Nb	Persons employed '000	%	Turnover US bn $	%	R
1. Foods	40	1650.1	14	147.4	13	4.7	20	171.2	5.2	41.1	6.7	1.7	58	1726.0	13	197.4	11.7	5.1
2. Auto's	21	1939.7	17	183.5	16	1.3	21	594.1	18	130.9	21.3	2.7	20	1705.1	13.0	240.7	14.3	3.6
3. Craft	6	227.8	2.0	18.7	1.6	2.1	0	0.0	0.0	0.0	0.0	0.0	18	1187.6	9.1	114.8	6.8	3.0
4. Chem.	38	1902.3	17	189.0	16	3.0	38	458.9	14.0	84.2	13.7	2.0	87	1581.2	12	206.6	12.3	4.1
5. Electr.	15	1708.1	15	107.3	9.2	2.7	19	1046.3	32	150.5	2.1	2.1	48	2150.5	17	186.5	11.1	3.3
6. Inform.	12	322.1	2.8	38.0	3.3	-1	8	202.4	6.1	25.8	4.2	3.2	41	1454.5	11	145.1	8.6	6.3
7. Mecha.	21	716.3	0.2	54.3	4.6	2.7	12	305.1	9.3	38.0	6.2	0	38	616.7	4.7	56.8	3.4	0.0
8. Petr.	29	685.5	6.0	234.0	20.0	3.3	13	103.5	3.1	71.4	11.6	2.6	34	1006.6	7.7	345.3	20.5	2.5
9. PHA	8	248.1	2.2	22.7	1.9	7.4	7	58.7	1.8	12.1	2.0	3.1	25	624.1	4.8	71.0	4.2	11
10. Steel	44	2104.8	18	175.5	15.0	-1	17	348.5	11	61.0	9.9	1.5	62	1000.0	7.7	118.6	7.1	-2
Sub-total	234	11504.8	100	1170.4	100	2.6	155	3288.7	100	615.0	100	1.9	430	13052.4	100	1682.8	100	3.7
Others	66	2798.3		169.6			10	86.5		21.7			105	1839.8		155.8		
	300	14303.1		1340.0			165	3375.2		636.7			535	14892.2		1838.6		
Average		47.700		4.47				20.456		3.86				27.836		3.86		

Note: R denotes profitability on sales.

Source: R. Linda, EC Commission (1987).

Tables 6-1 and 6-2 highlight some features of large-scale European business. In table 6-1 the 1,000 largest enterprises in the United States, Europe, and Japan are grouped in 10 large industrial sectors under headings of employment, turnover, and profitability. Of the 1,000 largest firms, the United States is the origin of more than half of them, Europe of 300, and Japan and other countries in East Asia of 165 firms.

Table 6-2.   DISTRIBUTION OF THE 50 LARGEST
               COMPANIES IN THE WORLD
               (N=Number, S=Sales, P=Profits)

TOTALS	1979			1983			1986		
	N	S	P	N	S	P	N	S	P
United States	22	539.7	27.6	23	678.4	35.9	21	668.4	28.5
Europe	20	375.2	17.7	20	422.2	8.9	20	469.6	13.1
Japan	6	75.0	2.1	5	79.8	2.8	6	131.8	4.1
Others	2	24.4	3.7	2	32.4	0.5	3	45	2.6
World total	50	1014.3	51.2	50	1212.9	46.7	50	1314.8	48.3

AVERAGES	1979			1983			1986		
	N	S	P	N	S	P	N	S	P
United States	22	24.5	1.25	23	29.5	1.56	21	31.4	1.36
Europe	20	18.8	0.89	20	21.1	0.45	20	23.5	0.66
Japan	6	12.5	0.35	5	16	0.56	6	22.0	0.68
Others	2	12.2	1.85	2	16.2	0.25	3	15.0	0.87
World Average	50	20.3	1.02	50	24.2	0.93	50	26.3	0.97
European share (% of world total)	40	37	35	40	35	19	40	36	27

Source: Based on Fortune, "The Largest Industrial
          Companies in the World."

A few things should be noted:

o   employment in the 536 U.S. firms is about the same as in the 300 European firms but their sales are 37 percent higher.

o   European large firms are on average somewhat larger than
     U.S. firms in terms of employment or sales, but their
     profitability lags behind that of large U.S. firms, though
     not behind that of large Japanese companies.

o   In 9 out of 10 large industrial sectors, U.S. large firms
     surpass their European and Japanese competitors. In
     sectors such as automobiles, aircraft, electronics,
     information technology, petroleum and pharmaceuticals,
     the U.S. large firms are distinctly more important than the
     European firms, in terms of profits.

o   Japanese large business is, comparatively speaking, of
     importance only in electronics, with a much larger
     turnover than in Europe, a similar rate of profits, but
     lower employment, which means a higher productivity per
     person. The foregoing remarks indicate that it is not so
     much size as productivity and value-added in which
     European firms underperform.

     Europe stands out in sectors like steel and mechanical
industry, of which the first, in particular, is of dubious value,
given the negative rate of return and the severe overmanning.

     Table 6-2 gives the distribution of the 50 largest companies
in the world, in terms of numbers, sales, and profits. As the last
row indicates, the performance of the European firms is below
average, and profitability has declined between 1979 and 1986.

Figure 6-2.   STANDARDIZED UNEMPLOYMENT RATES

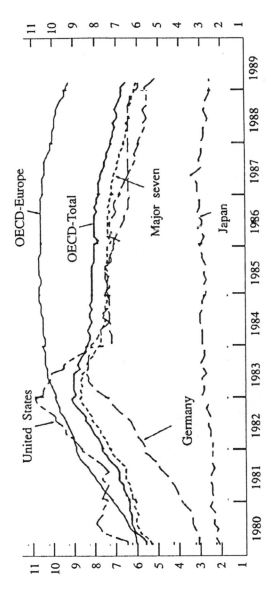

If we look to developments in small business, the European statistics are not pleasant reading either. Between the middle sixties and the years 1982-1985, the net growth of European small business was in total between 0 and 10 percent, with varying rates according to countries and regions. In northern Europe (Sweden, Denmark, the Netherlands, Belgium, Northern Germany, Northern England) net growth was negative or zero. In middle- and southern Europe (Southern Germany, Switzerland, France, Italy) there was more of a positive increase, but rates of growth in net firm formation were at best between 1 and 2 percent per annum. Contrast this European performance with that of the United States or Japan where net firm growth in the same period (middle sixties to early eighties) has been of the order of 30 to 40 percent, or over 2 percent p.a. on average. Net firm growth over such long periods accounts for births and deaths of firms, acquisitions and takeovers, withdrawals and the creation of large-firm subsidiaries, though the latter are quantitatively unimportant in comparison with the net growth of independent small firms. Therefore, this indicator can be used as a measure of entrepreneurial activity in the small and medium firm sectors because it reflects the development of the population of firms who are successful. The implications of a rising firm population for an economy are mainly twofold.

First, net firm growth creates employment, because on average a new firm that succeeds in business gives employment to some three to five employees directly and to one person indirectly. Since the middle seventies large companies have lost employment, in Europe as well as in the United States. In the latter country, for example, employment with the 500 largest U.S. firms was 15 million man/years in 1977; by 1984, it had receded to 14 million. Total employment in the EC was in 1984 on exactly the same level as in 1960, namely, 105 million man/years. U.S. employment, however, had increased from 65 million man/years to nearly 100 million man/years during the same period.

Figure 6-3.   INDUSTRIAL PRODUCTION AND LEADING INDICATORS

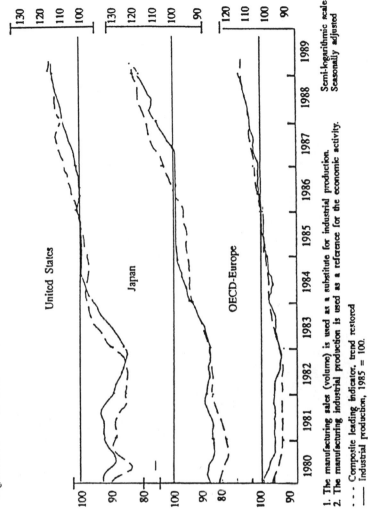

1. The manufacturing sales (volume) is used as a substitute for industrial production.
2. The manufacturing industrial production is used as a reference for the economic activity.

- - - Composite leading indicator, trend restored
—— Industrial production, 1985 = 100.

Semi-logarithmic scale
Seasonally adjusted

Figure 6-4.   GROSS DOMESTIC PRODUCT S.A.

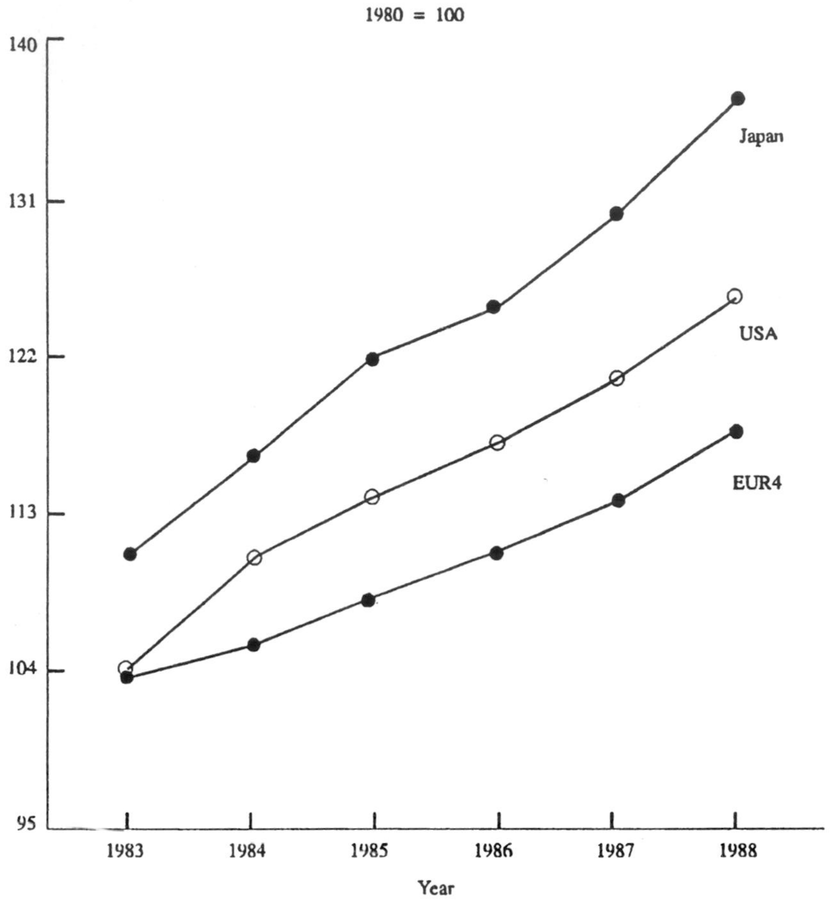

1980 = 100

Figure 6-5. Return on Investment, in Percent
for the EC and United States

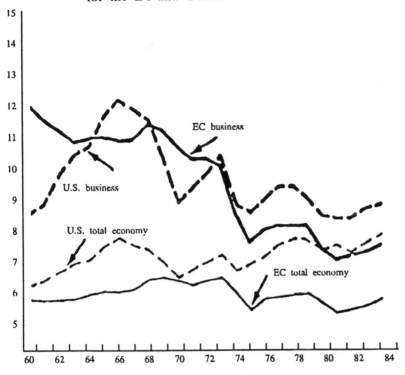

Source: EC (1984)

Second, one further implication of this failure of small business to create employment in Europe was that unemployment in Europe crept upward during the eighties, whereas the United States unemployment rate fell to about half the European rate. The costs of this differential both in terms of direct burdens (unemployment compensation, subsidies, and so on) as well as, indirectly, in terms of lost output, are appreciable.

In summary, macroeconomic indicators such as the growth of gross domestic product, industrial production, investment and employment, declining profitability in large business and the lackluster performance of small business in Europe converge to a similar pattern, which can be best be described as *relative stagnation*. Relative stagnation is no standstill: growth in an absolute sense is present in many sectors, and, in particular, as table 6-1 makes clear, European performance in several large branches of industry is satisfactory or good. In foods and drinks, motorcars, chemicals and pharmaceuticals, mechanical industry and petroleum, large European firms have more or less equivalent sales and profits to their American counterparts and easily outperform similar large Japanese businesses.

But relative stagnation also means a double disadvantage in comparison with the two major competitors. On the one hand, the share of the "low-demand" sectors (to use EC terminology) such as steel, textiles, clothing, and construction materials in the domestic market is high in Europe in comparison with the United States (though not if Japan is taken as a yardstick) whereas the share of the "high-demand" sectors was relatively lower than in the United States and Japan, as the EC Commission's study on competitiveness and industrial structures (1987, pp. 7 et seq.) brought forward. Consequently, the Community, with 44 percent of the combined population has only 33 percent of the market for high technology products, where growth, investments, and profits are above average; the United States with 37 percent of combined population represents 42 percent of the "high-demand" sectors, whereas for Japan the comparable figures are 19 percent and 25

percent, respectively. Relative stagnation also manifests itself in a
poor export performance in advanced goods and a rising import
penetration in those goods. The penetration rates -- that is, total
imports as a percentage of domestic demand -- for the period
1972-1984 are shown in Table 6-3.

Table 6-3 THE SHARE OF IMPORTS IN TOTAL DEMAND
(percent)

	Europe		United States		Japan	
	'72	'84	'72	'84	'72	'84
High-demand goods	9.7	16.5	5.8	11.0	4.0	4.8
Med.-demand goods	6.4	8.1	5.7	7.7	4.0	3.8
Low-demand goods	9.0	12.2	7.0	10.6	4.9	5.2

Source: EC 1987, pp. 50-52.

The European export market share in high-demand goods
deteriorated in those ten years, whereas that of Japan and the
United States improved. The Japanese export share rose most in
medium-demand goods, the European share in low-demand goods.
Thus, the relative stagnation in goods production which became
visible already in the early eighties is well documented.

In services -- where there are many obstacles to
international trade -- the situation is, however, less onerous for
the EC which has a relatively strong position in producer services.
Relative stagnation may be shown graphically by constructing the
sector profiles of economies, through the addition of the development stages of an economy's sectors (figure 6-6). Overall,
advanced sectors have a higher added-value, and show their peaks
more to the left in the figure, whereas medium- and low-demand
sectors have lower added-values and show peaks more to the right.
The European sector profile curve shows a tendency to move
toward the medium stage of development whereas the United

States   and Japanese curves tend to have peaks in the advanced stage.   The Japanese economy, as we noted earlier, besides being strong in high-demand sectors, also has a proportionately large share in low-demand sectors; that is, it exhibits a double peak, or saddle-type.   Note also that the United States peak in the advanced-stage sectors is more broadly based than in Japan, in accordance with the facts shown in table 6-1.

The Japanese competitive advantage is therefore (at least up till now) more narrowly based, and the task lying in store for that economy is to convert its lagging sectors (steel, shipbuilding, textiles, housing, construction and materials, agriculture, and so on) into advanced ones.

The picture as given by figure 6-6 is confirmed by tables 6-4 and 6-5 both based on data as provided by the European Commission.   Table 6-4 gives the dimensions of the domestic markets of the three economies in 1982.   The domestic market was figured out as output plus imports minus exports, and several sectors were distinguished, grouped in high-demand, medium-demand, and low-demand sectors (EC 1987, 47, annex 10). Putting the average representation for these sectors of the three economies combined at 100, the distribution is shown in table 6-4.

Table 6-4 REPRESENTATION OF SECTOR PROFILES
              (percent)

	Europe	U.S.	Japan
High-demand sectors	88.4	103.4	114.3
Med-demand sectors	105.4	109.3	75.3
Low-demand sectors	100.2	86.2	123.3

Source: EC 1987, 47 Annex 10. (by dividing
sector shares through overall economy shares).

Table 6-5 shows a decline in net added value since the middle seventies in all three economies, but especially in Japan.

Table 6-5 GROSS AND NET ADDED REAL VALUES AS RELATED TO THE NATIONAL PRODUCT 1960-1984

	Europe		United States		Japan	
	GAV	NAV	GAV	NAV	GAV	NAV
1960-1964	24.8	15.1	27.5	16.1	23.9	10.8
1965-1969	25.9	15.3	28.1	17.4	29.2	14.7
1970-1974	25.4	14.5	25.7	13.8	27.1	12.6
1975-1979	23.7	11.8	26.8	13.4	18.6	4.8
1980-1984	23.6	10.7	26.5	12.0	17.2	2.8

Source: Derived from tables in Appendix II. EC (1984).

This general decline probably reflects intensified world competition, but also capital deepening, as shown by the discrepancies between Gross Added Value (GAV) and Net Added Value (NAV). Although the low levels for GAV and NAV in the case of Japan may be overstated by the undervalued yen of those years (1975-1984), both tables support the picture of figure 6-6.

The European prospect follows clearly from figure 6-6: the EC needs to enlarge its high-demand sector shares and to reduce its still substantial medium- to low-demand sector shares. With respect to the first, it risks lagging behind the United States and Japanese advanced sectors. With respect to the latter, it risks (like Japan) being attacked by newly industrializing countries. How should this task be accomplished? The answer depends on the diagnosis of the causes that have brought about the present situation and upon the analysis of the ways advanced market economies work.

ENTREPRENEURIAL ACTIVITY AND CONTROLLED COMPETITION

In contrast to neoclassical, Keynesian, or Marxist theory, market theory, which focuses the attention on the interaction between structure and process, has traditionally emphasized the central role of the entrepreneur in the course of the market process. More than 230 years ago, the French-Irish economist Richard Cantillon wrote in his *Essay on the Nature of Trade* (1755) that the production and exchange of goods and services are set in motion and are being propelled by entrepreneurs, but in an uncertain way.[1] Entrepreneurs combine the resources they need, such as labor, capital, materials, transport, and distribution facilities, in the quantities and qualities they need and contract at prices which are fixed ex ante. Output, in the large majority of cases, has to be sold at fluctuating prices and the quantities produced likewise cannot be fixed beforehand. Thus, revenues ex post of the production process are uncertain. Yet, entrepreneurs are the prime movers of the market process.

Elements of Entrepreneurship

Later economic theories have added several important elements to this initial characterization of the entrepreneurial function. Neoclassical theory, before it assumed the static features of which it is so pregnant presently, and in particular Alfred Marshall emphasized the *organizational ability* of the firm's leader(s).[2] The most efficient combination of resources would bring about a reduction in average costs per unit of output, and, at a given output price and a satisfactory rate of utilization of those resources, a high rate of profitability would result. Organization for efficient production would tend to favor large-scale enterprise, though small- and medium-sized firms could survive by means of adroit product differentiation and specialization in remaining corners of the market. For half a century or more the economies of scale argument in favor of large firms had a central position in European thinking.

The theory explaining the entrepreneurial function by means of *uncertainty* got a new push in the interwar period, when a distinction was made between risk and uncertainty by Frank Knight (1921). Risks are insurable if they occur regularly and can be grouped or bundled; thus, in several cases (fires, price fluctuations of raw materials, foreign exchange rates are some examples) the risks connected with their occurrence can be converted into costs through payment of premiums. Those risks which can not be so treated are the "pure uncertainties" and it is the function of the entrepreneur to face them, internalize them, bear the responsibilities, and earn profits from an efficient handling of those pure types of uncertainties.

Schumpeter -- the main author in the third tradition -- stresses the *innovative element*. A combination of resources which is objectively new and by means of which a new product, a new production process, or a new type of organization is introduced, secures simultaneously profits for those firms who introduce the innovations and losses for those firms who are loath to do so. This is the process of "creative destruction" going on in market economies and giving rise to investment waves and economic cycles of various duration.

These elements of organization, pure uncertainty, and innovation are important in understanding the entrepreneurial function and the market process; however, it may well be questioned whether they can be rated as more than necessary conditions. Organizational ability may be indispensable for the efficiency of a firm, but as such it does not secure profitability: the most perfect organization can be upset through the unforeseen developments of markets, in particular the actions of competitors, and result in a loss-making affair. Also, organizational capacities can be hired, the expenditure of which may then be reckoned as a cost. It is the owner of a firm, hiring the organizational capacities of a competent manager, who nevertheless pockets the firm's net profits or losses.

The element of uncertainty is unmeasurable, which implies that the rate of profit is undetermined; also, if the entrepreneurial function was determined exclusively by uncertainty, the activity of the entrepreneur would, in principle, equally result in profits as well as in losses. However, in nine out of ten years, businesses are able to make profits, which leaves at least the largest part of them unexplained. Again, innovations, however important they may be for the long-run development of many firms, fail to explain the sometimes appreciable profits earned because of brands, entry barriers, institutional arrangements, and exogenous circumstances, which may cause monopoly rents and windfall profits (e.g., in the oil industry between 1975 and 1985). It is part and parcel of the entrepreneurial function to anticipate, to cope with, and to benefit from these circumstances, which may have little relationship with innovative activity.

Value Creation and Regulated Competition

If we do view the three elements mentioned as necessary but not sufficient conditions, the missing link may be provided by the entrepreneur's ability to create surplus value by means of such a varying combination of resources that the output value of production is higher than the value of the inputs. A lower valued combination is turned into a higher valued result because someone sees the opportunity to benefit from such a value conversion while others are altogether blind for it or arrive too late on the spot. In a number of cases, entrepreneurs do *make* a market by means of their innovative actions; in many more cases, they *follow* the trends in market demand, riding on the wave generated earlier or caused by exogenous factors. In reverse, those exogenous factors may restrain entrepreneurial activity through a reduction or even the elimination of the opportunities available to effectuate the creation of surplus value. In other words, the supply of entrepreneurial capacities -- most probably distributed according to a frequency curve in normal societies -- may well be available in a given society, but it can be suppressed by rules, traditions, and institutions limiting full operation. In the most extreme cases -- those of the command economies of the Eastern bloc -- the negative effects on the process of surplus value creation are visible in whole economies, because central planning subdues the free initiatives and blocks the value creation process. Still, the mixed economies, such as were built up in postwar Europe and especially during the seventies, as well as the nationalistic interferences with the market process within the emerging Common Market, likewise have contributed to this raising of the barriers to entrepreneurship. It is noteworthy that those barriers derive from power and the exercise of power in opposition to the freedom of economic activity: insurance companies are prohibited by force to effect direct transactions in foreign countries, airlines are forbidden to open new routes between member states, shops are not allowed to be open beyond certain hours, bids from foreign telecommunications equipment suppliers are refused, foreign car registrations are limited, goods and services are subsidized, cheap imports prohibited, and so on. So the real controversy is between entrepreneurial value creation and the restraints to such activity based on power, that is, between free and controlled competition. European society nowadays -- in contrast to the decades following the postwar period -- is full of those power-induced restraints, based on state, municipal, labor union, and other interest groups, including, last but not least, those of vested managerial positions.

Remedial Movements

If an economy suffers from a lack of entrepreneurial initiatives, if such initiatives are blockaded or are made too costly by interventions, it should be visible in relative stagnation. In reverse, economic stagnation in a relative sense is a sure sign that the market process is blocked. Controlled competition means that the economic structures are not commensurate to the market processes which are increasingly of an international nature. Steps have been taken to rearrange a number of insufficient European structures or such restructurings have been announced. Let us briefly review them before paying attention to the trends in the new dimensions of international competition.

1.   Since the early eighties a broad movement has manifested itself with respect to the role of the state in the European economies. After more than half a century of growing state intervention and increasing public ownership it was increasingly recognized that the state is not a good entrepreneur. In the prosperous years of the fifties, sixties, and early seventies, state enterprises achieved a much lower rate of profitability than private firms and did not pioneer new economic activities -- or only exceptionally when they could behave autonomously as did IRI and ENI in Italy. When adverse times came -- as since 1973-1974 -- many nationalized firms ran into heavy losses and were far from being able to stabilize the economy, through countercyclical investments, as had been proclaimed by their proponents. Instead, in countries like Britain, Italy, Spain, and France, public enterprise of the non-monopoly type became a drag on the beleaguered state finances. Whereas state deficits in the EC rose from zero to 5 percent of the GDP between the early seventies and the early eighties, state investments declined from 4.1 percent to 2.9 percent of GDP. In addition, the force of international (technological) competition made the choice unavoidable between a massive modernization program for public enterprise or a sliding back into obsolescence. Starting with Britain, several European states opted for a large-scale privatization, which meant an important restructuring (De Jong, 1989).

2.   Spurred on by businessmen's initiatives, the EC came to realize that the inner European deadlock, based on protectionism, subsidization, and nationalistic exclusivity, could not continue indefinitely without causing

irreparable damage. The breakthrough came with the ratification of the Single European Act in July 1987, imposing a system of majority voting within the Community. Since then, the air is full of promises, fed recently by the Cecchini Report. This report puts the gains from a removal of trade and production barriers at some 2.5 percent of GDP, the gains from exploiting economies of scale more fully at 2.1 percent and the gains from intensified competition at some 1.6 percent, summing up to some 4.5-7 percent of GDP. Also, there would be the creation of additional employment and a downward pressure on prices and costs. Whatever the value of such estimates, the urge for free competition is valuable.

3. A third area where restructuring has been taking place is in the regrouping of business firms. Mergers, takeovers, management buyouts, joint ventures, R&D agreements and the like are increasing in importance (as figure 6-7 shows). The number of mergers and takeovers among the 1,000 largest European business firms has more than doubled between 1982 and 1987; likewise, the number of joint ventures has risen substantially. One should not be too rash in linking these activities to the prospect of a unified, free European market in 1992; these restructurings were well underway before the 1985 document on the Internal Market was published. Similar activity had -- somewhat earlier -- started in the United States. And third, as in all previous merger waves, the buying and selling of companies is not a general phenomenon but concentrated in a limited number of sectors: chemicals, mechanical industry, electronics, foods and drinks, publishing, and the financial sector (banking, insurance, brokerage). The explanation for this sudden increase in merger and takeover activity, therefore, has to be sought in the rising intensity of international competition, in accordance with the idea of the competitive cycle: mergers, takeovers, and joint ventures

are a reaction against the increasing pressures of international competition, in periods when a relative measure of price stability prevails and the prospects for business are positive. It would be difficult otherwise to square the three basic, firmly documented tendencies of such firm restructurings: first, that mergers and takeovers tend to occur in waves (1890-1910; the twenties and the sixties and, now, since 1982); second, that they occur disproportionately strongly in particular sectors of industry; and third, that merger intensity rises with the size of the firm. However, it is not true that mergers and takeovers are always successful. The evidence we possess indicates a heavy failure rate; perhaps up to 40 to 50 percent. The explanation may be that businessmen -- especially during merger waves -- are incompletely informed about the firms they buy and pay too much for them. Also, they may be inclined to "entertain the absurd presumption to believe in their own good fortune," as Adam Smith said long ago, underrating the difficulties of effectively combining several firms, especially when they operate in different trades.

4.   A fourth area of restructuring is closely connected with the internal organization of large firms. Periods of rising intensity of competition bring about, or at least go parallel with, structural breaks in the development of branches of industry. Then, big companies are finding themselves in dangerous waters: overcapacity, innovations, and shifts in relevant markets bring about crosscurrents in market demand, of which it is difficult to predict the future trends. Such uncertainties provoke a number of different responses:

     o   a "back-to-the-core" of the business mood, inspiring sell-offs of noncore parts as well as purchases of businesses which can be fitted into the core.

Figure 6-6.   Sector Profiles of the Three Major Economies

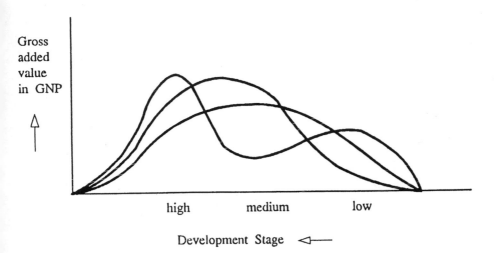

Gross
added
value
in GNP

high   medium   low

Development Stage   ⟵——

Figure 6-7. MERGERS IN THE EEC, 1973-1988

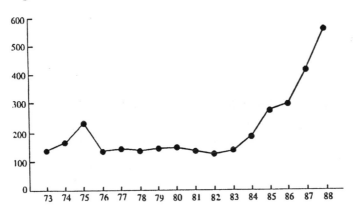

Source: EC Competition Policy Reports

o   some diversification where it has become clear that the original main business has no future; also speculative purchases occur, mostly by adventurous entrepreneurs.

o   decentralization of too centralized structures: the "flat organization," with the much reduced overhead costs as well as the promotion of so-called endogenous competition, that is, competition between similar companies or plants within the same group (de Jong, 1986, pp. 93-95).

o   vertical disintegration, a pruning of suppliers and the promotion of management buyouts.

Such measures aimed to streamline the often top-heavy organizational structures of groups, by instituting decentralization and responsible profit centers at the level of the firm. A case in point would be the Coats Viyella group, Europe's largest textile business, which, after the merger between Coats Patons with Vantona Viyella in 1986, faced the challenge to create a management structure capable of steering a huge group. A three-tier structure was adopted, in which each of the 250 subsidiaries is run by a managing director, reporting to a divisional head. The divisional head, in turn, sits on the main board. Every company is now a profit center in its own right (*Financial Times* , September 3, 1988). The whole operation is meant to improve the process and the group's performance, necessary to cope with the increased competition.

SECTORAL COMPETITION

So far I have discussed the idea of the competitive cycle at the macro and micro levels. However, it is probably most applicable to the sectoral level. Let me illustrate this with a most modern branch of industry, which a few years ago generated high hopes of rosy prospects with "the factory of the future," that is, manufacturing automation equipment. These comprise computers used on the shop floor, in production control and engineering (CAD/CAM systems), robots, and automated guided vehicles, flexible manufacturing systems, and so on, which are sold to the motorcar industry, aerospace companies, electrical and electronics firms, as well as the software and service companies linked to them. This automation market has grown fast since the seventies, but suppliers coming from all quarters rose even more. There are large integrated producers in this market like Siemens, Matsushita, and Toshiba, but also machine tool makers, computer manufacturers, software houses, process and contract engineering companies, process control suppliers, and the like. This is not different from other industries in their early years, but the crowding of suppliers has meant tough competition, narrow profit margins, and many failures and withdrawals. Now, volatile alliances are being formed to take on large projects by combining several specialists in temporary partnerships. Increasingly also, takeovers and permanent joint ventures are underway. They may aim at (1) securing a dominant position, in one or more sections of the market, (2) increasing the spread of capabilities, (3) building up networks with linkages to other manufacturers to cover a wide field of activities (e.g., IBM selling Dassault designed CAD/CAM systems, or the IBM-Measurex joint venture). The best position would be to become the dominant systems integrator of several specialists for big projects.

This discussion of the manufacturing automation industry highlights the importance of both market share and the surplus value of the product or system. The latter is based on the differentiation that a supplier can achieve in comparison with competitors, resting on innovation, superior quality, a systems product, a brand reputation, or technical specialty. The differentiation gives the producer an advantage in the eyes of the buyer/consumer and is expressed in a positive price differential with respect to goods or services in the same category. But this price differential is not absolute: a lower relative price difference will give the supplier a larger market share because, given the quality advantage, buyers feel the good is cheaply priced. In reverse, a high price differential restrains the supplier's market share.

There is, consequently, a tradeoff between market share and the relative price difference of the respective goods/services, and, because buyers entertain divergent estimates of the surplus values involved, the relative price differences have no exactly determined magnitudes. They occur within bands, which themselves have a tendency to shift in time and with the course of events. Adroit entrepreneurs capitalize on these phenomena and choose their strategies accordingly.

The Tradeoff Between Market Share and Price Differential

On this basis, we can distinguish four main types of industries (figure 6-8). First, there are industries which produce standardized mass production goods with very modest differentiation possibilities, mostly in terms of sale (type A in figure 6-8). Demand for most of these goods in Western developed market economies is stagnating or declining, exceptionally slow growing. Steel, paper, cement, fertilizers, basic fibers, ethylenes and basic plastics as well as basic foodstuffs and standard cars offer examples. Overcapacity promoted by economic cycles is often a prolonged affair. For firms in such markets, the tradeoff between relative price and market share offers only slight possibilities for gains: a higher price than that of competing products will quickly reduce market share, and a seller's lower price is immediately followed by others. European producers in these industries therefore have to work hard on paring their costs, shift more production abroad, purchase parts and materials in cheaper countries, and increase automation. For example, Volkswagen at Wolfsburg has already 25 percent of the final assembly of "Golf" cars automated by means of computer-controlled, robot-equipped assembly lines. Also, the formation of partnerships as well as takeovers and mergers for consolidation purposes are important. Mass car producers in high-cost West Germany like Volkswagen,

Ford, and Opel import their small, low-profit margin cars wholly or partially from abroad, where labor costs are far lower. In contrast, BMW and Mercedes Benz who have upgraded quality cars for sale do not produce outside of their domestic market to preserve the quality differential. There is another dimension of competition in mass production type industries, particularly in fast growing sectors, and it is illustrated by the microchip industry. Over half of the semiconductor market is for standardized products, the so-called "commodity chips." There is some differentiation, namely, in different speed chips and in quality control at which the Japanese companies excel. Yet, with sharply rising R&D costs -- now estimated 15 percent of annual turnover -- and with soaring capital investments -- 30 percent of turnover is spent on new plant each year -- semiconductor companies have no choice but to increase their volume of sales to recoup these overhead costs.

Marginal costs of chips are, therefore, very low and keep falling, and competitive gluts are a recurring phenomenon in this highly cyclical industry. However, because the chip is an essential input to various consumer electronics, computers, and telecommunications, none of the big companies in those markets can leave chip production to the open market. Vertical integration compels them to join the race toward smaller, more powerful chips, and they are (1) restructuring, for example, in research-oriented tie-ups between Philips and Siemens or the merger between SGS of Italy with the semiconductor operations of Thomson of France; (2) increasing their pressure for government subsidies and protection; and (3) sidestepping the commodity market by the formation of ES2, the pan-European group, which aims to make semi-custom chips in limited volumes but with rapid turnaround times.

Figure 6-8.   THE TRADEOFF BETWEEN MARKET SHARE
                   AND RELATIVE PRICE DIFFERENCE

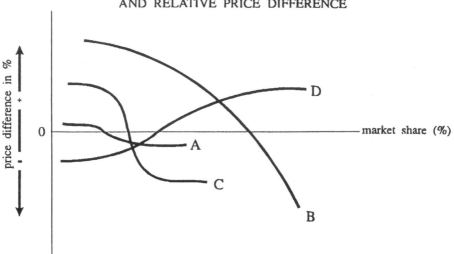

Second are the type of industries where products can be
differentiated (dotted C-line in figure 6-8).   Special foods and
drinks,   pharmaceuticals,   household   and   personal   products,
electrical domestic appliances are cases in point.   Within those
industries brands are all-important, because a well-established
brand is costly to achieve, takes a long time to build up, and has
the ability to command higher margins than commodity-type
products or goods sold under retailers' labels.   The costliness of
brands   results   from   the   high   television   advertising   rates,
advertising being necessary to persuade the large, multiple retail
chains to stock the goods.   A wide range of brands thus affords
manufacturers negotiating strength.

As a second factor, the internationalization of products and consumption habits and the wearing away of national and regional preferences is extending the relevant markets. To increase (or even hold) their market shares in these extending markets, branded goods producers would either have to (1) reduce sharply the relative price difference, which is costly and might spoil the whole game (figure 6-8, dotted line) or (2) build up new brands, which is time-consuming and insecure or (3) take over a company owning established brands. The latter way -- though not cheap either -- at least proceeds fast and includes few uncertainties, which is why the competition for those brand-owning companies has made so much headway in European and American markets. Generally such markets are stable; they do not grow fast, but belong to the medium range types which are broadly represented in the United States and European economies (figure 6-6). The entrepreneurial quest for surplus value and market share is therefore played by means of takeovers, several of them of the transatlantic type: Unilever buying Chesebrough Pond, BSN's acquisitions in pasta and dairy markets, the fights for the famous liquor brands, Nestle's and Suchard's battles over control of Cote d'Or and of Rowntrie, respectively, the Belgian and British producers of successful chocolate brands, and so on. (See R. Linda in de Jong (ed.), 1988.)

One encounters these strategies not only in goods production, but also when the service element increases or becomes dominant. The dilemma of growing by means of risky starts, unsuccessful price competition, or costly but fast takeovers or merger operations presents itself. Bertelsmann, the largest media group in the world, had a costly flop in the early eighties by trying to launch an American version of the glossy German magazine *Geo*. So in 1986, it bought Doubleday and RCA music in the United States. This was a jump, costing $800 million and boosting the group's sales by over one-third. Similarly, major accounting firms are merging into larger groups because the Continental type of firm -- being only auditors -- is under assault from the Anglo-American firm, offering a range of services: accounting, tax and business advisory work, systems work, and so on, besides auditing. With the spread of their multinational clients, networks have developed as loose groups, benefiting from referred work passing between national firms. Those groups could offer close control over the standards of operation of national member firms, but the next logical steps are international profit-sharing or even merger, as was the case in the Peat Marwick and KMG firms' creating KPMG, which was twice as large as its next rivals in Europe. Institutional rules, such as those of Consob, Italy's securities regulator, which rebuked Andersen earlier this year for offering other services than auditing to a bank, may delay the process, but are unlikely to hold it up.

The third type of industries are the systems products: type B in figure 6-8. In these types of industries, heavy entry barriers are important because the product in question is a system instead of an individual product. A system is a number of different products, linked into an operating whole, which means it is evaluated by users not only on the qualitative performance of the parts but also on the integrative value of the whole. Indeed the latter is more important and creates the surplus value. The prime example is IBM in the computer industry: IBM has not been the innovator of transistors, micro processors, semiconductors, personal computers and other breakthroughs, but the integrator, combining hardware, software, services and equipment into an operating system. The system creates heavy entry barriers: large capital requirements, captive customers because of their loyalty to the system, possibilities for price discrimination, nontransparency of markets, and the leasing of hardware instead of sales. The system, of course, has high overhead costs, but these are compensated for by a substantial market share and high profit margins. American companies, benefiting from a large domestic market, have been able to write off these overhead costs against massive sales, whereas European firms have had to operate in fragmented national markets. Systems products likewise work to their disadvantage in markets like telecommunications and pharmaceuticals. Once established, a system works like a glacier table, in which a rock is supported by frozen snow, melting away except for the column under the rock, which is protected by the rock's shadow. Ultimately, the sun's rays will also undermine the column as it grows longer but this may take quite some time. Thus, it took some 25 years to halve IBM's share of the total United States and European data processing markets to, respectively, 35 percent and 22 percent. In the meantime, the company made enormous profits, being the only one in the United States market to make profits until 1980. The tradeoff between market share and price differential in a systems market is like curve B in figure 6-8.

A systems market need not be the exclusive domain of huge, dominant firms. The Swiss watch industry offers the example of a combination of small to medium-sized firms, specialized in particular operations, joining together in common activities like marketing, training, cooling rooms (where watches are stored so as to preserve the fluidity of machine oils), buying operations, and the like.

Like the glacier table the private system economy may last long, but it will break down ultimately under the influence of a major innovation, which, like the sun's rays, cut the pillar from under the rock. In watches this was the invention of the digital watch, and in computers it may well have been Intel's Central Processing Unit, launched at the end of 1971, by means of which the microprocessor, combining switching, computing, and control in one small unit, revolutionized the industry.

These innovative assaults on systems products nearly always come from outside the industry. Why? Systems producers, because of the complexity of the system, the heavy entry barriers, and their attractive profits, have a tendency to develop monopolistic attitudes. They command markets (the Swiss had 70 percent of the world's market for watches) and are often lazy innovators. However, as private systems producers they can be contested and be forced to adapt, even though they are as mighty as IBM. With public systems producers like nationalized industries, the fourth category of industries (PTTs in their role of telecommunications suppliers, regulated airlines, and so on) it is different. Here the controlled competition preserves for them a nearly unassailable monopoly, and it has been made palatable to public opinion for a long time by speaking of "natural monopolies."

CONCLUSION

The implication of this concept is that the system as developed by these public organizations is unique and duplication of it would be immensely wasteful. So why competition? The remarkable fact is that these natural monopolies of a public nature show the same tradeoff curve (D, in figure 6-8) as the private, innovative firm: the higher the market share, the more they can raise the positive price differential. From a pure market point of view, the innovations of a free competitive market resemble the monopolies of controlled competition. But from a social point of view the difference is that the first open new roads, whereas the second close them. The first ones promise progress, the others lead up to relative stagnation. Again public telecommunications and regulated airlines in Europe underline my point. Whereas in limited national markets and with a relatively stable technology, one could speak of natural monopolies with some reason, current technical developments combined with market integration make this concept increasingly dubious. Therefore, liberalizing Europe's trade by means of the creation of a unified integrated market is only part of the answer. It should be complemented by deregulation and privatization of large parts of European public enterprise. Only free competition can break the European predicament.

Notes

1. Market theory has a long tradition in Continental European economics, as I have outlined in De Jong and Shepherd (1986).

2. Marshall (1919), like J.B. Say before him, stressed the organizational role of the entrepreneur, so that the terms *businessman, manager, entrepreneur* came to be interchangeable. However, that is to gloss over fundamental differences, which, moreover, have great effects on the operation of the economy, as Schumpeter rightly maintained in his *Theory of Economic Development* (1911).

References

Cantillon, R. *Essay sur la nature du commerce en général* (1755). Paris: Edition de l'INSED, 1952.

European Community (ed.). *European Economy*, No. 10, July 1984.

European Community. *Competitiveness and Industrial Structures*. Brussels, 1987.

de Jong, H.w. "The State as Entrepreneur. The Rise and Fall of an Idea in the Economic Experiences of European Countries," in H. St. Seidenfuss (ed.), *Deregulierung - eine Herausforderung an die Wirtschafts- und Sozialpolitik in der Marktwirtschaft*. Berlin: Schriften des Vereins fuer Socialpolitik, Band 184, 1989, pp. 173-193.

de Jong, H.w. (ed.). *The structure of European Industry*. (2nd ed.). Dordrecht: Kluwer Academic Publishers, 1988.

de Jong, H.w., and W.G. Shepherd (eds.). *Mainstreams in Industrial Organization.* Dordrecht: Kluwer Academic Publishers, 1986, Volumes I and II.

Marshall, A. *Industry and Trade.* London: MacMillan and Co., Ltd., 1919.

Murphy, A.E. *Richard Cantillon: Entrepreneur and Economist.* Oxford: Clarendon Press, 1986.

Knight, F.H. *Risk, Uncertainty and Profit.* Boston and New York: The Houghton Mifflin Company, 1921.

Schumpeter, J.A. *Theorie der Wirtschaftlichen Entwicklung.* (2nd ed.). Berlin: Duncker und Humblot, 1926.

Chapter 7

MNEs, Technology, and the Competitiveness of European Industries

John H. Dunning and John A. Cantwell

University of Reading

This chapter discusses some aspects of the changing role of multinational enterprises (MNEs) as producers, transferers and disseminators of technology and technological capacity,[1] and ways in which their activities may affect the international competitiveness of European countries. The argument adopts the theoretical framework of the eclectic paradigm of international production (Dunning, 1988), and relates it to the concept of technological cumulation.

The central theme of the chapter is that the steady growth of MNEs, especially since the 1950s, has been associated with new (and closer) relationships between the international creation and dissemination of technology. Such creation and dissemination may occur across or within the national boundaries, and within or between firms.[2] Within the EEC, it becomes one of the most powerful instruments affecting, and being affected by, the competitive position of industries and countries.

The chapter begins with a brief historical review of the changing nature of technological innovation. In particular it examines the proposition that there has been a fundamental shift of emphasis from technology being perceived by the firm as a specific and single-purpose input, requiring little coordination with other technologies, toward its being more general and multipurpose, and often needed to be used with other technologies for its effective deployment. The rise of such technological interdependence means that it is no longer appropriate to think simply in terms of a sequence that runs from technology production to transfer and diffusion. The successful creation and application of new technology is becoming increasingly dependent upon its ability to relate to other similar technologies developed elsewhere by other firms. It is also difficult to separate individual innovations from the way in which they are organized by firms; and from the multiple use of the same technology to produce different products or processes across national boundaries. This is one major reason why the product cycle (Vernon, 1966, 1979) and the industry technology cycle (Magee, 1977) type of hypotheses are inadequate today in explaining the complex modern role of the MNE as both a source and a recipient of innovative change.

The next section considers the recent behavior of MNEs in greater detail. In particular, it is contended that the extent to which they create and disseminate technology and technological capacity depends upon their international competitive position, and the extent to which their production and marketing activities are globally integrated. Some evidence on the significance of technology creation as a competitive force behind the international expansion of MNEs (through generating new ownership specific (O) advantages) is reviewed. The evidence of the relationship between this and technology transfer and dissemination is more tentative.

The influence of the foreign investment strategy of MNEs on internal and external technology dissemination is next discussed. A distinction is drawn between resource-based, import-substituting, and rationalized types of MNE activity. The part played by these different activities in the European operations of the MNE concerned will affect the degree and form of technology dissemination between subsidiaries. In addition, it is contended that the strength of local competitors, the nature of the linkages with local firms, the structure of the relevant domestic markets, and host country government policies are among the determinants of the amount and speed of technology transfer and diffusion.

The chapter concludes by examining some of the implications of the increasingly footloose nature of many kinds of economic activity for individual European countries that wish to create and sustain indigenous technological capacity. It also argues that, due to the shift towards technological systems or galaxies, the growing linkages between technological developments are likely to entail an increasing interdependence between innovation in different countries. The way in which these developments are allied to patterns of cumulative causation in the competitiveness of industries and the growing integration of European economies is discussed from a UK perspective and with reference to two sectors -- motor vehicles and pharmaceuticals.

THE HISTORICAL TREND TOWARD TECHNOLOGICAL SYSTEMS

The production and efficient deployment of technology lie at the heart of the growth of most MNEs. Historically, product and process innovations are an essential source of the competitive advantages of firms. Since they arise from the exclusive or privileged possession of a specific asset, they have also been called "asset" advantages. There is considerable evidence that many MNEs that maintained successful foreign manufacturing facilities abroad before 1914 depended upon specialized product or process innovative strengths. Sanna Randaccio (1980), Buckley and Roberts (1982), Archer (1986), and Wilkins (1988) consider the case of European direct investment in the United States before

1914, while Wilkins (1970) describes the foreign expansion of U.S. MNEs in the same period.

The success of the modern MNE also rests on its ability to create, or acquire, advantages of a transaction cost minimizing kind. In the present context, this type of advantage arises from the role of the firm as a coordinator of economic activities requiring different technologies, rather than a producer of a single product using one particular technology, and can only be exploited by it producing at different points of the value-added chain or on different value-added chains. The technological complementarity that exists between certain groupings of products and processes is a case in point. Here, Rosenberg (1981) has described how innovative success in related activities, and how the possibility of new applications of any particular innovation, may stimulate complementary innovations. However, close links are required between the creation and use of technology (which is an iterative process), and these links are often maintained more efficiently within the firm or the MNE. Historically, MNEs have increasingly been able to provide such linkages, and to benefit as a result from transaction cost or governance advantages, as the costs of managing larger and more complex firms have fallen.

In the past, the relative significance of asset-based (Oa) and transaction-cost based (Ot) advantages in MNE activity has depended on the overall rate of product and process innovation, and the comparative efficiency of markets and hierarchies as transactional agents. At times, when the pace of new innovations has been especially strong (as it was in the industrialized world in the 1890s and in the 1950s), then Oa advantages played a more prominent role in the internationalization of firms and industries. However, in other periods, the extent of the leadership of particular MNEs over their rivals, in terms of specialized technological strengths, have become more dependent upon other Oa advantages, or upon a more careful coordination of their international activities.

However, apart from such fluctuations in the balance between Oa and Ot advantages, there has been an historical shift toward the latter in the organization of MNEs. Inter alia this is associated with the development of integrated technological systems by MNEs, which, to be properly exploited, need to be under the control of the same hierarchy. In part, this is the natural outcome of the growth of such industrial firms, and the progress of technological innovation itself, which continually forges new links between established productive experience and potential new applications for the underlying skills and process technology. Moreover, not only has technology become less activity specific, but it has increasingly affected the capacity of firms to coordinate different and/or geographically diversified activities. In other words, the organization of technology has become a generic competitive advantage, not very different in kind to management or entrepreneurship.

This transformation in the extent to which technological innovation is organized within the firm or MNE can also be attributed to changes in the international economic and political environment. In a purely technological sense, there may well have been benefits from a closer international integration of production in the interwar period, especially between Europe and the United States. However, in these years, such a development was inhibited by the height of protectionist barriers (and their increase in the 1930s), and by the political and exchange risks encountered by any MNE that coordinated production across potentially hostile countries. Since 1945, the liberalization of trade in manufactured goods between the industrialized countries (particularly within Europe), and the relative political stability of the same regions, has helped to encourage the establishment of global networks of trade and production, covering the industrialized and the newly industrialized world.

The change in the international environment has further compelled a move toward integrated technological systems. The advantages that stem from such centralized coordination have helped to strengthen the position of many MNEs vis-a-vis national firms, who are constrained to follow seriously only those activities in which their own countries have an existing or potential locational advantage. In turn, those MNEs which have remained strongest in the creation of new technology, as well as in its use and dissemination, have generally been those best able to sustain the fastest growth rates of all. The best illustration of this is the emergence of many Japanese firms as important MNEs, which developed a unique capacity for linking import and dissemination of foreign technology to the creation and transfer of new indigenous technology. While Japanese firms have accounted for 9.1 percent of all patents granted in the United States to foreign residents in the period 1963-1969, they accounted for a massive 36.5 percent in 1983[3]; and this improvement was matched by an increase in the Japanese share of the sales of the world's largest 483 industrial firms, from 6.0 percent in 1962 to 12.1 percent in 1982 (Dunning and Pearce, 1985). Innovation has now been clearly tied to technology creation, transfer, and use.

THE DEPENDENCE OF INTERNATIONAL TECHNOLOGY TRANSFER AND DIFFUSION ON THE STRUCTURE OF INDUSTRIES

The extent of international technology dissemination will vary between an industry in which one leading MNE predominates (say, IBM in computers), and an industry in which groups of major rivals coexist (say, pharmaceutical MNEs based in the United States, Germany, Switzerland, and the UK). In the former case, technology will be rather more centrally controlled, and its dissemination tends to run in just one direction. Innovation diffusion outside the MNE is limited to a range of more specialized companies, which typically compete in market segments in which the leader is less involved. In the latter case, the transmission of technology within the MNE may well run in more than one direction, and it may further diffuse to other MNEs as an input to their own technology creation and transfer.

The location of poles of innovative capacity in an international industry may affect the nature of the competitive advantages of firms (determining which countries are sources of the strongest MNEs), as well as influencing the location of MNE activity. A shift in the location of innovative capacity will strengthen the position of the firms, which will increase their stake in the creation of technology. An example of this in recent years is the gradual movement of Japanese firms from the adaptation of existing, to the innovation of new, technology in a number of sectors (such as motor vehicles and consumer electronics).

Meanwhile, in the last decade many MNEs based in Europe and the United States have tended to place an increasing emphasis on the adaptation rather than the creation of new technology. This required them to give greater weight to better organizing and managing technology, one consequence of which has been a trend toward the rationalization of international activity (creating advantages of a transaction cost kind through improved coordination). The implication is that although U.S. and European MNEs may have slowed down their technology creation (at least relative to Japanese firms), their use and dissemination of technology -- both cross-border and within the countries of their affiliates -- may well have increased. Firms that become more competitive through their ability to locate and relocate productive activities to the best advantage, while developing the benefits of the common governance of their full range of activities, may well need to increase the transfer of technology between activities and locations. Whether this increases the international dissemination of technology depends, in part, on the capabilities and the location of competitors, suppliers, and customers.

Despite this shift, most MNEs continue to link technology transfer (and imitation or diffusion from other firms) to efforts toward fresh innovation. In a study, based on some field research (Wyatt et al., 1985), when 95 leading MNEs were asked to rank different means of maintaining their international competitive advantage, technological superiority was believed to be most important for the sample as a whole. Using data on their patenting activity in the United States, it is also possible to identify the sectoral pattern of the technological advantages of the firms for each industrialized country, using data on their patenting activity in the United States (Soete, 1980). From these data, it is also possible to indicate the types of sectors in which particular countries appear to have particularly strong technological advantages, relative to their major foreign competitors. Cantwell (1985), for example, has shown how, in the early 1980s, established technological advantage calculated in this way has remained especially important in the competitive success of firms from Germany, the UK, the United States and Japan. For the companies of these four countries, the index of technological advantage is significantly correlated with the industrial distribution of their share in total international manufacturing activity.

We have suggested that the extent and speed of international technology dissemination by MNEs depends upon the structure of the industry in question, the strengths of the constituent firms, and their geographical configuration. Consider first an industry that is located in a number of countries, each of which is home to a group of highly innovative firms. This base of technology creation helps to support a network of exports and international production in each case, though, for the reasons outlined above, each firm also becomes dependent upon the coordination of connected activities. Over the last 25 years, this is the kind of industry that has been characterized by the rise of the cross-hauling of investments between these countries harboring the strongest firms. Such countries become hosts to the greatest levels of international production as well as being home to MNEs of their own. We have offered some explanations for this phenomenon in a previous chapter; such intra-industry trade and production are also usually accompanied by intra-industry technology flows as well.

It is in this kind of industry that those countries that have become poles of innovation tend to build up a position of absolute competitive advantage in international trade or as host to foreign based MNEs. This position is achieved by the continuous innovation and growth of production of its own firms and also of the affiliates of foreign MNEs, which adapt their technology in the light of local knowledge and customer requirements. Indeed, one reason why MNEs may invest heavily in such an advantaged country is to take advantage of the agglomerative economics offered by a flourishing innovative environment. By so doing they may advance the technological capacity of the country. The firms of each country tend to embark on a path of technological accumulation which has certain unique characteristics (Pavitt, 1987). Moreover, the kinds of linkages that grow up between competitors, suppliers, and customers in any one country are also, to some extent, peculiar to that country, and imbue the technology creation of its firms (which depends on such linkages) with distinctive features. For these reasons, other MNEs often need to be on-site with their own production and their innovative capacity if they are to properly benefit from the latest advances in foreign technological development.

By contrast, where the technological capacity of a host country is weak in the sector concerned, the investments of MNEs may drive out local competition and reduce local technological capability still further. Foreign-owned affiliates tend to import a higher proportion of their inputs than do indigenous firms, particularly in the early years of their operations, or where they constitute part of a globally integrated network. Even where host governments set targets for a gradual increase in the local sourcing of components -- particularly those which involve high value-added activities (e.g., tubes for TV sets, wafers for microchips, chemicals for pharmaceuticals, etc.) -- subsidiaries of foreign companies supplying the parent MNE may be established to fulfill this function.[4] While this may result in a greater international dissemination of technology, it is quite possible that the design, research, and development work remains concentrated in the parent company. Indeed, in supply activities upstream from the original investment (e.g., in the motor vehicles or electronics components sectors), this is potentially very serious, as the expanding global sales of supplying MNEs allows them to increase their own technological capacity at the expense of local suppliers who are then driven out even more effectively.[5]

In today's international economic environment, MNEs that operate in industries characterized by strong, oligopolistic (or technological) competition normally need a direct presence in each of those countries that hold leading positions in the development of their industry and of associated technologies (Ohmae, 1985). Whether or not this is achieved depends on the strength of the existing technological capacity of the countries, the policies of these countries to inward trade and investments, the strategy and competitive position of the individual MNEs, and the economics of the location of research and development. By contrast, MNEs that are among the technology leaders are not so concerned to try and feed off parallel technologies developed by other firms. Insofar as they need to do so, they are content to imitate promising new ventures, or in the limit, perhaps to butt out a smaller but innovative competitor. In the case of this kind of MNE, insofar as R&D facilities are decentralized at all, they tend to be located primarily in accordance with cost considerations, and there may be little immediate dissemination of technology. The latter situation is today rather more prevalent among U.S. MNEs (and perhaps in the future among Japanese MNEs) than it is among European MNEs. As a rule, European MNEs (and, of course, Third World MNEs) are most likely to want access to a range of alternative technologies generated outside their home countries, to link together more firmly the creation and dissemination of their own technologies.

THE DEPENDENCE OF INTERNATIONAL TECHNOLOGY CREATION AND DISSEMINATION ON THE GLOBAL INVESTMENT STRATEGY OF MNEs

For MNEs to be successful in technology intensive industries, they must not only be productive innovators but successful commercializers and users of that technology. This suggests that they must have or be able to acquire the complementary assets needed for commercialization (Teece, 1986) and be able to disseminate among its user subordinates. However, the form that this dissemination takes is closely allied to the prospects for its diffusion to other firms producing in the host country. The implications of transferring technology by way of a cooperative agreement with another firm (whether this takes the form of a joint venture or some kind of contractual agreement such as the licensing of an unaffiliated company) will be different than the implication of a transfer controlled within the MNE.

The reasons that MNEs may enter into collaborative arrangements are discussed by Cantwell and Dunning (1985) and Contractor and Lorange (1988). Broadly speaking, MNEs more readily transfer technology in this way where their main O advantages derive from their possession of a specific asset of grouping of assets; and where the local partner has some synergistic contribution to make (which might include some technological contribution, especially in the case of joint ventures or cross-licensing agreements between MNEs); where the technology is of a mature or standardized kind and is easily codified, or is of secondary concern to the major activities in which the MNE is engaged; or where political pressure encourages such arrangements. In the first three cases, the diffusion of technology from the affiliates of MNEs to other local firms is likely to be more pronounced due to the very conditions which brought about a cooperative agreement in the first place.

To put this in context, it is important to understand why technology transfer is more frequently internalized within the

MNE. Firstly, where technology is not mature or standardized it is not easy to determine its price in an external market (that is, the MNE wishes to ensure that it appropriates a full rent on its O advantages of an asset kind). Secondly, technology dissemination may well involve external economies to the rest of the owning firm which require close coordination and feedback between the parties concerned (so the MNE is able to benefit from O advantages of a transaction cost kind). This second factor has become increasingly important, and it is bound up with the need of the MNE to retain control over technology transfer in order to link itmore effectively to technology creation through drawing on the feedback that it receives from the transferee. Third, there may be risks (e.g., of infringement of property rights) associated with an arm's length transaction which the selling firm is not prepared to bear.

The costs of technology transfer are more significant than is commonly thought (Teece, 1977), and, as market failure may be greater across borders than within a country, the costs of international dissemination between independent firms is especially high. In international dissemination the technology must be adapted to conform to foreign work practices and existing technology, and to accommodate differences in the infrastructure of the countries within which it must function. In addition, there may be high travel and communication costs involved in the initial establishment of a new technology acquired from abroad (Hirsch, 1976). These costs can be reduced where transfer takes place within the MNE. One reason is that the implementation of technology and the transfer of know-how is greatly facilitated by a close cooperation between the creators and users of technology. One aspect of this is the interactive links between capital goods producers and users that is built into the infrastructure of all industrialized counties (Rosenberg, 1976).

The efficient creation and/or absorption of technology can only be achieved if the environment offers the right market conditions for the supply and use of inputs necessary to it.

Innovation is an ongoing process, and it must be sustained to make technology viable at each stage; any given technology is not a static blueprint to be taken off the drawing board and applied at will. This connection between the design, production, and use of technology requires a coordination that the market is not well suited to achieve. However, if the transfer of technology by an MNE to its subsidiaries is then to give rise to its diffusion within their host countries, then this requires some capacity on the part of these countries to absorb and utilize this technology. This is the main reason why innovation diffusion is often harder to achieve in a less developed country.

External technology diffusion is more likely to occur where some related technological capacity already exists among local firms. Otherwise the presence of MNE subsidiaries may act solely as low value satellites of their parent companies. With reference to the "Le Defi Americain" Servan-Schreiber, 1968) that threatened the long-term competitiveness of European firms in the 1960s, Cantwell (1985) found that a necessary condition for indigenous revival in Britain, Germany, and France was the existence of strong technological advantages on the part of local firms. In such cases, inward direct investment led to technology diffusion, and the competitive stimulation of a new wave of local innovation; the pharmaceutical industry provides an excellent illustration.

In these instances, the investments of U.S. MNEs in Europe were mainly of an import-substituting kind, and by example and competitive stimulus, technology was diffused to their local competitors. Indeed, it was often the potential for such diffusion or imitation which gave the impetus to the displacement of U.S. exports by local European production on the part of U.S. MNEs in the first place. However, import substituting investment also carries with it the possibility of innovation diffusion to local suppliers and customers. It is usually associated with backward technology dissemination from assembly operations to their local component suppliers. This happened in the 1950s and 1960s; and also more recently in the case of recent Japanese investment in the UK, especially in the consumer electronics sector (Dunning, 1986). As innovation diffusion proceeds, subsequent inward MNE investment (or subcontracting arrangements) takes place in more technology-intensive or higher value-added activities at an earlier stage of the vertically integrated chain.

A similar pattern of increased local vertical integration as diffusion proceeds is sometimes observed in the case of MNE investments of a resource based kind. However, resource-based investments normally lead to the forward rather than the backward diffusion of technology, e.g., into secondary processing activities which may be established locally. This is particularly the case where the cost of transporting the raw materials is greater than the cost of transporting the intermediate or final products. This is more likely to be achieved through national technology diffusion and subcontracting (as opposed to an extension of MNE investment and technology transfer) where the MNE has some monopolistic power, and where the coordination with further processing and marketing is not difficult to accomplish.

The exception in the case of resource-based MNE investment is that undertaken in export processing zones, in which the "resource" being exploited is cheap labor. This is akin to import substituting investment inasmuch as any subsequent technology diffusion is likely to be upstream in further preparation for the MNE's marketing network abroad. However, MNE investments that are aimed at taking advantage of cheap labor, or the availability of other local resources in developing countries, have not often led to much technology diffusion to independent firms, except in the electrical and electronics goods sector. All too frequently the technology transferred from MNEs to their subsidiaries and the spillover effects of the latter's presence are confined to low value-added activities; indeed, where such investment inhibits the development of indigenous firms, which might have produced at other points along the value-added chain, it may actually diminish local technological capacity.

This type of export platform investment in the developing countries is a special case of rationalized investment, in which the affiliate in question is integrated into a global network of activity within the MNE. This type of investment has been on the increase since the early 1970s, as MNEs have increasingly come to rely on O advantages of a transaction cost kind through global organization and management. Although international technology dissemination may sometimes be greater within such a system, the extent of diffusion through linkages with host country firms is likely to be less than in the case of import substituting or most resource-based investments. This is because the main linkages of the affiliate are with other parts of the MNE, and in this sense inter-border corporate integration may be at the expense of intra-border sectoral integration.

However, even in the case of a rationalized investment, it is quite possible that certain activities may be subcontracted locally to other firms. In this situation, it might be supposed that technology diffusion (in both directions) will be greater where the component suppliers are themselves MNEs. Hence, with reference to recent Japanese involvement in the UK color television sector, the component suppliers such as Phillips and Plessey are as powerful as the cable television companies to whom they sell, unlike in Japan where subcontractors tend to be small and highly specialized. However, much depends upon the strength of the O advantages of the competitor firms. One of the complaints frequently voiced by the UK component suppliers is that they are inhibited from being global (and hence competitive with other MNEs) because they are prevented from having full access to one of the main growth markets, namely, Japan (Dunning, 1986).

The extent to which to which technology diffuses to other firms in consequence of an MNE investment depends upon the impact on competitors that have local operations, and upon the impact on suppliers and customers, which in turn relates to the strategic decision of the MNE to buy in certain inputs locally rather than importing them. It also depends upon which products

the MNE decides to produce locally, and the technology it chooses
to use in its local operations. The potential for domestic diffusion
may be greater where it locates more technology-intensive or
higher value-added activities in the host country, and this kind of
decision may well be influenced by the state of local industry and
by the industrial policies of the local government.

In summary, technology dissemination will be affected by
the number and strength of indigenous competitors, the form of
linkages with local firms, the structure of the relevant domestic
market's host country government policies toward sourcing inputs,
and encouragement of a higher local proportion in value-added,
local technological capacity and infrastructure, local managerial
skills, and the destination of exports from the MNE affiliate.

THE POLICY IMPLICATIONS OF THE CLOSER RELATIONSHIP BETWEEN THE INTERNATIONAL CREATION, TRANSFER, AND DIFFUSION OF TECHNOLOGY

The Concept of Cumulative Causation and Technological Competitiveness

The emergence of globally oriented MNEs, within which the
international dissemination of technology is now more linked to its
creation, has led to an increased mobility of certain types of
economic activity -- and particularly that in medium and high
technology-intensive activities.

The increasing footloose nature of international production
and of innovative activities is likely to reinforce patterns of
cumulative causation within countries. Those countries which are
growing more rapidly, upgrading their industrial structures, and
devoting more resources to the encouragement of indigenous
technological capacity (e.g., by a well-formulated industrial
strategy and an educational policy designed to meet this strategy)
are more likely to attract inward MNE investment in technology-
intensive activities, and to benefit from the dissemination outside

the recipient affiliates.   By contrast, countries that are losing international competitiveness are more likely to attract MNE satellites concentrated in assembly and low value-added activities; however, since these affiliates are able to import the O advantages of their parent companies, they may still be able to drive out their local competitors.   In so doing they reduce the technological capacity of indigenous competitors (and that of their suppliers) and, hence, reduce their capacity for domestic technological dissemination consequential upon inward investment.   It is this possibility which in the case of recent Japanese direct investment in the UK and the U.S. has been labeled the "Trojan horse" effect.

Approaching the argument from the role of outward direct investment, where domestic firms hold an internationally strong competitive position, they can usually afford to invest more in technology creation, which through backward linkages may benefit their domestic suppliers.   This, in turn, will strengthen the latter's competitive capacity to supply the affiliates of foreign firms requiring their products.   More subcontracting work is then given to domestic suppliers by foreign affiliates which further strengthens their technological capacity.   In this scenario, outward and inward investment are complementary forces making for an improved international competitive situation of the country concerned.   But the link to this success is technology creation and dissemination via the MNE.

In summary, then, where economies become convergent in their technological capabilities, aided and abetted by intra-industry trade and production, MNEs may assist in the transfer and diffusion of technology between them.   Through cross-investments and spillover effects there is more international diffusion of technology, while technology creation in each country becomes more closely intertwined.   Thus, in the context of national economic policy, the MNE may play a dual role.   On the one hand, it may serve to increase technological divergences between countries; but, on the other, it may strengthen the technological linkages between them.   Whether countries are brought closer together or pushed farther apart, the interdependence between them is increased, and the development of technological systems or galaxies within the MNEs reinforces such interdependence between innovation in different countries.

Consider now how the technological activities of MNEs may intensify cumulative causation, but operating in different directions in different industries in the same country.[6]

MNEs and a 'Virtuous' Cycle of Increasing Technological Capability. Inward MNE investment is likely to be attracted into innovative industries caught up in a virtuous circle, and is likely to be associated with local R&D facilities and an increase in indigenous technological capacity. In doing so, it may increase competition, spurring local rivals to a higher rate of innovation. Indeed, this type of sector is also probably home to outward MNE activity, and such activity plays a similar role to inward investment of foreign MNEs. By locating research-intensive production in other important centers of foreign innovation, and/or assembling or processing manufacturing abroad, the firms of the most dynamic countries sustain more effectively the global basis for increased research activity at home. They are able to integrate complementary foreign technologies and to devise more broadly based technological systems in their domestic plants. Thus the activities of domestic and foreign MNEs, and the spillover effects following from them, may aid in the development of a country's technological capacity.

MNEs and a 'Vicious' Cycle of Declining Technological Capability. By contrast, inward direct investment may still take place in declining sectors, but it is likely to be in low value-added subsectors of the industry, importing the more high value-added intermediate products. By dint of their higher efficiency, or by deliberate strategy, the foreign affiliates may cut in the markets of local competitors. Indeed, the foreign MNE may be able to finance an increased level of R&D within its parent company from its increased global sales, including its greater market share in the host country. Meanwhile local firms whose markets are cut back may lack the resources to "go global" themselves, and are consequently compelled to cut back their R&D expenditure. If, in addition, the government of the home country of the MNEs prohibits or creates obstacles against investment by foreign firms in its own domestic market, then this constitutes the type of "technological protectionism" of which the Japanese are sometimes accused (Spencer and Brander, 1983). In these circumstances, inward direct MNE investment is liable not only to drive out local competitors, but also to restrict the technology creation of local suppliers, even if more technology disseminates to them from the MNE.[7] For both these reasons, domestic technological capacity is reduced.

However, the notion of a vicious circle just described needs some qualification. Assume, for example, that the firms of a country whose technological capacity in an industry is low or declining are no longer competing effectively with the MNEs of the strongest countries. In this case, inward investment of foreign MNEs may help to stem a vicious circle by raising the technical capacity of the host country by linking it with a dynamic MNE network of activities, rather than by promoting indigenous research. In this case, local innovation is likely to take the form of the upgrading of local skills, incremental process improvement, better production engineering, new quality control procedures, and so forth, even though fundamental research and development capacity is located abroad.

Some Empirical Evidence from the UK. Studies of U.S. direct investment in Europe in the 1950s and 1960s, and/or Japanese investment in the UK, provide ample evidence of cases where new competitive stimulus helps set in motion a vicious circle of increasing dependency on external sources of supply. Much depends on the initial technological capacity and international competitiveness of the country and sector in question, and this influences the motivation underlying the MNE investment. Until now, the the literature on MNEs and international technology dissemination has not paid attention to this issue, preferring to concern itself with the immediate form or impact of technology transfer in a static framework, rather than the unfolding dynamic process that it opens up.

Let us illustrate the role of the location of technological activity by MNEs in cumulative causation by reference to the UK motor and pharmaceutical industries.[8] Though there have been some impressive inward investments in the UK motor vehicle industry in the last 20 years, until the advent of Nissan, the UK was not an attractive European location for foreign companies. Take one very telling set of statistics. The UK content of cars sold in the UK by the multinational producers fell from 88 percent in 1973 to 46 percent in 1984 in the case of Ford, 92 percent to 42 percent in the case of Talbot, and 89 percent to 22 percent in the case of General Motors. More generally, over the same period in trading terms, the motor vehicle industry experienced the greatest deterioration of any British manufacturing sector; between 1978 and 1984, for example, vehicle exports rose by 13 percent (in value terms) while imports increased by 118 percent. In volume terms, the exports of all the major UK producers fell quite dramatically in the early 1980s. Britain's share of the global research and development expenditure by motor vehicle firms, which was always lower than its production, and substantially lower than its consumption, of vehicles, has slumped even further since the mid-1960s. Until the mid-1980s, at least, the motor industry was not one of the British success stories.

Moreover, as inward investment fell and became less directed to high value activities, this further weakened the industry's ability to compete. Multinationals were choosing not to produce in Britain because the supply capabilities were perceived as inadequate, while the environmental stability (especially in terms of of industrial relations) was thought to be inferior to that offered by Continental competitors. Only the most generous incentives and the most persuasive efforts of UK Government

Ministers induced companies like Ford to make the huge new investments they did in Wales and the North West. The fact that Nissan and, to a lesser extent, Honda and Toyota have expressed their faith in the British economy and British work force has undoubtedly been a shot in the arm for the industry. Maybe it will see a turning of the tide.

By contrast, the tale of the pharmaceutical industry is one of almost uninterrupted vitality and vigor. From the early 1950s, foreign producers have acted as a competitive challenge to an already quite strong indigenous sector. The reputation of the UK scientific community, its professional system of drug registration, its patent system, its clinical testing procedures are all excellent. Its industrial relations and contacts with universities and the medical profession are second to none; and the government, through the PPBS scheme, has offered a stable and fair reward system for the pharmaceutical companies, as well as providing them with good incentives to engage in innovative activities.

The results are shown in a variety of indices. First, the pharmaceutical industry is a substantial net contributor to the UK balance of payments; in 1986, it exported nearly twice the amount it imported. Second, the UK is one of the two or three leading centers for pharmaceutical research and development in the world. At the end of the 1970s, it was estimated that while only 3 1/2 percent of the world's drugs were bought by UK consumers; 5 percent of the world's production was undertaken in the UK and 11 1/2 percent of the industry's global research and development (Dunning, 1988). Success breeds success: though foreign companies account for about 45 percent of the drugs supplied by the National Health Service, this figure has remained fairly constant over the years. British multinationals are among the world's leading drug producers and in the forefront of technological advances. Between them, foreign and domestically owned firms have generated a critical mass of physical and human innovative capacity, which separately neither could have ensured.

The agglomerative economies so gained are in total contrast to those lost in the motor vehicle industry.

The Impact of Economic Integration

The geographical dispersion of research-intensive and other production in global MNE networks is further reinforced when operations are located in an economically integrated region. When trade barriers between countries are lowered, it increases the incentives to organize an international division of labor in which productive activity in each country becomes more highly specialized. This implies that when a customs union is created or extended, in the following period industries will be gradually restructured. For any given industry, countries that are homes to strongly innovative firms will find that local research is further encouraged as local firms increase their market shares elsewhere in the region (through exports and international production), and foreign MNEs find it a more attractive location for their research-intensive production. In countries in which local technological capacity is weak it will be further undermined as indigenous firms lose domestic market shares, both from increased imports from more dynamic parts of the region, and from the local assembly activities of foreign affiliates that are linked up with MNE networks elsewhere in the region.

This suggests that following the economic integration of a region that in any particular industry, the investments of MNEs from outside the region will have beneficial competitive effects in some countries, and damaging anticompetitive effects in others. In countries in which local firms have reserves of technological strength in the industry in question, new MNE entry may act as a catalyst, helping to set in motion a virtuous circle of an increasing proportion of research-intensive activity and a faster growth of output. In other cases it is likely to drive out local firms and set in motion a vicious circle of increasing dependency on external sources of supply and technology. Much depends upon the initial technological capacity of local enterprise in the sector concerned, and this influences the motive underlying the MNE investment and hence the form that it takes. Models that embody an implicit assumption that foreign MNE entry is either inherently competitive or anticompetitive are misleading or at best only tell part of the story; these two opposite effects in different locations are interdependent with one another.

However, there may be industries in which MNEs from outside the region are especially strong relative to firms from within the region. In the European Community electronics is a case in point, in which U.S. and Japanese firms are the world leaders. Where this happens research may remain quite highly centralized in the parent companies, except perhaps in certain specialized sub-sectors. It is then possible that a country within the region whose own firms have little innovative capacity in the relevant sector may act as a regional center for foreign MNEs. The choice of country in these circumstances depends upon the skills of the local work force, wage rates, the provision of government incentives, and the like. Where local firms are technologically weak this kind of foreign entry may have beneficial production and employment effects, even if it is not associated with a (restoration of) fundamental research capacity.

The existence of an economically integrated region strengthens the trend toward a joint determination of production decisions in different countries by MNEs operating within the region. Many MNEs have moved closer to a regionally integrated strategy in their European activities. The creation and enlargement of the EEC has played some part in increasing specialization in innovation and production between European countries. In each European industry there are centers of innovation, and there is a tendency for them to attract an increasing amount of the research-intensive and allied production of MNEs.

The question that arises next is, What is likely to be the effect of the second round of market liberalization in the EEC brought about by the removal of nontariff barriers in 1992? The answer will be partly industry and partly country specific. The most significant impact of the internal market is likely to be felt by those industries in which nontariff barriers (including national regulation) are now important obstacles to product and process specialization and cross-border trade. These include most service sectors and some manufacturing sectors: e.g., pharmaceuticals, industrial machinery, and many food and drink products. The countries most likely to gain are those that currently have a comparative advantage, a strong indigenous technological capacity, and in which both foreign and domestic MNEs have an important stake. In terms of the analysis just set out, we would expect the polarization of innovative activity to be intensified with MNEs playing a more rather than less important role in affecting the location of these poles. But this is an area in which much more research needs to be done before any definitive answers can be given to these important questions.

Governments and the Restructuring of the Domestic Economy

To our mind, these two case studies encapsulate the conditions necessary for successful inward direct investment. We are all rehearsed in the reasons why foreign firms invest in Europe, and we also know why they choose (or do not choose) the UK as a European location. What, perhaps, is not as well appreciated is the value placed by foreign investors on a strong and vibrant industrial economy; and the crucial role that governments have to play in bringing this about. Inter-country differences in wage, raw material, and transport costs no longer are the crucial locational factors. They have been replaced by the quality of economic management, and an educational, technological, and industrial policy which promotes entrepreneurship, innovation, and efficiency; a realistic and positive attitude of mind toward work, rewards and competitiveness; and a unity of commercial and social purpose. These are all important influences which will determine, for example, how much R&D companies like Sony, NEC, Sharp, and

Nissan will eventually undertake in Europe and where they will locate their laboratories. Equally to the point, they are shaped, if not directly determined, by the actions or non-actions of governments.

There is a lot of misunderstanding about the role of government in a modern industrial economy. All schools of thought seem to agree that governments have a responsibility to set the right economic climate, and that there are some functions that only governments can perform. But as soon as one talks about industrial strategy, the positions diverge. The free market protagonists preach "let the discipline of the market decide"; governments are not technically competent to make the right decisions on who should provide what; much better leave it to those who know and are prepared to bear the consequences for their action. The opposing view is that imperfections and distortions in the market system, and differences between private and social benefits and costs, require some intervention by governments in the allocation of resources. A third school of thought -- the structuralists -- argue that the market mechanism as conceived by the non-interventionists is inherently incapable of dealing with many of the demands of the modern economy, and particularly with the high transaction costs associated with uncertainty and coordinating interrelated activities.

The fact is that in today's global economy, many firms and particularly those supplying markets dominated by international oligopolists, cannot compete effectively unless they are able to reap the full economies of scale and scope of their activities. At the same time the costs of structural adaptation to new patterns of consumption and technological advances are often too great for individual firms to bear.

The principle of comparative advantage and the invisible hand was initially based on the assumption that the wealth or assets of a country consisted of its natural resources. But, increasingly, the prosperity of modern industrial economies rests

142   MNEs and European Competition

in their ability to create new technology and human capital, and to provide the appropriate institutional machinery and incentives to foster wealth-creating activities. These are not things a laissez faire philosophy or "hands-off" approach to resource enrichment or allocation can readily do. The provision of an adequate education, transport and telecommunications infrastructure laws, rules and regulations that affect human and physical capital formation and technology development, the promotion of an efficient market system, taxes and incentives, policies that affect savings, consumption, and investment patterns, and industrial relations are, at the very least, the responsibility of both government and the private sector, and some would argue the major onus lies with the government.

History suggests that almost every industrial country has needed, and still needs, the active support of its government for its economic restructuring. The instruments used range from protectionism of one kind or another, to well-defined and holistic industrial strategy, within which firms (who are still the main arbiters of resource allocation) produce. If the Japanese have taught the West anything at all, it is the need for the unity of purpose and strategy between the various contributors to the value-added process, -- workers and managers, suppliers and customers, the private sector and governments. The European country whose government promotes the type of macro and micro economic policies that ensures domestic and foreign investors the right environment for growth will, most likely, be the one that will both attract the bulk of inward (and especially) investment in the 1990s and benefit most from it.

CONCLUSIONS

The major policy implication of the analysis contained in this chapter for European governments is that they need to reappraise their industrial and technological policies in the light of the activities of MNEs. Technology is not a natural resource; it has to be created. Increasingly, governments, by a variety of policies, are determining the amount of technology produced and designated in their territory. A government that creates a basis for the domestic location of investment and living standards should also have some guidelines for the way in which domestic industry can be restructured in the light of its previous experience. This is the kind of outlook that has been embodied in Japanese (and more recently that of the Singaporean and South Korean) government policy, in order to engineer the continual upgrading of domestic industry and the further progression of its technological development. Investment in "sunrise" sectors is welcomed through favorable institutional arrangement, while firms in "sunset" industries are encouraged to relocate their activities in other South East Asian economies at an earlier stage of development. Clearly if other governments were to follow a similar course of action, the selection of "sunrise" industries would differ between countries, depending not only upon their stage of development but also upon their existing technological strengths with a capacity to support further innovation.

Countries can encourage new investment and technology dissemination in those activities in which the prospects for innovation diffusion are greatest, while allowing MNEs to strengthen innovative linkages between technology creation in the domestic economy and other countries which have similar or related advantages. What is clear is that governments cannot ignore the implications of recent developments both in international innovation and in the cross-border organization of its fruits, in which technology creation and dissemination have become progressively more intertwined, with globally oriented MNEs at the forefront of this process.

Notes

1. By technological capacity we mean the assets required to produce technology. Technology is a flow of ideas, information, and knowledge generated from this capacity. Technology is itself defined as the ability to create output or produce a given output more effectively. It embraces the *how* of the production process throughout the value-added chain.

2. Note that some commentators distinguish between international transfer and diffusion. Wilkins (1974), for example, suggests that a technology transferred across national boundaries by an MNE (whether to an affiliate or to a licensee) is only diffused to other firms if it "spills over" to suppliers or customers in the host country, or if it is imitated by other, indigenous firms. We shall treat this international diffusion as a particular type of dissemination that takes place within a country and between independent firms.

3. According to the U.S. Office of Technology Assessment and Forecast, unpublished data.

4. As a result of Nissan's investment in the UK, several Japanese component suppliers are setting up plants.

5. Recent studies on the effects of MNEs on the local firms that supply their affiliates are provided by Lall (1980), Landi (1985), and Dunning (1986).

6. The following section summarizes an argument that is set out in greater detail in Cantwell (1987).

7. In the language of the eclectic paradigm, inward investment will be attracted where there are strong specific advantages of the host country for the generation of technologically oriented O specific advantages possessed by foreign

owned MNEs. Inward direct investment will help create or sustain a virtuous cycle when it interacts with local competitors to add to indigenous production and technological capacity; it will intensify a vicious circle, which not only drives out local competitors, but, by concentrating the high value activities (e.g., innovative) in the home countries, reduces the production capabilities and hence the L advantages of the host country.

8. Other UK industries in which there is a substantial amount of inward investment fall in between the two extremes but veer toward one or the other. As a broad generalization, the impact of both inward and outward direct investment seems to have been most favorable in the processing industries and least in the fabricating industries. Whether the recent Japanese investment in motor vehicles and industrial electronics changes this position remains to be seen.

References

Archer, H. "An Eclectic Approach to the Historical Study of UK Multinational Enterprises." Ph.D. thesis, University of Reading, 1986.

Buckley, P.J., and Roberts, B.R. *European Direct Investment in the USA before World War I*. London: Macmillan, 1982.

Cantwell, J.A. "Technological Competition between European and U.S. Companies in the Post-War Period." Report submitted to the EEC, October, 1985.

Cantwell, J.A. "The Reorganization of European Industries after Integration: Selected Evidence on the Role of Transnational Enterprise Activities," *Journal of Common Market Studies*, December, 1987, 26(2), pp. 127-151.

Cantwell, J.A., and Dunning, J.H. "The New Forms of Involvement of British Firms in the Third World." Report submitted to the OECD, Paris, 1985.

Contractor, F.J., and Lorange, P. *Cooperative Strategies in International Business*. Lexington, Mass.: Lexington Books, 1988.

Dunning, J.H. *Japanese Participation in British Industry*. London: Allen & Unwin, 1986.

Dunning, J.H., and Cantwell, J.A. "The Changing Role of MNEs in the Creation and Diffusion of Technology," in *The Diffusion of New Technology*. (eds.), Arcangeli, F., David, P.A. and Dosi, G. Oxford: Oxford University Press, 1988.

Dunning J.H., and Pearce, R.D. *The World's Largest Industrial Enterprises, 1962-1983*. Farnborough: Gower, 1985.

Dunning, J.H., and Webster, A.D. (eds.) *Structural Change and the World Economy*. London: Routledge, 1989.

Hirsch, S. "An International Trade and Investment Theory of the Firm," *Oxford Economic Papers*, 1976, **28**, pp. 258-70.

Lall, S. "Monopolistic Advantages and Foreign Involvement by U.S. Manufacturing Industry," *Oxford Economic Papers*, 1976, **32**, pp. 102-22.

Magee, S.P. "Information and the Multinational Corporation. An Appropriability Theory of Foreign Direct Investment," in *The New International Economic Order*, J.N. Bhagwati (ed.). Cambridge, Mass.: MIT Press, 1977.

Ohmae, K. *Triad Power*. New York: The Free Press, 1985.

Pavitt, K. "International Patterns of Technological Accumulation," in *Strategies in Global Competition*, (eds.), N. Hood and J.E. Vahlner. Chichester and New York: John Wiley, 1987.

Sanna Randaccio, F. "European Direct Investments in U.S. Manufacturing," M.Litt, Thesis, University of Oxford, 1980.

Servan-Schreiber, J.J. *The American Challenge.* London: Hamish Hamilton, 1968.

Spencer, B.J., and Brander, J.A. "International R&D Rivalry and Industrial Strategy," *Review of Economic Studies*, 1983, **50**.

Teece, D.J. "Technology Transfer by Multinational Firms: the Resource Costs of Transferring Technological Know-how," *Economic Journal*, 1977, **87**, pp. 242-61.

Teece, D.J. "Transaction Cost Economies and the Multinational Enterprise," *Journal of Economic Behavior and Organization*, 1986, **I**, pp. 21-45.

Vernon, R. "The Product Cycle Hypothesis in the New International Environment," *Oxford Bulletin of Economics and Statistics*, 1979, **41**, pp. 255-67.

Vernon, R. "International Investment and International Trade in the Product Cycle," *Quarterly Journal of Economics*, 1986, **80**, pp. 190-217.

Wilkins, M. *The Emergence of Multinational Enterprise: American Business Abroad from the Colonial Era to 1914.* Cambridge, Mass.: Harvard University Press, 1970.

Wilkins, M. "The Role of Private Business in the International Diffusion of Technology," *Journal of Economic History*, 1974, **34** (1).

Wilkins, M. *Foreign Investment in the United States*, Cambridge, Mass: Harvard University Press, 1988.

Wyatt, S.M.E., Bertin, G. and Paritt, K. "Patents and Multinational Corporations: Results From Questionnaires," *World Patent Information*, 1985, 7, pp. 196-212.

Chapter 8

Competition Dynamics Behind the Mask of Maturity

C.W.F. Baden Fuller, F. Dell'Osso, and J.M. Stopford

London Business School

Over the last 15 years there has been a profound crisis in many European "mature industries": firms associated with success in the 1960s have been doing badly in the late 1970s and early 1980s. This has given rise to a number of searching questions, the most important being: Is strategy choice important? and Must strategy be altered over time?

A number of recent writers have shown that it is possible for a firm to do well where its competitors do badly. A recent paper by Cubbin (1988) highlights this point; it examines a sample of 243 UK companies and shows that between 1962 and 1967 about half of profits could be attributed to the choice of industry, and that for the period 1972 to 1977, the choice of industry had no measurable effect on firm performance. Using the PIMS data base, Buzzell and Gale (1987) also show that industry effects are swamped by firm effects. These findings highlight something well known to strategists: strategy choice matters a great deal, usually far more than choice of industry.

That strategy choice matters does not mean that there is a universal strategy valid through time; on the contrary, there is

strong evidence that a successful strategy in one period does not
transmit into success in another period.   Casual evidence on the
crisis in European manufacturing is supported by case study
evidence on European mature industries.

    Most UK cutlery firms successful in the 1960s failed in the
1980s because they failed to adjust their strategy (Grant and
Downing, 1985) one firm, Richardson, which did change with the
economic circumstances has been very successful (Grant and
Baden Fuller, 1987).   Courtaulds, once a star in the knitwear
industry, has done badly in recent years by sticking to an outdated
strategy, whereas Benetton, a new arrival adopting a different
strategy, has done very well.

    In this chapter we highlight the case of European washing
machines; among other things we show that   Hotpoint was
unsuccessful in making appliances in the 1970s but, upon changing
its strategy, became spectacularly successful in the 1980s (Green,
1988).   In contrast, firms such as Zanussi and Indesit were very
successful in the 1970s but have been close to bankruptcy in the
1980s by not changing their strategy (Baden Fuller and Stopford,
1988).

    The central finding of our case study is that a mature
industry can be dynamic, not static, and that a successful strategy
in one period may be inappropriate in another.   This contrasts
sharply with the conventional literature. Writers such as Hedley
(1971), Buzzell, Gale, and Sultan (1975), Porter (1985), Hall
(1981), Hambrick (1983), and Hambrick and Lei (1985) suggest
that there are some stable successful strategies in a mature
industry that prevail through time. We suggest that the source of
the difference between the conventional literature and our
observations lies in the assumptions behind "maturity."

    The commonly accepted meaning of the word *maturity* is
demand and product stability; however, the critical assumptions
behind most models in the literature go further. Demand stability

is assumed to be accompanied by segment stability: a well-established product manufactured by a well-established production process, and change, if any, that evolves slowly (Hofer, 1975; Scherer, 1980, pp. 98-100).

In the following description of the European washing machine industry, we show that a mature industry need not be static. Within a stable overall sales pattern the structure of demand preferences has shown significant changes over time, and although the product has been well established since the mid-1960s the source of cost advantage has also changed from scale driven to non-scale driven factors.

In tracing the history of this industry we examine two key dimensions of strategy choice expressed as the following pair of dilemmas: on the demand side, is it better to suppress variety, simplifying the organization's systems, or to accept complexity and exploit consumer preferences providing variety? At the same time, on the supply side, is it better to replicate existing production systems to exploit economies of scale or to concentrate on reorganizing the production process looking for non-scale cost advantages?

Choices have to be made about which pair to emphasize as it is rarely possible to do everything simultaneously. Consider first the question of variety versus homogeneity. If the firm caters to the customers' demands, the product range proliferates, and so do the ranges of support services; variety could be due to customers wanting products delivered more frequently. Satisfying them requires a high cost even if it does not affect the actual production process.

The opposing choice of homogeneity need not be as extreme as Ford's "you may have it any color as long as it is black," but it indicates the emphasis on standard product types and service. Such a strategy allows a simplification of the organization of the firm, lowering costs and hence prices; consumers, however, might still prefer more choice.

On the supply side, the dilemmas of ways of reducing costs for a given range of products and services can be most vividly seen in the production process. Scale economies are achieved by expanding the production process allowing specialization. When it expands it can specialize its machines and labor. Reorganizing the production process relies on redesigning the configuration of men, machines, and materials without consciously expanding the rate of production.

Economies of scale in the production process to attain cost reductions is typified by the Taylor principles practiced by Ford in the manufacturing of automobiles in the 1920s. Reorganization of production, on the other hand, is described by Abernathy, Clark, and Kantrow (1983). It is widely practiced in Japan and to a lesser extent in some Western plants, and it is best known as "just in time" and "total quality" systems.

Specialization (scale) and reorganization are, in most situations, substitute strategies rather than complementary ones.

The choice of solution to the dilemmas has important repercussions for the competitive position of the firm as it will both reflect and influence the nature of competition in the industry. For example, if the competitive advantage is fashion and low costs are achieved by internal reorganization rather than by scale, then the basis of competition is small units providing variety - a situation not dissimilar to that of "monopolistic competition".

In sharp contrast, if competitive advantage is achieved by producing a standard product exploiting scale economies, the basis of competition is an oligopolistic industry of large players, essentially that discussed in many of the traditional models. Combining homogeneous products with non-scale cost advantages gives rise to yet another form of competition, as does combining product variety with the exploiting of scale type advantages.

In this chapter we argue that many existing theories of competition in traditional industries need modification because it is wrong to use a single static model to describe the whole of the mature phase of an industry's life cycle. The example of the European washing machine industry suggests that competition in mature industries is dynamic.

Even if overall demand does not change much, the product is well established, and overall costs move slowly, there may be rapid and frequent shifts in the structure of demand (variety vis-a-vis homogeneity) and in the structure of the cost advantages (deriving from scale vis-a-vis non-scale production). These changes, driven in part by external factors and in part by the actions of the players in the industry, give rise to the changing dynamics of competition, and the inability of firms to adjust to these changes can give rise to rapid alterations in their fortunes. In the last section we discuss the generalizability of our findings.

THE EUROPEAN WASHING MACHINE INDUSTRY

The washing machine industry in Europe embraces a wide variety of firms differing in size, degree of diversification, vertical integration, and internationalization. Our data come from combining information on the strategies of both successful and unsuccessful assemblers and marketers of machines, with independent data on cost and demand factors, and information from published studies.

We define firm strategy by outcomes, not intentions, and hence we use measures such as the scale and location of plants and the producer's marketing activities (brands, models, and countries), relying extensively on information supplied by top managers in the principal firms. Despite the wealth of data, conflicting stories, gaps, and other worries forced us to make some guesses.

In figure 8-1 we show data on the consumption of washing machines in four major countries: Italy, France, Germany, and the UK. In spite of the data gaps it can be seen that the market first matured in Italy in the 1960s and matured last in the UK about 1972. Between 1950 and 1965, there was rapid growth in all countries. Crude data on unit costs (proxied by prices) revealed in figure 8-2 show a similar picture, with costs falling rapidly in the early period and more slowly there after. We can see that for many years, this industry has the outward signs of maturity.

Figure 8-1. SALES OF WASHING MACHINES IN
ITALY , GERMANY, FRANCE, AND UK.
(000s) - (1956-1987)

	Italy	Germany	France	UK*
1956	54	n/a	n/a	405
1959	164	n/a	n/a	1255
1960	189	n/a	n/a	872
1965	1136	n/a	n/a	782
1969	1102	n/a	485	625
1970	1357	n/a	1016	750
1971	1265	n/a	1168	887
1972	1438	1497	1185	1231
1973	1635	1484	1325	1572
1978	1598	1653	1365	1441
1980	1663	1550	1568	1435
1982	1669	1415	1583	1591
1984	1284	1518	1489	1763
1987	n/a	n/a	n/a	1753

* Includes non-automatics. In the UK market, in 1964
sales of automatics were 100,000, in 1969 200,000,
and in 1976 650,000.
Source: Centre for Business Strategy (LBS)

Competition has not remained static over the period, and figure 8-3 captures the essence of what is described in more detail in the following pages. It says that in the period up to the 1960s, the industry was emerging; from the early 1960s to the mid-1970s, maturity was setting in. In that period there were a number of mergers within countries. The product was becoming homogeneous, large plants were the source of low costs. The European market was dominated by Italian producers.

Figure 8-2. EUROPEAN WHOLESALE PRICES FOR WASHING MACHINES IN ITALY, UK, AND GERMANY (1960-1977)

	Italy	UK	Germany
1960	100	100	100
1961	n/a	96	96
1962	99	92	94
1963	83	86	91
1964	67	81	86
1965	54	76	84
1966	52	75	80
1967	49	72	76
1968	44	67	72
1969	40	61	69
1970	39	61	66
1971	38	59	62
1972	36	55	60
1973	34	53	58
1974	40	50	58
1975	35	48	58
1976	37	47	56
1977	36	50	n/a

Source: Owen (1983)

In the late 1970s, scale became less important as medium-sized firms found other ways of reducing costs. In the mid-1980s, demand fragmented, and competition patterns were not very dissimilar from that of monopolistic competition, with national players being the most profitable. Finally, in the late 1980s, pan-European mergers among firms were creating a more oligopolistic industrial structure. Demand in the market remains static, yet tastes are increasingly influenced by fashion trends.

The Emerging Industry of the 1950s

Corley (1966), Hatch (1970), and Balloni (1978) describe the period immediately postwar until the 1950s as one when shortages of both materials and skilled labor were not uncommon; taxes on consumer durables were high throughout Europe, as were tariffs and transport costs. The automatic washing machine was still in a phase of development, the market was very fragmented and costs and prices were falling rapidly due to technology developments in the production process (Owen, 1983).

Most producers were operating within national boundaries, producing short runs of few models substantially different from those offered by the competition. Most of the leading firms in the industry were large enterprises which had diversified into domestic appliances from light engineering, like GEC in the UK, Fiat in Italy, and AEG in Germany. Clearly the industry was not yet mature.

The Maturing Industry of the Mid-1950s to Early 1960s

Hatch (1970), Balloni (1978), Owen (1983), Green (1988), Bianchi and Forlai (1988) describe the rise in consumer incomes through the 1960s and how this helped expand the market for automatic washing machines. At the same time, the methods of production shifted from batch process to continuous assembly; the largest plants had the capacity of around 250,000 units a year.

Figure 8-3 CHANGES IN THE EUROPEAN AUTOMATIC WASHING MACHINE INDUSTRY

PERIOD	THE SUPPLY SIDE:	THE DEMAND SIDE:	THE DYNAMICS OF COMPETITION:
	Nature of Process Typical New Plant Size (units/year)	Type of Demand Market Size	
Pre-50s to Mid-50s	Batch Process Less than 50,000 Local markets	Luxury good No standard product	Emerging industry Local markets within national boundaries
Mid-50s to Early 60s	Continuous assembly 200,000 to 300,000	Emergence of a mass market stimulated by rising incomes	Maturing industry Increase in standardization within some national markets
Early 60s to Late 70s	Exploit replication Homogeneous Production; growing plant size to 1,000,000	Deep penetrating first-time buyers replacing twin-tubs leading to a replacement market	Breakdown of national barriers. European wide competition. Emergence of dominant firms offering standard products
Late 70s to Early 80s	Reorganization of plants with smaller scale; 300,000 - 500,000	Replacement market Rising incomes Particular preferences emerging	European market with some increase in brands and models. Scale no longer main determinant of cost
Mid-80s	Continuous flexible production 400,000-700,000	High disposable incomes; Product almost subject to fashion	Fragmentation of market into national and international niches Increasing product differentiation
Future Trends	Network Systems?	Product subject to innovations and fashion	Common ownership of "networks" of local and international niche producers

Run lengths, formerly quite small, rose sharply. Learning effects were exploited and this allowed prices to fall, further stimulating demand. There was a notable trend toward increasing the homogenization of the product to achieve low costs, especially in the lower priced segments of the market. Examining the individual firms' strategies within this period, it is apparent that not all followed the changes suggested by the industry's economics and, of those that adjusted, some were quicker in doing so than others.

The most successful firms were founded by Italian entrepreneurs not previously involved in the manufacture of washing machines: principally Zanussi, Fumagalli, Zoppas, and Borghi. Unlike the incumbent competitors, they had not yet committed their plants to any particular production strategy, and they foresaw the mass-market potential of the product. They adopted a low-cost strategy based on heavy investment initially building plants producing around 300,000 units per year (Owen, 1983). Apart from lowering the costs and hence the price of the product, they were also able to introduce important design modifications simplifying the product and making it more appealing, thus increasing its potential market.

By 1960, this latter group of enterprises began to reap the benefits of their investments. They continued to expand their plants to gain economies of scale, particularly in assembly, with capacities of about 1 million units per year. They established themselves as market leaders in the Italian domestic market. With plants typically 30 percent larger than the foreign competition they began to penetrate successfully into other European markets.

Some firms, such as Hoover and Hotpoint in the UK, were slower in implementing volume strategies, and they remained behind the Italian leaders in terms of costs and profits. It is unclear whether these firms failed because of lack of commitment to copying Italians (when Hoover expanded its plants to produce 400,000 units in the early 1970s, Zanussi was already producing

1.1 million units a year) or whether they suffered second mover disadvantages and were shut out by the dominant players.

Some failed to adjust to the changes in the economics of the industry, persevering with their old production and marketing strategies adopted in the previous period, apparently viewing the washing machine as a luxury good with a limited market and seeing no role for economies of scale in production. Finding themselves unable to compete successfully in the market, many such as Fiat, in Italy, and English Electric, in the UK, left the industry.   Others were bailed out by their governments who intervened, encouraging mergers and takeovers of smaller firms and enlargements of plants creating enterprises such as AEG in Germany and Thompson in France.

The changes within the industry in the decade from the early 1960s were dramatic. In Italy, in 1960, there were 50 producers of washing machines, by 1964 they had decreased to 18; in France their number decreased from 40 in 1965 to 5 by the mid-1970s; in Germany only 5 main producers were left in the market in the mid-1970s from over 50 in the 1950s.

The Early 1960s to the Late 1970s

The early 1960s to the early 1970s saw a continual increase in the size of the European market as incomes continued to rise. By the late 1970s the market was mature. Decreases in transport costs, the elimination of tariffs within the European Community, and the elimination of some of the external tariff with EFTA helped to homogenize the European market.

According to Balloni (1978), Owen (1983), Bianchi and Forlai (1988), and executives from the industry, building larger scale plants continued to be a source of reducing costs. Many of the leading firms expanded through horizontal takeovers of rivals within their own country.   These necessitated the appropriate management and coordination of purchasing market share, restructuring and selling assets peripheral to the company's strategic goals, and rationalizing the whole operations.

GEC's acquisition of Hotpoint and English Electric achieved mixed success. Hotpoint got into trouble when it attempted the transition to an export-led strategy the problem arose from the firm's inability to capture sufficient internal resources to implement the changes (Green, 1987). The white goods division of Electrolux succeeded in securing control of the domestic market (which it defined as Scandinavia rather than just Sweden), through a careful acquisition program (Electrolux annual report). From a firm domestic base it expanded into other national markets in the 1970s. In the same period, AEG in Germany also tried to expand through acquisitions, but it ran into devastating losses and it had to abandon the strategy. Thompson of France also had mixed success.

Most of the large Italian firms like Indesit, IRE, and Zanussi grew by internal expansion, sometimes supplemented by mergers (e.g., Zanussi's acquisition of Zoppas). According to some executives, Italian producers benefited not only from scale but also from lower wages and export subsidies. Limitations on management resources encouraged the firms to concentrate on a limited number of products and penetrate foreign markets by selling through private labels, overcoming local distributive and market barriers. Candy spent even longer concentrating on the domestic market and was similarly successful in gaining market share at the expense of the foreign competition. Merloni was a late entrant in the washing machine market, having had previous experience in cookers.

The Late 1970s and Early 1980s

The late 1970s and early 1980s heralded an important turning point for the industry. Demand fell due to the economic recession, and new competition emerged from the Eastern bloc countries and Spain; prices were low by historic standards, excess capacity emerged, and many producers saw their profits falling.

As is described in Bianchi and Forlai (1988), Green (1988), Hampden-Turner and Baden Fuller (1988), and Baden Fuller and Stopford (1988), there was no consensus among the producers about the correct strategy. Because of exit barriers caused by low scrap values, high costs of laying off workers, government subsidies, and management inertia, the excess capacity was not leaving the industry rapidly.

The actions of Hotpoint are worth noting. In the mid-1970s, the new chief executivo -- Schreiber -- ordered the abandoning of overseas networks and rebuilding of plants with a capacity of less than 500,000 units a years -- far smaller than that suggested by industry beliefs at the time. Although it had expanded its plant, this move was not an attempt to replicate the large scale of the Italians. Hotpoint's goal was to seek low costs through a reorganization of its operations, a major innovation being the use of prepainted steel, which eliminated many steps in the production process.

Other firms were also experimenting with smaller plants. A cross-sectional survey for the early 1980s revealed some startling conclusions (Stopford and Baden Fuller, 1987); there were very substantial productivity differences between assembly plants and these productivity differences were not scale related (see figure 8-4).

Some of the highest productivity levels were achieved in medium-sized plants (400,000 units a year). Further work suggested that productivity was not related to gross investment. The evidence strongly pointed to a change in the economics of production similar to that described by Abernathy, Clark, and Kantrow (1983) in cars. Here the source of low cost was the reorganization of the production process, rather than the expansion of output.

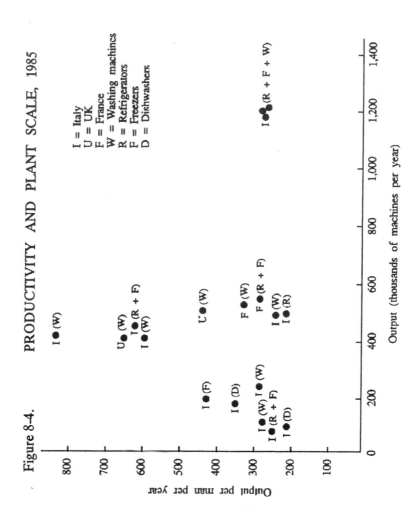

Figure 8-4.

PRODUCTIVITY AND PLANT SCALE, 1985

The Mid-1980s

By the mid-1980s, the pattern of competition within the industry had changed again. The number of brands, models, and models per brand increased from 1980, indicating heterogeneity on the demand side. Figure 8-5 highlights these trends for the UK market. The number of brands increased by 13 percent from 1976 to 1979 and by 44 percent from 1979 to 1987. The increase in the models on the market was even more marked; in 1976 there were 52 models, rising to 73 by 1979, an increase of 40 percent. In 1987 the number had increased to 201; a rise of 175 percent since 1979. The product was being matched more to the consumers' continuously changing taste than ever before.

Figure 8-5 BRANDS AND MODELS OFFERED IN THE U.K. WASHING MACHINE MARKET   1976-1987

Year	1976	1977	1978	1979	1980	1981	1982	1983	1984	1985	1986	1987
Brands	22	23	23	25	28	34	34	38	37	35	37	36
Models	52	67	68	73	77	107	121	140	152	171	189	201
Models per Brand	2.36	2.91	2.96	2.92	2.75	3.15	3.56	3.68	4.11	4.89	5.11	5.58

Source: UK Consumer Association Reports

Figure 8-6 highlights that tastes were not changing just within national boundaries, but also at a European level. Even only concentrating on two characteristics, spin speed and type of loading, it can be noted that within Europe tastes were diverse. For example, Germans, Italians, and British consumers chose front loaders; the French opted for top loaders. Spin speed preferences also differed widely across Europe: for example, in Italy low spin speeds (about 600 rpm), were favored, while Germans opted for spin speeds of more than 1,000 rpm.

164

Figure 8-6.

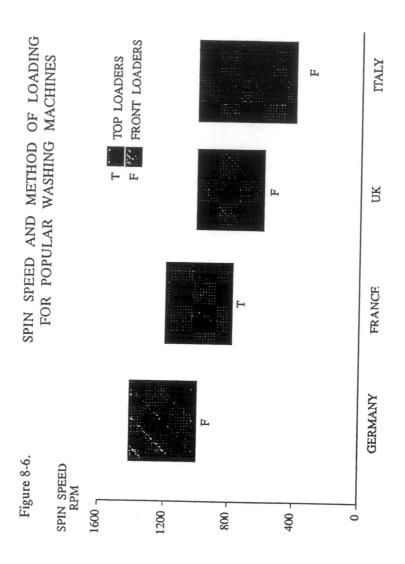

SPIN SPEED AND METHOD OF LOADING FOR POPULAR WASHING MACHINES

On the supply side large plants were at a double disadvantage. Not only were the smaller reorganized plants more efficient but they were much better at coping with demands for variety and short model runs. Many firms such as Zanussi, Indesit, Hoover, and AEG failed to adjust to this change and the success they had enjoyed in the previous periods degenerated into financial losses. In addition, some manufacturers were able to succeed by exploiting international premium market niches. Miele was one of these firms that avoided long runs of mass-market products and focused on bespoke segments such as the built-in kitchen and relatively high priced, quality washing machines. With such a strategy, Miele succeeded in placing itself in a highly profitable position.

Baden Fuller and Stopford (1988) surveyed profitability among the major firms of the Western Appliance industry. Figure 8-7 documents how the large firms declined in profitability and how firms focusing on national markets were relatively more successful. Hotpoint, TI Creda in Europe are good examples of such a trend. In 1985, they all achieved a return on capital (ROCE) of between 10 to 20 percent higher than any of the large, global players like Electrolux, Zanussi, and Philips. Their ROCE was also higher than the exporters like Merloni and Candy.

Future Trends -- From the Mid-1980s

The dynamics of competition seem to be changing again, principally due to the takeover activity of Electrolux and Philips. Electrolux has become a global player through buying the white goods businesses of Tappan and White in the United States, Zanussi in Italy and Thorn-EMI in the UK. By the late 1980s the Swedish company's share of the European white goods market was about 23 percent. In the early 1980s, Philips acquired Bauknecht, increasing its share to 19 percent of the European market. It has now sold out to Whirlpool, a U.S. company.

The evidence seems to suggest that heterogeneity of demand is a continuing and increasing trend. The major players in the industry appear to be experimenting with different patterns of production without necessarily reducing the number of plants. Firms in similar markets in other parts of the world appear to be choosing different production systems.

One idea receiving serious consideration is to copy the systems used by some Japanese and European firms, particularly the textile giant Benetton. To solve the conflict between standardization and diversification the production system can be organized as a network, and it is not improbable that such an option could be adopted in the European washing machine market in an attempt to solve the dilemmas of what the optimum levels of variety and scale are in this industry.

DISCUSSION

It is obvious that the maturity of demand of washing machines has masked a dynamically changing industry. If we ignore the 1950s when the industry was emerging, we suggest that there are four models -- each corresponding to different eras and different demand and cost conditions.

1.   In the 1960s and early 1970s competitive advantage within the industry was achieved by Italian firms using mass production techniques to manufacture relatively homogenized products. Competitive advantage and profits were derived from a large market share. Such a scenario is captured in what we might call the "traditional" type of models extensively used in strategy literature. Porter (1980, 1985) advocates the low cost strategy; the Boston Consulting Group emphasizes the value of market share in reducing costs; and Buzzell and Gale (1987) focus on the value of both market share and scale in creating profits.

2. Numerous case studies appear to confirm the power of this type of model in those circumstances where variety is suppressed and scale economies are an important source of cost reduction; the most famous being Abernathy and Wayne's (1974) description of Ford's automobile strategy in the 1920s. Other well documented studies include the Boston Consulting Group's study of motor cycles (HMSO, 1975).

3. In the mid-1970s companies like Hotpoint decided to reverse the trend to large scale plants. Although demand was homogeneous, scale differences were not the principal cause of cost differences. Firms lowered costs significantly by reorganizing the process of production and logistics using different combinations of skills. Interfirm cost differences were determined by specific actions which were either hard to copy or their relative importance was not understood by the competition. The "non-scale low cost" type of models of Nelson and Winter (1982) and Lippman and Rumelt (1987) come quite close to explaining this type of market environment.

4. Our industry is by no means an isolated example: Abernathy, Clark, and Kantrow (1983) vividly document how the Japanese car industry gained advantage over the U.S. auto industry in this way. In the early 1980s, contrary to popular opinion, factor prices were relatively unimportant, as Japanese wages were not material different from those in the United States; rather, the cost differential arose from diverse skill bases leading to important cost savings in time and inputs. Grant and Baden Fuller's (1987) description of the use of electronics in the grinding processes of Richardson, the UK knife manufacturer, is another example.

5. In the late 1970s and early 1980s, we saw that the washing machine industry had changed again. Demand was

becoming more heterogeneous, and average plant scale of the successful enterprises was about half that in the late 1960s. The success stories in this period are provided by firms like Hotpoint in the UK and Thompson in France. Models of "monopolistic competition" described by Spence (1976) and Dixit and Stiglitz (1977) capture part of the competitive dynamics of this period of the washing machine industry.

6.   Competitive advantage was achieved by concentrating on getting closer to the customer by offering variety and (something missing in the economists' models) by exploiting the technological advantages outlined above. Large-scale linear processes were broken down into shorter, more parallel processes similar to those used in the car industry (Bianchi, 1984), and in many cases this diminished the comparative cost advantage of the bigger units. More significantly, price competition was muted by product differentiation, and the single-product traditional firm strategy appeared to fail.

7.   Finally we commented that, at present, the washing machine industry is undergoing some fundamental restructuring with pan-European mergers and acquisitions and subsequent reorganization dominating the scene. Although it is not yet clear what the industry competitive pattern will look like, we suggested that one possible scenario is provided by "network systems" models described by Ornati and Lorenzoni (1988) and Jarillo (1988) where identifying a breadth of international and national customer niches is the key to achieving competitive advantage in this setting. Here success may be achieved by the ability to coordinate a network of specialized operating units resolving the conflict between a heterogeneous demand, favoring small production units and firms' continuous search for scale economies in organization.

Figure 8-7. PROFITABILITY (ROCE*) OF MAJOR
WESTERN APPLIANCE MANUFACTURERS
(1974-1985) (percent)

Company	1974-79	1980-84	1985
Global Players			
Electrolux UK	20.7	9.4	4.7
Zanussi	14.3	1.5	8.0
Philips IRE	11.4	10.1	4.2
Exporters			
INdesit	16.0	-10.0	n/a
Merloni	17.7	13.0	8.3
Candy	11.4	12.2	8.9
Hoover	11.8	3.5	14.7
Nationals			
Hotpoint	6.6	23.2	37.9
TI Creda	35.1	34.7	11.8
Lec	21.7	21.1	14.6
USA			
GE	n/a	28.7	33.3
Whirlpool	20.0	19.8	18.3
White	n/a	13.5	n/a
Maytag	n/a	36.6	37.5

*ROCE = Profits before interest and tax divided by
capital employed (for major appliance division).
Source: Published Records.

A single matrix incorporating the four types of models just discussed can be derived going back to the two dilemmas facing the firm -- scale versus non-scale and homogeneous product versus variety. Figure 8-8 shows such a two-by-two matrix.

In this final part we suggest that the dynamics of change, so notable in the washing machine industry, is a feature in some other industries. Figure 8-9 illustrates the history of the strategies adopted by knitwear firms from Carpi in Italy. In the 1950s they were producing a very limited range of colors and styles using large-scale plants. In the 1960s their operations became more fragmented, relying less on scale as a source of low cost but still producing a limited range of products.

In the 1970s, the size of their plants remained medium sized but, in adopting converging technology, the range of products increased considerably. After the success of companies like Benetton and Stefanel, more of the Carpi firms started to organize their operations as systems of networks. Figure 8-10 maps on to the framework the dynamics of the strategies of two other firms from different mature industries: Edwards High Vacuum, a British pumps producer, and Richardson, a British cutlery firm.

CONCLUSIONS

While we suggest that our framework is a useful dynamic tool for the analysis of the dynamics of competition in mature industries, we have used it on a very limited number of case studies, so it is vulnerable to the criticism that its generality has not been fully proved empirically. For example, it is possible that there are not many firms whose strategy changes can be traced through all four boxes. We are aware of this limitation and further research could be pursued in this direction.

However, one conclusion is clear from our studies and cannot be overemphasized. Maturity is a mask. Successful firms

Figure 8-8.   DIFFERENT WAYS OF ACHIEVING ADVANTAGE

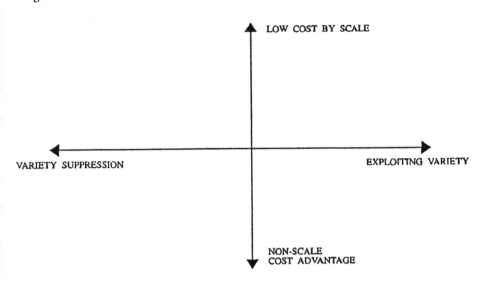

Figure 8-9.   DIFFERENT WAYS OF ACHIEVING ADVANTAGE

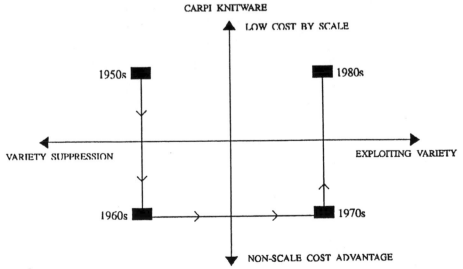

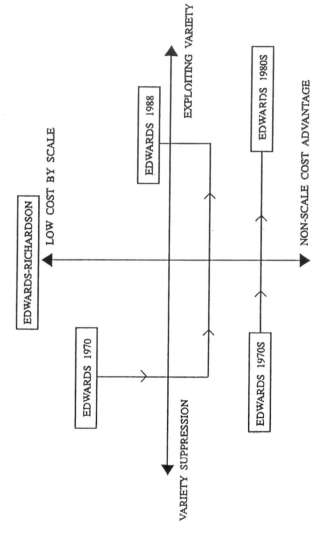

Figure 8-10.   DIFFERENT WAYS OF ACHIEVING ADVANTAGE

are those that adjust, recognizing the highly dynamic competitive nature of mature industries.

References

Abernathy W.J., Clark, K.B., and Kantrow, A.M. *Industrial Renaissance: Producing a Competitive Future for America.* New York: Basic Books, 1983.

Abernathy W.J., and Wayne K. "Limits of the Learning Curve," *Harvard Business Review*, Sept-Dec, 1974, pp 109-119.

Baden Fuller, C. and Stopford, J.M. "Global or National?" *L'Industria*, 1988.

Balloni, V. *Origini, Sviluppo e Maturita' dell'industria degli Elettrodomestici.* Il Mulino: Bologna, 1978.

Bianchi, P. *Divisione del Lavoro e Ristrutturazione Industriale.* Il Mulino: Bologna, 1984.

Bianchi, P. and Forlai, L. "The European Domestic Appliance Sector, 1945-1987." 1988.

Buzzell, R.D., and Gale, B.T. *The PIMS Principles: Linking Strategy to Performance.* New York: Free Press, 1987.

Buzzell, R.D., Gale, B.T., and Sultan, R.G.M. "Market Share - a Key to Profitability", *Harvard Business Review*, January-February, 1975, **53**, pp. 97-106.

Corley, T.A.B. *Domestic Electrical Appliances.* London: Cox and Wyman Ltd., 1966.

Cubbin, J. "Is it Better to be a Weak Firm in a Strong Industry or a Strong Firm in a Weak Industry," Working Paper Series, June 1988, No. 49, London Business School.

Dixit, A.K. and Stiglitz, J.E.   "Monopolistic Competition and
Optimum Product Diversity"   *American Economic Review*,
1977, **67**, pp. 297 308.

Grant, R., and Baden Fuller, C. "The Richardson Sheffield Story,"
Case Series, 1987, No. 2, London Business School.

Green, S. "The Hotpoint Success Story," Case Series, 1988, No. 3,
London Business School.

Jarillo, J.C.   "On Strategic Networks," *Strategic Management
Journal*, 1988, **9**, pp 31-41.

Hall, W.K. "Survival Strategies in a Hostile Environment," *Harvard
Business Review*, January-February, 1981, pp. 135-144.

Hambrick, D.C., and Lei, D. "Towards an Empirical Prioritization
of Contingency Variables for Business Strategy," *Academy of
Management Journal*, 1985, **28**(4), pp. 763-788.

Hambrick, D.C.   "An Empirical Typology of Mature Industrial
Product Environments," *Academy of Management Journal*,
1983, **26**,(2), pp. 213-230.

Hatch. "Competition in the British White Goods Industry
1954-1964."   Unpublished Ph.D., Cambridge University,
1970.

Hampden Turner, C., and Baden Fuller, C.   "Strategy and the
Managing of Dilemma,"   Working Paper, 1988, Center for
Business Strategy, London Business School.

Hedley, B. "A Fundamental Approach to Strategy Development,"
Long Range Planning, 1976, **6**, pp. 2-11.

H.M.S.O.   *Strategy Alternatives for the British Motor Cycle
Industry*. 1975.

Hofer C.W.   "Toward a Contingency Theory of Business Strategy,"
    Academy of Management Journal, 1975, **18**(4), pp. 784-811.

Lippman, S.A. and Rumelt, R.P.   "Uncertain Imitability an
    Analysis of Interfirm Differences in Efficiency under
    Competition," *Bell Journal of Economics*, 1987.

Lorenzoni, G., and Ornati, O.A.   "Constellations of Firms and
    New Ventures," *Journal of Business Venturing*, 1988, 3, pp.
    41-57

Nelson, R.R., and Winter, S.G.   *An Evolutionary Theory of
    Economic Change.*   Cambridge, Mass: Harvard University,
    1982.

Owen, N. *Economies of Scale, Competitiveness and Trade Patterns
    Within the European Community.* Oxford: Clarendon Press,
    1983.

Porter, M.E. *Competitive Strategy.* New York: Free Press, 1980.

Porter, M.E. *Competitive Advantage.* New York: Free Press, 1985.

Scherer, F.M. *Industrial Market Structure and Economic
    Performance* (2nd ed). Chicago: Rand McNally, 1980.

Spence, M.   "Product Selection, Fixed Costs and Monopolistic
    Competition." *Review of Economic Studies*, 1976,   43, pp.
    217-235.

Chapter 9

Reconceptualizing the Corporation and Competition

David J. Teece

University of California, Berkeley

Two somewhat independent shifts are causing academics, businessmen, and policy makers to rethink fundamental ideas about the corporation and competition. The first is the increased level of international competition, particularly from the Japanese and other developmental states which have relentlessly been challenging American and European corporations in the global marketplace. These competitive pressures are leading, at least in some circles, to a re-evaluation of American institutions and policies. The second and more subtle shift is occurring within economics and is driven by a dissatisfaction with orthodox theory. Textbook views of the corporation as a black box, or production function, are giving way to views of the corporation as an institution for economizing on transaction costs, for housing organizational learning, and for capturing value from technological innovation. In addition, some fundamental rethinking is occurring with respect to how corporations ought to cooperate and compete. This latter issue has not gone very far to date, but it will probably become an increasingly important consideration in the years ahead.

In this chapter, I briefly survey and interpret these recent developments and indicate the directions in which the new thinking might productively gravitate.

THE CORPORATION

Traditional Views

Economists and managers have had their own stylized view of the corporation in the postwar period. Each perspective is quite distinct and is examined separately.

Neoclassical Perspectives. Academic economists, relying on the classical economists and in particular Ricardo and Marshall, have always tended to view the firm as a mechanism for converting inputs into outputs, using known technologies in accordance with the dictates of marginal analysis. This view has proved to be useful as the underpinnings of a theory of production and enables much of traditional industry analysis as well as price theory to proceed.

The theory of the firm as developed by the classical economists has had a remarkable stability, with very few new insights provided until quite recently. But to view the firm as an input conversion mechanism is extraordinarily limited and often downright misleading. It has tended to focus attention on cost conditions and, in particular, scale and more recently scope economy issues. But in today's world if not in earlier periods, the key economic functions of the corporation relate to learning and innovation, to organizational control and coordination, and to economizing on the transactions costs that would be incurred if the economic activity which is internalized had to proceed between stand-alone firms in the market.

A key limiting aspect of the production function view is that it avoids governance and agency issues. How is the firm to be organized and managed, and how are the top managers going to be policed? These complex and real issues are not part of the basic conceptualization contained in the production function view, and to the extent they were dealt with at all, it was in special theories which were not successfully grafted onto the underlying theory of production.

Equally remiss has been the treatment of know-how and knowledge generation and retention with the business enterprise. The most common theoretical approach, evidenced in practically all of the textbooks on microeconomics or price theory, is to take technology as given, ignoring completely the fact that managers almost always have the option to invest in R&D in order to bring about improvements in products and processes. On the occasions when this pattern is broken by explicit attention to technological change, the treatment of states of knowledge and changes therein is usually simplistic and misleading. It is common to assume in models of competition that technology is available to all at zero cost. If proprietary, it is considered to reside in a "book of blueprints" that can be traded just like a bushel of wheat or a ton of coal. In reality, know-how cannot, except in some circumstances, be transferred at zero cost from organization to organization. The book of blueprints metaphor implies that know-how is codified, when more often than not it is tacit. The book of blueprints metaphor caricatures the development and transfer of know-how.

The inadequacy of the received orthodoxy is evidenced by the complete inability of the theory to explain the organization and structure of the modern corporation. There is nothing in orthodox theory, except chance, to explain why firms diversify and nothing to explain why the observed diversification is not completely random. Clearly, most firms do not diversify in a completely random fashion, and some firms, like IBM, are remarkably specialized. Nor is there anything, other than appeals to monopoly incentives, to explain vertical integration. Even explaining the size of the firm and limits thereto is beyond the means of neoclassical orthodox theory.

Hence, without too much exaggeration, one can say that the orthodoxy found in practically all the textbooks tells us virtually nothing about the modern multiproduct, multidivisional, vertically integrated corporation. It might constitute an acceptable model of the nineteenth century English farm, but nineteenth century agriculture is quite some organizational and technological distance from the modern postwar America or Japanese corporation.

As mentioned above, neoclassical orthodox theory even has trouble explaining the limits to firm size. Oliver Williamson (1985) has referred to this as a "chronic puzzle" in the theory of the firm. Primitive formulations of the theory of the firm appeal to exhaustion of scale economies; but while limits to production level economics may explain why plants reach a certain size, they do not explain why **firms** cannot expand indefinitely. Knight's (1965, pp. 286-87) answer was that a man could not "adequately manage a business enterprise of indefinite size and complexity" because of "effective uncertainty." Coase posed the question of "Why is not all production carried on in one big firm?" (Coase, 1937), but seemed unable to answer his own question.

Institutional-Managerial Perspectives. It is much more complex to characterize institutional-managerial views of the corporation. Institutionalists' and historians' concepts of the corporation have been shaped less by theory than by actual facts and circumstances.

Different methods for organizing work have shaped the corporation, both here and abroad. Early organizational forms included the putting-out system. The capitalist firm, personified by the putter-outer and his agents, supplied rural workers in the early nineteenth century with raw materials that would be processed in the home to produce woolen and cotton goods. The finished goods would then be collected and paid for at a previously agreed upon piece rate.

The putting-out system reduced the capitalists' fixed costs but did not provide control, and the ability to quickly introduce productivity-enhancing investments.   Also, division of labor was limited as the workers could only communicate with each other via the putter-outer and his agent.   The **factory** afforded a potential solution to throughput and productivity problems.   In capital-intensive activities like spinning, the mechanized factory system came in during the 1770s, and half a century later in weaving.

In the nineteenth century British factories, operatives took on functions now commonly thought of as management functions (Pollard, 1965, ch. 5).   They recruited and trained workers, and often acted as inside subcontractors.   Such shop floor control was later parlayed into powerful and enduring unions.   Senior adult workers utilized the management and apprenticeship system to play the major role in the development of the labor force.   The early British firms were thus akin to vertically specialized factories.   The reliance on skilled labor for managerial functions lessened the need to develop managerial hierarchies.   Regional concentration permitted external economies to be realized so that British industry was viable, even if scale was limited (Lazonick, 1987).

The 1920s witnessed a second industrial revolution, dominated by U.S. manufacturing companies.   The second industrial revolution was based on additional mechanization and on organizational innovation.   In the nineteenth century, a distinctive "American system of manufactures" had emerged in wood working and metal working, and particularly in armaments where long-term government procurement contracts justified investments in special purpose machinery (Smith, 1977; Hounshell, 1984; Lazonick, 1987).   These investments economized on skilled labor and lowered costs by achieving parts interchangeability.   The "Lowell system" of cotton textile manufacture similarly encouraged skills in cotton textile manufacture.   The trend toward mass production and vertical integration reached its full expression in

182

Henry Ford's giant River Rouge facility for manufacturing the model T.

Henry Ford, with his introduction of the moving assembly line and his perfection of interchangeability, was first and foremost an organizational innovator. Ford and his contemporary, Fred Taylor, made significant contributions to managerial thinking by stressing the need to share productivity gains with workers, and the importance of scheduling and coordination. However, both Ford and Taylor erred in treating human effort as purely an expandable marketable commodity. As the specialized capital required for efficient production expanded, so did the the need for commitment from the workplace. In subsequent decades, as their market power increased, American firms came to offer de facto extended employment through internal job ladders (Lazonick, 1983).

American managers were the first to learn how to structure large corporations to overcome control loss problems and to facilitate long-term planning. The multidivisional structure was developed in the 1920s and diffused rapidly thereafter. The separation of operational from strategic decision making which the M-form accommodated created a new concept of the business enterprise.

The passing of economic leadership from Britain to the Uinted States in the interwar years changed the institutional nature of global capitalism. The British model of the family firm was displaced by the American model of the large multidimensional enterprise with ownership separate from control. British business institutions ossified; the American ones continued to change. Craft control of the shop floor and the family firm structure in Britain impeded innovation and exchange. The superiority of American management over the the British was apparent to all by 1950. The British system, based on aristocratic values, the family firm, and the inability of the education system to offer the pre-employment foundations for management development could no longer compete in global products against a better system. The relative levels of living of the British had to decline, along with Britain's economic and political power.

However, the American epoch of economic prowess was to be short lived. The American concept of the corporation and strategy took on some distinctive properties -- some would say debilitating qualities -- during the postwar years. Diversification expanded and took on a conglomerate dimension during the 1960s. It was widely believed, and for a while the stock market seemed to bear it out, that the way to profitability was through growth and the fastest way to grow was to diversify, through mergers and acquisitions if necessary. This belief was fueled by an explosion in strategic management tools and, in particular, the product portfolio concept of the Boston Consulting Group (BCG).

The BCG held that, because of experience curve effects, the acquisition of market share was the key to profitability. Moreover, a firm had to have a balanced portfolio of businesses with different cash flow profiles. The cash generated by "cash cow" businesses ought to be used to finance new businesses, as if there was no venture capital market (there was not much of one in the 1960s), and as if mature markets could never be revitalized through reinvestment and innovation. The investment banking community facilitated and encouraged growth via merger and acquisition.

By the 1970s, however, it had become apparent that the American system was being challenged by smarter capitalists from across the Pacific -- the Japanese. Prominent institutional features of the Japanese industrial system include enterprise groups, consensus decision making, and permanent employment. The Japanese manager's concept of the corporation is very different from his American counterpart's. If the United States has a "control model" to accomplish hierarchical integration, then the Japanese have a commitment model. The transition from the first to the second requires transformation in both the traditional division of labor between managers and workers as well as in skills and attitudes of workers and managers.

Important and possibly critical differences in the relationship of finance to industry characterize the United States and Japan. The Japanese economy has grown largely independently of an active reliance on stock markets -- either as a major source of corporate capital or of discipline on corporation management (Gerlach, 1987). True, institutions have in Japan, as in the United States, replaced individuals as the primary controller of shareholdings. About 43 percent of shares of U.S. firms were held by institutional investors in the early 1980s, while the figure in Japan was 62 percent (Aoki, 1984, pp. 10-11). But the nature of this relationship is markedly different in the two countries. In the United States, nearly two-thirds of institutional investors are pension funds and personal trust funds. In Japan, equity is held instead by business partners. These equity links signify interfirm relationships that tend to be markedly stable over time.

New Perspectives

The Organizational Economics Perspective. Most applied economists have now abandoned the traditional production function view of the firm. A new perspective has emerged that views the corporation as simultaneously a mechanism for internalizing certain transactions which would proceed much less efficiently, if at all, were they forced into a market context and as a mechanism to facilitate path dependent learning.

The transactions cost perspective has its origins with Ronald Coase's seminal (1937) article on the nature of the firm. The perspective has been further developed by Williamson (1975, 1985) who has turned transactions costs reasoning into a theory of the firm by specifying the circumstances under which contractual linkages among unaffiliated parties are likely to break down, and when superior hierarchical alternatives exist. This theory points to the importance of the technological requirements of efficient production in determining desirable organizational arrangements. When efficient production requires special purpose equipment which is idiosyncratic to a particular set of buyer-seller relationships, or investment in firm or customer specific know-how, then firms will probably need to internalize these assets if they want production to proceed efficiently. Specialized assets turn out to be the key discriminating factor in the transactions cost theory of the firm, and they help explain complex forms of business organization and especially vertical integration.

But transactions costs approaches leave much about the corporation unexplained. Diversification is a case in point. Neoclassical concepts such as economies of scope cannot explain diversification either. Orthodox theory would imply that since economies of scope arise from the sharing of a common input, a specialist firm ought to be able to own the common input and rent its services to other specialist firms who would pursue their own particular product line strategy. Multiproduct firms would exist in the world of orthodox micro theory and frictionless markets, but only as flukes. Transactions cost reasoning, which emphasizes the shortcomings of contractual investments for leasing the services of specialized assets, can explain why firms might become multiproduct (Teece, 1982). However, additional factors must be introduced to explain observed reality, and particularly the fact that firms often start specialized and become diversified. There is nothing in orthodox theory, or in transactions cost theory, to explain why it is rarely observed that firms begin large and diversified and subsequently become specialized.[1] Generally, of course, firms are formed specialized and later diversify.

To explain such a phenomenon, one must reconceptualize the corporation. Firms need to be understood and their boundaries explained in terms of their **economizing** and **learning** capability, in terms of their **path-dependent growth**, and not their resources conversion capabilities as orthodox theory would have it. Important aspects of each are briefly examined next.

Important characteristics of **economizing** are the following. Internalizing economic activity is more efficient than the market alternative when efficient production requires highly (transaction) specialized investments in plant and equipment, in location, and in learning. Otherwise, there is a great risk that these investments will be stranded as a result of recontracting by unaffiliated parties whose prior contractual commitments are important to the profitability of the investment in question.

Important characteristics of learning inside the corporation are that it is cumulative, it involves the development of organizational rather than individual skill, and that the knowledge generated by learning is best conceptualized as residing in organizational structures and not in some mythical book of blueprints. The rate of learning is powerfully influenced by changes in the science and technology that underpin the industry.

It is also important to recognize that the growth of business firms is path dependent, being constrained by significant irreversibilities as well as forward constraints. There are several reasons for this. First, firms typically arise as governance structures to protect specialized idiosyncratic physical and human capital. These assets are not generic and generally cannot be deployed outside the line of business for which they were developed in the first place. Second, notwithstanding notable exceptions, there are cognitive limits on the capacities of managers which prohibit them from knowing all technologies and markets equally well.

Once reconceptualized along these lines, a rather interesting and empirically satisfying set of propositions emerge about the firm, its capabilities, and its boundaries. A firm is likely to have one or more "core businesses" defined by the technological and market paths it has historically traversed. The degree of coherence displayed among the firm's businesses will be a function of the interaction of learning, path dependencies, and the strength of the competitive environment in which the firm has operated.

With rapid learning, as in many high technology industries, and tight path dependencies, one should expect to see single product (specialist) firms growing rapidly. With slow learning and path dependencies, one can expect to see specialist firms displaying some degree of lateral integration. With high learning and low path dependency, fast-moving "network" firms and "hollow" corporations should be viable. Conglomerates may exist where there is low path dependency, slow learning, and weak competitive pressures. Learning, path dependencies, and the selection environment the firm occupies will thus explain the coherence of the corporation.

Institutional and Managerial Perspectives. Since the 1970s, a rather different view, or at least an alternative view, of the corporation has begun to emerge in America. Alfred Chandler (1977), basing his observations on the period before World War II, defined the modern corporation as follows: "Modern business enterprise...has two specific characteristics: it contains many distinct operating units and it is managed by a hierarchy of executives. Each unit...has its own administrative office....In contrast, the traditional American business firm was a single-unit business enterprise...."

But the modern American corporation in the 1980s is not necessarily of the type Chandler describes. A whole new class of specialized, fast-growing firms has emerged, usually in high technology industries. These firms possibly represent an alternative paradigm for organizing business. These firms also have a different ownership structure, displaying considerable employee ownership, and different corporate cultures. They sometimes have close links with established firms. For instance, the new biotechnology firms often have close links with established pharmaceutical companies. They are typically venture capital funded, with the venture capitalists playing important advisory and sometimes managerial roles.

These firms do not take their boundaries as given. Two key dynamics are whether technology should be developed internally or sourced from the outside, and whether manufacturing and other key vertical stages should be performed in-house or serviced externally. Technology strategy in these new companies is thus just not a question of how much to spend on R&D and on what, but also should the firm license in or license out, and should it commercialize innovation using in-house marketing and manufacturing, or should it collaborate and/or joint venture with firms better positioned in these complementary assets. These concerns are now a critical decision variable for big firms as well as small firms, but it is the newer firms that have been the most willing, possibly because of necessity, to consider their boundaries as a decision variable.

Larger traditional firms have in some instances attempted to adopt the small company model internally, creating new venture groups with considerable autonomy. Not many have been successful. What is evident, however, is a clear tension between the virtues of bigness and of smallness, of centralization and decentralization, of integration and contract. The challenge of management is to balance these properties and attempt to capture benefits from simultaneously maintaining some of each structure. This is what American management has experimented with in the 1970s and 1980s, so far with mixed success. Perhaps the internal logic of each form is so strong that mixed structural forms are not viable.

COMPETITION

Traditional Views

The basic tenet of received orthodoxy is that competition drives resource allocation toward efficient outcomes, while market power distorts and detracts. The image of competition that informs this view is that of the neoclassical perfectly competitive process. This model employs a long list of assumptions, including atomistic competitors with fixed technology and perfect foresight. In this model, the effect of monopoly is to reduce output, raise price, and create excess profit. If there is any redeeming virtue of monopoly, it is the case of "natural" monopoly, where the economies of scale gained through monopolization yield economies of great value.

In the orthodox formulation, price is considered to be the sharpest competitive weapon. Nonprice competition, through product and process innovation, "can have real effects but it is less direct and hard hitting" (Shepherd, 1979, p. 301). Cooperation is generally analyzed only in terms of its negative impact on economic welfare. Indeed, coordination of prices is often the only form of cooperation recognized in the textbooks. For instance, Shepherd (1979) has an entire chapter (chapter 15) devoted to the topic of "cooperation among firms" which is entirely a discussion of cartels, as if it were the only kind of interfirm cooperation. One must look in vain for analysis of interfirm collaborative research in the Western literature on research and development published before 1970 (Samuels, 1987). And in the economic literature, there is practically no mention of cooperative R&D, let alone analysis of it, until about the 1980s.

Embedded in the orthodox literature is a hostility toward cooperation, even when it involves R&D. Cooperation is feared because it would preclude multiple paths to invention and dull the incentives to be creative. Furthermore, collaborative habits might migrate from the laboratory to product development and marketing, with attendant antisocial consequences.

The conceptualization of competition informs competition policy in North America. It leads to a hostility toward many forms of business conduct, particularly if agreements with competitors are at issue. It also informs industrial policy in many Western nations. Economies are often sought and protected in the formulation of public policy; however, because economies of scale are practically the only economies recognized in orthodox theory, the avenues in which government can assist industrial development, and the matters upon which the government should restrict business behavior, tend to be construed narrowly. For instance, notions of "critical" or "strategic" industries cannot find a foundation in received orthodoxy -- nor can the strategic use of trade barriers or the use of export promotion mechanisms. The result is a world in which governments, particularly in North America, restrict complex forms of business behavior, such as the exchange of competitor information and collaboration with respect to new product commercialization, while finding nothing objectionable about conglomerate mergers, even if they are efficiency destroying.[2]

Challenges to Orthodoxy

A reconceptualization of competition, and in particular horizontal collaboration, would appear to be warranted. In many circles, not much is new with respect to the fashion in which competition and cooperation is assessed. Nevertheless, elements of a new approach can be identified.

The underpinnings of a new approach can reside in the observation that an essential aspect of economic organization is the need to coordinate economic activity and, in particular, investments. It is the essence of the private enterprise economy that although its individual members are independent, their activities are nevertheless interrelated. Any single investment will, in general, only be profitable provided, first, that the volume of competitive investment does not exceed a limit set by demand, and, second, that the volume of complementary investment reaches the correct level (Richardson, 1960, p. 31).

However, orthodox theorists often fail to recognize that there is no special machinery in a private enterprise, market economy to ensure that investment programs are made known to all concerned at the time of their inception. Price movements, by themselves, do not generally form an adequate system of signaling. Indeed, Tjalling Koopmans (1957, p. 146) has been rather critical of what he calls "the overextended belief" of certain economists in the efficiency of competitive markets as a means of allocating resources in a world characterized by ubiquitous uncertainty. The main source of this uncertainty, according to Koopmans, is the ignorance that firms have with respect to their competitors' future actions, preferences, and states of technological information. In the absence of a complete set of forward markets in which anticipation and intentions could be tested and adjusted, there is no reason to believe that, with uncertainty, competitive markets of the kind which American antitrust laws seek to foster can produce efficient outcomes.[3] The information-circulating function which economic theory attributes to competitive markets is quite simply not discharged by any existing arrangements with the detail and forward extension necessary to support efficient outcomes (Koopmans, 1957, p. 163).

Today, there is no arena in which uncertainty is higher and the need to coordinate greater than in the development, and possibly the commercialization, of new technology. In many industries, the stupendous foreshortening of product life cycles and the tremendous escalation of development and commercialization costs have increased the technological, managerial, and financial resource requirements for marketplace success. Moreover, the sources of innovation have become geographically and organizationally more dispersed. A related development is that imitation and idea borrowing are becoming increasingly easy and common. Most scientific know-how and new product concepts are available to all firms willing and able to invest in the relevant information collection activities. Low cost travel and telecommunications means that the natural protection of distance and language has all but evaporated. While intellectual property law is migrating in a direction that favors innovators, the instruments of the law (patents, copyrights, trademarks, and so on) are inherently weak and cannot protect any ideas, only some of their manifestations. Appropriating the benefits from investment in new technology is thus inherently difficult. Accordingly, the incentives to coordinate via collaboration have markedly escalated. In the global environment of the 1980s and 1990s, collaboration (horizontal and vertical) is a necessity in many industries.

Not surprisingly, some analysts are coming to realize that collaborative research activities among firms which may be competitors in product markets is likely to improve economic welfare. There are several forms in which such cooperation may take place. At one extreme, firms may simply combine their total activities, including R&D, through acquisition or merger. At the other extreme, one firm could perform under contract all of the R&D needed by both. Intermediate solutions include collaborative behavior, where firms could simply pool their research activities, in whole or in part, or R&D joint ventures, where a separate entity could be established in which joint R&D activities could be conducted (Pisano, Russo, and Teece, 1988, pp. 4-16).

Both research joint ventures and research collaborations can assist firms in overcoming appropriability (technology leakage) problems because research costs can be shared, and also because the set of firms receiving the benefits is likely to include a greater portion of firms that have incurred R&D costs.[4] The effect of greater appropriability is, of course to stimulate greater investment in new technology. It is well understood that competitive markets tend to underinvest in new technology because those firms which support R&D have limited capacity to extract "fees" from the imitators (free riders).

In addition, collaborative research reduces, if not eliminates, what William Norris, Chief Executive Officer of Control Data Corporation, refers to as "shameful and needless duplication of effort" (Davis, 1985, p. 42). Independent research activities often proceed down identical or near-identical technological paths. This is wasteful and can be avoided if research plans are coordinated.

The manifold benefits from collaboration activity have been recognized abroad and, more recently, in the United States as well.[5] One assessment of the United States is that "up until now, however, we have taken it for granted as an article of faith that no cooperation should be permitted, that it is best that we keep companies apart from one another" (Ouchi, 1984, p. 103). Japanese competitors have engaged in deep cooperation for decades and have received de facto exemption from Japanese antitrust laws to do so. Japanese cooperative activity is in the form of not only R&D joint ventures, but also R&D collaboration. For instance, by the end of 1971, the entire Japanese computer industry (six firms) was paired in order to compete with IBM and its System 370 (Ouchi, 1984, p. 105). While the research was done in existing cooperative labs, there was intense interaction and information sharing. Another celebrated example of Japanese collaboration was the VLSI (Very Large Scale Integrated Circuit) Research Association which was an R&D joint venture formed in 1975 with the capital contributed by NEC, Toshiba, Hitachi, Mitsubishi, and Fujitsu[6]. At the successful conclusion of the project in 1979, the laboratory was dissolved and the scientists went back to their sponsoring companies.

Since the National Cooperative Research Act of 1984, which limits, but does not eliminate antitrust risks, some interest has been shown in R&D joint ventures in the United States Well known R&D joint ventures include: the Microelectronics and Computer Technology Corp. (MCC) in Austin, Texas; the Semiconductor Research Corporation (SRC) in Research Triangle Park, North Carolina; and Bell Communication Research (Bellcore). These joint ventures are restricted to R&D up to the prototype "stage." For instance, MCC's objective is to engage in advanced long-term research and development in computer architecture, semiconductor packaging and interconnect, software technology, VLSI, and CAD. Its numbers include AMD, Boeing, Control Data, Harris, Motorola, Sperry, and others. (IBM is conspicuously absent as are Japanese and European-based firms.)

The only form of cooperative research that receives special antitrust treatment (but not exemption) in the United States is the R&D joint venture. Other forms of collaborative R&D activity, such as the pooling of R&D projects and the sharing of development data, are subject to deep antitrust exposure. Cooperation using existing facilities is thus perceived to be exposed to serious antitrust risk, particularly if participating firms have significant market shares. Beneficial collaboration in R&D is thus likely to be circumscribed in the United States if participating firms are world class competitors.

In order to go beyond laboratory activity and commercialize new technologies, a more challenging and typically more investment-intensive set of tasks must be successfully conducted. The commercialization of technologies is perhaps even more challenging than their initial development. The requirements for cooperation here are also strong.

In idealized treatments of the innovation process, it is common to represent the various steps as being largely sequential but with significant overlaps. In the textbook treatment, one does basic/applied research, then prototyping or pilot plant design, production planning and manufacturing setup, manufacturing startup, and marketing startup. The impression is often left that one step mechanically leads to the next. Feedback loops from manufacturing to research, from sales and marketing to manufacturing, and from sales and marketing to research are often omitted, particularly in treatments of the innovation process by policy analysts (although managers generally know better).

The innovation process is, however, decidedly nonlinear. The reason is that with incomplete information available at the outset, there are shortcomings and failures that demand rapid, accurate feedback with followup and redesign. Radical, or revolutionary, innovation prospers best when provided with multiple sources of informational input. Ordinary, evolutionary innovation requires iterative fitting and trimming of the many necessary criteria and desiderata. In either case, feedback and trials are essential. An implication of this is that it is difficult to organizationally separate R&D from commercialization. Hence, antitrust statutes that view collaboration with respect to R&D sympathetically, but collaboration with respect to commercialization antagonistically, are inherently in conflict.

Moreover, the successful commercialization of technology often involves collaboration among firms that have different pieces of the puzzle. The relevant manufacturing capacities need not be resident within the firm responsible for the other activities in the innovation process. In order to capture value from the innovation, it may therefore be necessary for a number of firms to collaborate, with different firms being responsible for different activities (Teece, 1986). In some cases, these firms may be horizontal competitors and antitrust may block desirable collaboration.

Strictures on collaboration after the prototype stage and pursuant to earlier involvement in an R&D joint venture also create technology transfer burdens even if the prototype is fully optimized. The reason is that key personnel from the R&D project will drift back to their particular companies where they will be inaccessible to competitors for post-prototype consultation. One can therefore predict that the various R&D joint ventures which have recently taken root in America, such as MCC, will face a considerable challenge in transferring technology back to the sponsoring companies, and successfully commercializing it. The fact that communication among the sponsoring companies is cut off, or at least attenuated by antitrust constraints, once commercialization commences must limit the productivity of R&D. In short, public policy, which cautiously permits R&D joint ventures but maintains hostility or ambiguity toward other forms of R&D cooperation and extreme hostility toward collaboration with respect to commercialization activities when the firms involved are significant market players is unlikely to promote satisfactorily long-run economic welfare.

It is thus apparent that while a pragmatic case for adopting a new vision of competition, and of public policy toward competition and cooperation, is required in several Western nations, the intellectual-theoretical case has yet to be fully articulated. This reflects inherent shortcomings in the body of orthodox economic theory which many analysts bring to bear on economic problems. These deficiencies are particularly embarrassing when matters of innovation and adjustment are at issue. Unfortunately, it is these conditions which are at the essence of today's global economy.

CONCLUSION

The corporation and the nature of competition have changed. Traditional conceptualizations of each have always been inadequate, but those inadequacies are particularly hazardous as a guide to policy in today's global environment. The corporation today is an animal quite different from the textbook caricature. Moreover, the population of corporations is rather different from what existed barely two decades ago. Giant enterprises are becoming islands in a sea of smaller, entrepreneurial technology-based enterprises, located especially in California and the northeastern seaboard. Some of these corporations are "hollow" in the sense that they contract out for manufacturing and other key services. Others take on more traditional levels of vertical integration. Larger companies often purchase technology from them or develop it with them. These smaller companies often have nontraditional control structures with flat hierarchies and significant equity ownership by employees. Economic theory and perhaps management theory as well has a way to go if it is to incorporate key features of these new institutions into mainstream theory.

Likewise, American economists and policy analysts must reconceptualize competition in order to reconcile theoretical tensions between cooperation and competition. While much antitrust law has been revised in recent years to produce relaxed standards with respect to many vertical issues, cooperation among competitors is still regarded with suspicion in North America. Elsewhere, nations recognize that competitiveness in the global marketplace may require close collaboration with respect to matters ranging from R&D to standardization. The Japanese in particular have a different view of competition, and see collaboration as ultimately pro-competitive in many important circumstances. Economic theory, and perhaps managerial theory, needs to be unshackled from orthodox paradigms so that an appropriate competitive policy can be fashioned for today's global economy.

Notes

1. It is true that many specialized firms adopted diversification strategies and then divested many of their former acquisitions (e.g., International Telephone and Telegraph).

2. By assumption they could not be because if they were, no manager would seek to execute one. At least, this is the reasoning advanced by many orthodox financial economists.

3. Koopmans (1957, p. 147) goes on to point out that because of this deficiency economic theorists are not able to speak with anything approaching scientific authority on matters relating to individual versus collective enterprise.

4. If the R&D is industry specific and all firms in the industry participate in funding, the appropriability problem will be substantially solved, particularly if a coordinated marketing program is also put in place.

5. According to William Norris, United States corporations were not willing to give collaborative research a try until "these

companies had the hell scared out of them by the Japanese"
(Davis, 1985, p. 42).

6. A Japanese government laboratory was also involved.

References

Aoki, M. *The Economic Analysis of the Japanese Firm.*   North
    Holland, 1984.

Chandler, A.D. *The Visible Hand: The Managerial Revolution in
    American Business.* Cambridge, Mass: Belknap Press, 1977.

Coase, R. "The Nature of the Firm," *Econometrica*, 1937, **4**, pp.
    386-405.

Davis, D. "R&D Consortia," *High Technology*, October, 1985.

Gerlach, M. "Business Alliances and the Strategy of the Japanese
    Firm," *California Management Review*, Fall, 1987, 30(1).

Hounshell, D. *From the American System to Mass Production,
    1800-1932.*   Baltimore: Johns Hopkins University Press,
    1984.

Knight, F.H. *Risk, Uncertainty and Profit.* New York: Harper &
    Row, 1965.

Koopmans, T. *Three Essays on the State of Economic Science.*
    New York: McGraw-Hill, 1957.

Lazonick, W. "Technological Change and the Control of Work," in
    H. Gospel and C. Littler (eds.). *Managerial Strategies and
    Industrial Relations.* Heinemann, 1983.

Lazonick, W. "The Social Determinants of Technological change: Innovation and Adaptation in Three Industrial Revolutions." Unpublished manuscript, Barnard College - Columbia University, August, 1987.

Ouchi, W. *M-Form Society*. New York: Avon Books, 1984.

Pisano, G., Russo, M. and Teece, D. "Joint Ventures and Collaborative Arrangements in the Telecommunications Equipment Industry," forthcoming in D.C. Mowery (ed.), *International Collaborative Ventures in U.S. Manufacturing*. Washington, DC: American Enterprise Institute, 1988.

Pollard, S. *The Genesis of Modern Management*. New York: Penguin Books, 1965.

Richardson, G.B. *Information and Investment*. Cambridge, England: Oxford University Press, 1960.

Samuels, R.J. "Research Collaboration in Japan," MIT-Japan Science and Technology Program Working Paper No. 87-02, April, 1987.

Shepherd, W.G. *The Economics of Industrial Organization*. Englewood Cliffs, N.J.: Prentice-Hall, 1979.

Smith, M.R. *Harper's Ferry Armory and the New Technology*. Ithaca, N.Y.: Cornell University Press, 1977.

Teece, D.J. "Towards Economic Theory of the Multiproduct Firm," *Journal of Economic Behavior and Organization*, March, 1982, pp. 39-64.

Teece, D.J. "Profiting from Technological Innovation: Implications for Integration, Collaboration, Licensing and Public Policy," *Research Policy*, December, 1986, 15(6).

Williamson, O.E. *Markets and Hierarchies.* New York: Free
    Press, 1975.

Williamson, O.E. *Economic Institutions of Capitalism.* New York:
    Free Press, 1985.

Chapter 10

Collusive Behavior, R&D, and European Competition Policy

Alexis Jacquemin

University Catholique de Louvain

Over the past few years, the traditional view that market structure largely determines the conduct (or behavior) of firms in a market, and industry structure determines the industry performance, has lost ground. The "New Industrial Organization" literature insists on the central role of market conduct, the necessity of detailed analysis of business behavior, and the usefulness of well-defined microeconomic models to understand the complex relationships characterizing the structure-conduct-performance paradigm.[1] Given the dynamic nature of strategic competition, each firm knows that over time its behavior can have an effect upon the other firms and that its best plan of action depends upon the plans chosen by its rivals. Firms must then be conceived as actors able to modify to some extent their environment instead of being subject to it. In this perspective the configuration of industrial structures and organizational forms is as much the outcome of deliberate strategies as of initial conditions and predetermined rules of the game.[2]

One crucial strategic choice for a firm is between collusive and non-collusive behavior. While collusion is generally expected to raise a firm's profits, it is also in the interest of each firm to let its competitors pay the cost of cooperation and to gain a "free-ride" by acting as an independent outsider. From the point of view of public interest, the question is also complex, and there have been many changes in academic thinking and antitrust policy. At times it has been fashionable to emphasize the negative effects of collusion, such as deviations from marginal-cost pricing, which reduce welfare. At other times, emphasis has been put on the dynamic effects such as the provision of new technologies and new products which could be fostered by cooperative behavior. For example, Article 85 of the Treaty of Rome condemns agreements between firms and concerted practices which may affect trade between Member States. On the other hand, the White Paper *Completing the Internal Market* (1985, p. 34) states that: "The removal of internal boundaries and the establishment of free movement of goods and capital and the freedom to provide services are clearly fundamental to the creation of the internal market. Nevertheless, Community action must go further and create an environment or conditions likely to favor the development of cooperation between undertakings. Such cooperation will strengthen the industrial and commercial fabric of the internal market. ... The Commission will seek to ensure that Community budgetary and financial facilities make their full contribution to the development of greater cooperation between firms in different Member States."

The purpose of this policy paper is to suggest that too much collusion, tacit and explicit, can be expected in many domains where noncooperative, non-collusive behavior would be socially more efficient, and that too little collusion can occur in activities where socially desirable outcomes might arise from cooperation, R&D being a case in point. In the first part, we deal with the general problem of collusion. We first identify, on the basis of recent models, various situations facilitating the adoption and stabilization of collusive behavior. We then discuss the public view of collusion in light of European competition policy which, contrary to the U.S. approach, provides an "efficiency defense" for some collusive actions. In the second part of the chapter, we consider cooperative agreements in R&D. A discussion of the private costs and benefits of joint R&D leads to the conclusion that specific characteristics of R&D, mainly the difficulty of approaching the results of the joint efforts, tend to impede and destabilize many agreements in this domain. A brief public cost benefit analysis suggests in other respects that cooperative R&D can sometimes improve efficiency. This provides support for the 1985 permissive European regulation allowing cooperative research whereby members firms agree to share the costs and the fruits of a research project.

COLLUSIVE BEHAVIOR AND EUROPEAN ANTITRUST POLICY

The conventional wisdom underlines various intrinsic difficulties at each state of the collusive process: reaching an agreement, detecting cheating, punishing credibly the defector. This could lead to the view that the probability of collusion, tacit or explicit, is very small. But in fact collusive arrangements are common practice, and every year a great number of cases are brought to the European Commission and the European Court of Justice (see the Annual Reports on Competition Policy published by the European Communities). Recent models have suggested some explanations of this paradox.

Factors That Facilitate Collusion

Various factors tend to make collusion successful. Let us consider infinitely repeated oligopoly games and suppose that each player chooses its quantity of production[3] in order to maximize its discounted stream of profits. Then

$$s_i = \sum_{t=0}^{\infty} w^t \pi_{it}$$

where π_{it} is the the ith firm's profit in period t and $w = 1/(1+r)$ is the discount factor (r being the discount rate). Denoting by π_i^* the firm's profit under a tacitly collusive equilibrium, firm i earns $\pi_i^*/(1-w)$ by cooperating permanently.

Let us assume that, on the contrary, if one of the players defects, it will induce noncooperative behavior in all the subsequent periods. Calling π_i^d the defector's profit during the one period in which is deviates from the collusive scheme and π_i^c the noncooperative profits following its deviation, the defector's overall payoff in the game is given by $\pi_i^d + w/(1-w)\pi_i^c$. Tacit collusion will be the outcome so long as the profit obtained by colluding is no less than the profit obtained by defecting. The corresponding well-known condition is:

$$ w \geq \frac{\pi_i^d - \pi_i^*}{\pi_i^d - \pi_i^c} \ , \ i=1,\ldots,n. $$

This equation allows us to identify several conditions for tacit collusion:

1. If w is close enough to unity, i.e., if firms give enough weight to the future, noncooperative collusion can be sustained. As a high w means that successive periods payoffs are highly valued, this condition also implies that the scope for tacit collusion is great when detection lags are short. This suggests that "policies designed to make secret price cuts possible are valuable in undermining tacit collusion or conscious parallelism. And industry practices that inhibit secret price setting should be subject to close antitrust scrutiny" (Shapiro, 1986).

2. Profits from defection must be bound ($\pi_i^d < \infty$ for all i) and the smaller these profits, the higher the supportable level of collusive profit π_i^*.

3. Only mild punishments ($\pi_i^c < \pi_i^*$) are needed. And moreover the more severe the punishment is (the lower π_i^c is), the higher the level of π_i^* that can be supported as an equilibrium.[4]

Note that there are various ways to sustain the collusive outcome non-cooperatively. In the previous model, firm j cooperates with i unless and until i defects, in which case j is triggered into perpetual noncooperation. An alternative and less severe strategy is "tit-for-tat" (Axelrod, 1984), according to which each firm starts by playing friendly and then chooses in the current period what the other player chose in the previous period.[5] More generally, Abreu (1984) has been able to characterize what he calls "optimal penal codes," i.e., the most effective credible strategies for punishing deviations from collusive behavior. Within the class of symmetrical punishments (punishments which assume that all firms act identically), he shows that the optimal punishment has a two-phase structure: if a firm deviates from collusive behavior, there would immediately be one period of punishment, followed by a return to the most sustainable collusive configuration.

Collusion might also occur non-cooperatively in the finitely repeated game, once we relax the artificial assumption of complete information and suppose instead that a firm has a small degree of doubt about the end of the game, the factor w may be interpreted as the probability that the game will continue into the next period. When this probability is sufficiently high, any individually rational outcome can be sustained as a credible Nash collusive equilibrium of the repeated game.[6]

The rapidly growing literature suggests that the number of possible tacitly collusive strategies and outcomes is indeed very large and that it is not very easy to make the solution determinate. If the equilibrium is not unique, then "at least verbal assent will be required on which equilibrium among those possible will be chosen. Such discussion might be considered tantamount to collusion even if no explicit coordination is needed after that preliminary decision" (Waterson, 1984, p. 46).

This leads us to the case of explicit collusion or cooperative behavior. Again, many difficulties have been mentioned in the literature about cartels (Osborn, 1976; Jacquemin and Slade, 1986): locating the contract surface, i.e., the points or set of points providing maximum profits to the cartel; sharing activities and results between members; maintaining members in the cartel and controlling nonmembers (either firms already in the industry or entrants attracted by the high profits); and detecting breaches of the agreement and deterring effective breaches through various types of penalties.

Various answers can be given to these problems.[7] We should like to focus on one important aspect.

Once the explicit formation of a cartel has been decided, stability of this cartel does not necessarily require coercive mechanisms or side payments. Thus d'Aspremont, Jacquemin, Gabszewicz, and Weymark (1983) have shown that there is always stability for a cartel establishing the leading price if the s of firms is finite. To illustrate the argument, let there be a set of n identical firms, k of which form a cartel that fixed the price in such a way that profits are maximized for each firm in the cartel, given that production of competitive firms is determined by the equality between the fixed price and their marginal cost. Because all firms sell at the same price and because the firms in the fringe choose without any constraints the output that maximizes their profit at this price, we have

$$\pi^f(n,k) \geq \pi^c(n,k)$$

where $\pi^f(n,k)$ and $\pi^c(n,k)$ denote the profits of firms in the fringe and the cartel, respectively.

Two types of stability are then defined. A cartel made up of k members has internal stability if $k \geq 1$ and if $\pi^f(n,k-1) \leq \pi^c(n,k)$; it has external stability if $k \leq n-1$ and if $\pi^c(n,k+1) \leq \pi^f(n,k)$. The cartel is called stable if there is internal and external stability at the same time. d'Aspremont et al., then wrote a simple algorithm showing that there is always a stable cartel. Having established that the profits of each firm in the cartel increase with the size of the cartel, they assumed that the cartel with $k=1$ has internal stability. If the case $k=1$ also has external stability, then a stable cartel has been found. Otherwise, the case $k=2$ is considered: this has internal stability, or else the process would have stopped at $k=1$. If $k=2$ has external stability, the search for a stable cartel has ended. According to the algorithm, either a stable cartel is found with $k<n$, or the algorithm reaches $k=n$. In this case, $k=n$ has internal stability, and because all the firms are included, the monopoly cartel is stable. Building on d'Aspremont et al., Donsimoni (1985) examines the impact of variations in cost and demand conditions on the structure of the stable cartel. In her model, demand and cost functions are linear and costs vary across firms. As before, with a finite number of firms there always exists a stable cartel. In addition, the members of the stable cartel are the efficient firms (those with low costs). Finally, the size of the cartel is a decreasing function of the industry elasticity of demand.[8]

From this section, it appears that a private firm's cost benefit analysis of collusive behavior is a complex matter. But several factors can in general promote cooperation: making the future more important than the present, making the interactions between firms more durable and more frequent, improving the firm's ability to recognize defection when it occurs, changing the payoff structure so that the punishment for defection is greater and the gains from mutual cooperation higher and more easily appropriable, recognizing the effects of its own action on the structure of the market.

In the light of the European Competition Policy, we shall see in the next section if the existence of the often observed collusive behavior has positive or negative connotations from the point of view of social welfare.

Collusion and European Competition Policy

Article 85 of the Treaty of Rome contains a broad prohibition of explicit and tacit collusion where it is likely to affect trade between Member States and has as its purpose or result the prevention, restriction, or distortion of competition within the Common Market. Such collusive agreements are void unless EC Commission is notified of them and grants an exemption.

A priori, such a broad prohibition could be based on one or several goals which are traditionally at the core of competition policy. One eventual goal is the diffusion of private economic power, the protection of individual freedom and individual rights. The use of cartels can then be seen as a radical departure from such an individualism.[9] This aspect, which was originally basic to antitrust legislation, still occupies an important place, although perhaps more at the level of public opinion than at policy level.

A second eventual goal of competition policy may be to protect the economic freedom of market competitors. Here the protection of competitors takes precedence over the defense of the competitive process as such. Attention will be directed toward abusive practices such as coercion, discrimination, refusal to sell, boycotts, and cartels through which powerful firms might endanger the existence of weaker competitors. This type of approach is particularly in evidence in European countries in the national laws of "unfair competition."[10]

A distinction is then usually made between competition policy concerning efficiency and market injury, and competition law concerning unfair conduct and private injury to one or a few firms. In most instances, like the law on boycott, fairness and efficiency require the same outcome, but there are situations where a conflict could arise. An especially important one in the domain of cartels concerns exclusive dealing agreements. The basic principle expressed in the Beguelin/G.L. Import Export case (Judgment of the Court, 25/11/71, in the Court of Justice of the European Communities, Reports of Cases Before the Court, 1971, Part II, pp. 949-972) is that an exclusive dealing agreement is liable to affect trade between Member States, and may have the effect of impeding competition if, owing to the combined effects of the agreement and of the national legislation on unfair competition, the dealer is able to prevent parallel imports from other Member States from entering the territory covered by the agreement. On this occasion the Court of Justice clearly confirmed that the European rules of competition were not formulated to give protection to individual competitors on the basis of fair practices. If there is a conflict between a national law on unfair competition and the European competition rules, the latter predominates.[11]

The third type of goal of competition policy is dear to the hearts of economists. Competition policy is one of the main instruments to assure consumer welfare through both allocation and productive efficiency. The neatest affirmation of a purely efficiency-directed competition policy has been made by Bork (1967). According to his view, antitrust law must challenge inefficient conducts. A necessary (but not sufficient) attribute of inefficiency is a restriction of output beyond levels which would prevail under competitive conditions. Conduct not so identified must be presumed to enhance efficiency, and should not be the subject of legal sanction.[12] On the contrary, price-quantity cartels create inefficiency which can be measured by the well-known formula for deadweight loss D

$$D = \frac{1}{2}\sum_i \epsilon^i \Delta q^i \Delta p^i$$

where p^i, q^i and ϵ^i are price, quantities, and the price elasticity of demand in the ith sector, the symbol Δ representing a change due to monopoly pricing.[13]

However, in recent years new research in industrial organization has shown that simple formulas for efficiency appear to be deceptive and misleading.

An important example in the domain of collusive behavior is the sharing of information by oligopolists. It has been shown that the incentives for information-sharing and its welfare consequences depend crucially on the type of competition, the nature of the goods, and the degree of product differentiation. Clarke (1983) demonstrates that with Cournot competition and homogeneous products, there is never a mutual incentive for firms in the industry to share information unless they plan to collude. But Vives (1984) finds that in Bertrand competition or if the goods are not close substitutes, the results are reversed.[14] More generally, "free competition" can lead to too much or too little information, product variety, R&D, entry, and so on,[15] according to the characteristics of the game.

The main implication is that once the neoclassical paradigm is abandoned, there is no longer the kind of general theorem about the Pareto optimality of the methods of strategic competition that we have for perfect competition. The results are at best ambiguous. Furthermore, with the various types of nonprice competition, consumer welfare becomes more multidimensional and includes aspects such as the quality of the product, the speed and security of the supply, and so on. Most of these aspects are not measurable. Value judgments are necessary to determine, for example, whether allocating a greater amount of resources to activities which result in technological change or product variation than would be allocated under a more "classical" form of competition contributes enough to consumer welfare to outweigh the possible losses resulting from static inefficiencies. On the whole, a precise definition of the "efficiency" criterion is more apparent than real and most of the time requires a delicate appreciation of complex tradeoffs.

In contrast to the U.S. tradition,[16] such tradeoffs are explicitly accepted by the Treaty of Rome in Article 85, paragraph 3, according to which some collusive behavior restricting competition in a nonminor way may be exempted because of sufficient beneficial effects. Four conditions are required:

1.   the agreement must contribute to the improvement of the production or distribution of goods or promote technical or economic progress;

2.   it must allow ultimate buyers a fair share of the resulting benefits;

3.   the restriction must be necessary for the attainment of the objective;

4.   the firms concerned must be unable to eliminate competition in respect to a substantial part of the product in question.

What Williamson (1968) calls a "naive tradeoff model" for mergers is a good way of illustrating these conditions. This model tells that in order to appreciate whether the cartel can benefit from the "efficiency defense," it is sufficient to compare the surface corresponding to the "deadweight loss," i.e., the loss of consumer welfare which is not otherwise compensated, and the surface corresponding to the savings in resources which become available for alternative use.

This "naive" static partial equilibrium model, with its cost-benefit analysis limited to two-dimensional terms, requires a number of qualifications that strongly reduce its applicability. These qualifications include matters of timing, nonprice competition, X-inefficiency, income distribution effects, second-best considerations, as well as the inference and enforcement expenses needs to prove the existence of economies.[17] What is, in fact, suggested by such a model is the difficulty of identifying precisely the efficiency consequences of a business business conduct and of advocating fine-tuned optimal antitrust rules. The conditions of Article 85, paragraph 3, cannot rely on a strict welfare analysis and will often require political compromises between conflicting and incommensurable values.

These dangers can be reduced in two ways. The first one would be to rely more on the use of a reasonable test in applying Article 85, paragraph 1.[18] On the basis of the general presumption that an antitrust policy augmenting competitive forces is needed to enhance efficiency, a pragmatic interpretation of Article 85, paragraph 1, could broaden the number of cases where economic behavior can be said to comply with Article 85 without having to resort to the criteria and procedures of paragraph 3. For example, this interpretation might allow some type of vertical agreements which could appear to represent a restriction of competition, but which actually do not impose an unreasonable restraint on competition or even increase it in the relevant dynamic and uncertain framework. Given the previously mentioned theoretical works of the New Industrial Organization, it is evident that this approach will not eliminate the ambiguities nor offer strong legal security to businessmen. Nevertheless, this interpretation is less demanding than the tradeoff system of Article 85, paragraph 3, which requires notifying and disclosing all doubtful matters to the Commission in order to obtain an exemption.[19] A pragmatic application of Article 85, paragraph 1 could reduce information and transaction costs,[20] and allow the Commission to use its limited resources to formulate general policies and prosecute important cases.

The second way which has effectively been used to reduce the burden of the tradeoff is to implement Article 85, paragraph 3, not so much on a case-by-case basis, but by granting group (or block) exemptions dealing with important types of agreements for which there exists a presumption that a situation of market failure can occur. This system of exempting certain classes of agreements from the notification requirement avoids the necessity of a detailed analysis of each conduct. It creates codes of conduct that can increase the credibility of the policy and limit the discretionary power involved in the Article. At the same time, it preserves the Article's valuable message that antitrust policy must be sensitive to economies and that in some circumstances cooperative behavior can restrict competition in a non-negligible way and still produce socially desirable results.[21]

A clear illustration is the block exemption regulation of R&D agreements, which came into force in March 1985. This new regulation leaves intact the 1986 notice on cooperation between enterprises, which states that cooperation agreements relating only to R&D normally do not fall under Article 85, paragraph 1. But it extends this favorable treatment to R&D agreements which also provide for joint exploitation of the results. To appreciate its content, it is necessary to examine in some depth the role of cooperative R&D.

COOPERATIVE AGREEMENTS IN R&D

In this second part, we shall first identify the main private advantages and disadvantages of R&D cooperation, then their main public costs and benefits. The paradox that will emerge is that there are more obstacles to cooperative R&D than to collusion in other areas, in spite of the positive social welfare effect often associated with such cooperation. The policy option taken by the European Commission in its Regulation 418/85 will then be discussed.

Private Cost-Benefit Analysis of Cooperative R&D[22]

Three types of private potential benefits of cooperative R&D can be identified. First, cooperative agreements are <u>an alternative to either pure market transactions or integration within the firm</u> under a single administrative structure. Its choice could, therefore, indicate that it is perceived as a compromise between commitment and flexibility.

On the one hand, in-house developments or mergers tend to create very rigid structures without easy mechanisms for switching research capability, strategy, and partners over time. This can call into question a company's ability to innovate or respond to innovation, and impede access to know-how which it cannot develop internally or can acquire only with irreducible delays in developing and testing products in-house.

On the other hand, arm's-length transactions do not allow for long-term relationships, which are generally crucial in technology. Frequent switching is costly and inefficient because the process of R&D, as well as technology transfer, require prolonged interaction and experience between partners to exploit or develop complementaries which affect the costs and benefits of innovations. Furthermore, market transactions are expected to be affected by moral hazard and adverse selection. Indeed the domain of R&D and innovation is a typical case where the agent's action is not directly observable by the principal, and the outcome is a random variable whose distribution depends on the action taken. A cooperative research arrangement can then reduce the problems of asymmetric information and opportunism, as well as the vagueness of monitoring by relying on easily measured R&D inputs.

A second potential advantage of cooperative R&D is to <u>accelerate the speed of invention and innovation with less risk.</u> On the one hand, what often matters is the speed at which firms can deploy the necessary resources and enter into new markets, first over advantage depending upon an ability to do it more quickly than rivals; on the other hand, the absence of a complete and perfect set of contingency markets makes useful joint actions which permit risk-spreading, i.e., sharing the benefits and costs of a project among a number of firms, and risk-pooling, i.e., pursing more technological avenues and (relatively) independent projects.

Finally, the <u>pooling of various complementary resources</u> in R&D can provide financial capital at better conditions if capital markets are imperfect, spread the high fixed costs of technology development, and produce synergistic effects by the combination of research information, teams of scientists, technological and marketing know-how, and so on.

Despite the previous arguments, cooperative agreements in R&D are not very frequent. When they exist, empirical evidence shows that they are fragile and unstable arrangements confronted with various difficulties, which generally lead to early breakups, buyouts, or mergers. This situation is aggravated within Europe where the majority of R&D arrangements are multicountry and where divergent objectives, strategies, domestic regulations, and institutions often combine with socio-psychological factors such as nationalistic feelings, fear of a loss of identity, and clash of corporate cultures.

Arrangements relating only to R&D have a number of important handicaps. At a first stage, <u>partner selection and the possibility of defining well-balanced contributions</u> is an important barrier. The fear is that one partner will be strengthened by the technological cooperation in such a way that it will become a dangerous competitor at the level of the product market. This situation is, of course, more probable for horizontal agreements than for vertical ones. In the later case, complementarities allow the benefits to be distributed according to the respective activities and products. In the case of cooperation between competitors geographical partition is the most obvious way of trying to solve the problem but it has a side effect on existing competition. The compromise between collaboration and independence is reflected

in the organizational structure of the arrangement, which is often
ambiguous, complex, and implying heavy transaction costs of
negotiation.

At a second stage, the management of existing cooperative
agreements and the sharing of the benefits are also difficult.
First, in the absence of an efficient system of management, the
transaction costs of coordination and cooperation may outweigh
the benefits, especially when a large number of actors is involved.
Second, even with lengthy contracts containing explicit clauses
concerning confidentiality and transmission of information, patent
licenses, trademark, and copyright, there are fundamental limits
on the ability to protect intellectual property, given that scientific
knowledge has many aspects of a public good, that its results are
not easily incorporated, and that the speed of incorporation will
vary from one firm to another. In fact, there are often close
connections between the effectiveness of basic research,
conventional R&D resources, and marketing and manufacturing
resources. Von Hippel (1982) and Flaherty (1980) have shown the
multiple interactions of technological advantages with conventional
business resources in various fields. Their analyses imply that the
full exploitation of the results of cooperative marketing to sell
products which embody these results. Successful achievement of
first-mover advantages in research depends upon an ability to
bring quickly new products and techniques to the market where
the greatest potential strategic payoffs are encountered.

Limiting cooperation to pure R&D or to the so-called
"precompetitive level", will then exercise a strong deterrent effect
on the emergence of such cooperative arrangements.[23]

Public Cost-Benefit Analysis of Cooperative R&D and the European Regulation

The main arguments in favor of socially beneficial effects of cooperative research is based on a problem of market failure, bound to the appropriability of returns.[24] The starting point is that the amount of research made by private firms and the diffusion of the knowledge generated by them may be socially inefficient over a broad range of market structure including competition. Two situations can be distinguished.

Assume first that there are no spillovers or externalities so that each firm's R&D influences only its own costs. Nevertheless, as long as firms in the pre-innovation market would not expect a perfect discriminating monopoly in the post-innovation market, appropriation of the entire social value from innovation will not be expected. Even the pre-innovation monopolist would not generally invest the socially optimal amount in R&D. A fortiori when price competition in the post-innovation market intensifies as the number of R&D competitors in the pre-innovation market increases, it is more likely that the value of the surplus of total R&D revenues above post-innovation costs will fall short of the social value. Moreover, the knowledge generated by the R&D of the individual firm will be priced incorrectly. Given the existing degree of appropriability, diffusion of this knowledge will not be priced at the marginal cost of its dissemination (which is often close to zero), but at higher prices. This may lead competing firms to wasteful duplication of research.

Now suppose that there are substantial R&D externalities or spillovers: the benefits of each firm's R&D flow without payment to other firms. This leads to underinvestment in R&D relative to the social optimum and to a structure of knowledge supply which is determined by the different degrees of appropriability of the various types. Incentives to innovate will also be reduced as the potential innovator knows that competitors will be freely strengthened by its own R&D investments.

It can then be argued that cooperative R&D can improve both situations and alleviate the tradeoff identified by Spence (1984).

According to this tradeoff, the incentives of a firm to do R&D require a sufficient degree of appropriability of the benefits and thus a limited diffusion of knowledge; but, on the other hand, a near perfect appropriability (whether created by circumstances or policy) impedes spillovers of the results of R&D to other firms, at no cost, and hence does not allow a sufficient decrease in aggregate R&D costs for achieving a given level of cost reduction.

Cooperative R&D can then be viewed as a means of simultaneously internalizing the externalities created by significant R&D spillovers -- hence improving the incentive problem and limiting wasteful duplication -- and providing a more efficient sharing of information among firms.[25]

Katz (1986) has rigorously established the conditions under which a cooperative agreement could raise welfare through its effects on the equilibrium level of R&D and on the cost of achieving a given R&D level.

o   "...cooperative R&D is most likely to have beneficial incentive effects in markets that have strong spillovers in the absence of cooperation;

o   when firms have flexibility in their choices of both R&D cost-sharing and R&D output-sharing rates, cooperative R&D arrangements are most likely to have beneficial effects in markets where a high rate of between-member spillover or R&D sharing is feasible, such as in basic research" (p. 542).

This leads us to mention briefly a second argument for permitting or encouraging cooperative R&D.

In certain high technology industries, such as the next generation of mainframe computers, firms are producing, under increasing returns of scale, differentiated products on which basic research can lead to production of a higher quality product. In such industries, equilibrium is characterized by the presence of a limited number of firms, each of which makes positive profits (net of any fixed costs). In this case the neoclassical competitive paradigm does not apply, as "natural" oligopolies are dictated by the exogenous conditions of supply and demand. If certain potential entrants in such markets enjoy an advantage as a result of a cooperative agreement, this may then favor equilibrium outcomes in which cooperating firms are able to enter while certain of their independent rivals decide otherwise.

By promoting R&D cooperation between European firms, the European authorities could then succeed in giving these firms a better base for oligopolistic competition against foreign rivals and in getting a larger share of high-return industries.

Contrasting with these potential advantages of cooperative R&D, effects leading to a harmful reduction of competition must also be considered. This question could be explored on the basis of a model having the standard two-stage form, with R&D expenditures in period one affecting the parameters of the second period output/price game. Solving the latter yields profit functions (gross of R&D costs) that are dependent upon the earlier R&D choices. The shapes of these functions depend, among other things, on the nature of competition: for instance, noncooperation in R&D and in output, cooperation in R&D and in output, cooperation in R&D and noncooperation in output, noncooperation in R&D and cooperation in output.[26]

In the absence of a model reflecting the complete picture, let us simply distinguish between two situations.

First, let us assume that it is feasible to limit the extent of the agreement solely to aspects of R&D and to exclude coordination at the level of the final product (*precompetitive level*). The dangers of anticompetitive consequences are then strongly reduced. Still, one danger is that cooperative R&D could be a way for a dominant firm to avoid competition through innovation, by co-opting potentially very innovative rivals and by controlling and slowing down the innovation race (Reinganum, 1983). Coordinating the R&D process so as to avoid duplication can reduce initiative and lead to inflexibility and to waste in dead-end research, when multiple, not perfectly correlated research strategies could have been feasible. At the other extreme, incumbent firms with market power can, through concerted pre-emptive operations, excessively accelerate their programs of R&D and innovation in order to exercise a dissuasive impact on potential entrants (Gilbert and Newbery, 1982). In the situation of integrated firms, cooperative agreement for the purpose of knowledge exchange could also lead to barriers to entry downstream and foreclose firms who are not members of the agreement from some segment of the market. Firms being at the frontier of technological change could, for example, jointly determine standards for future products and processes, making new entry more difficult.

A second situation involves an extended collusion between partners, resulting from their action in R&D and creating common policies at the product stage (*competitive level*). Discussions about R&D can, for example, spill over into illegal discussions of pricing policy. Cooperative R&D can also provide a ready mechanism for side payments in the event that it is useful for cartel members to redistribute the revenues earned by the firm as a result of product market division. What makes these dangers probable is again the difficulty of appropriating technological breakthrough. As discussed earlier, partners who have achieved inventions want to control the processes and products which embody the results of their collaboration, in order to recapture jointly, and as quickly as possible, their R&D investments. If the firms are prevented from such a joint exploitation, and if the benefits of cooperative R&D are expected to be very quickly dissipated through intense product market competition, firms will be tempted either to avoid R&D cooperation and to maintain wasteful competition in the pre-innovation market or to use their cooperation to limit unduly their R&D. If this is true, *a regulation of R&D cooperation excluding any cooperation at the level of the final markets could discourage or destabilize many valuable agreements. However, allowing an extension of cooperation from R&D to manufacturing and distribution encourages collusive behavior which impedes competition. This is precisely the dilemma faced by the European Antitrust Authorities.*

The text of the regulation 418/85 expresses the compromise that has been adopted. It covers joint research and development of products or processes and <u>joint exploitation of that R&D.</u>

Art. 1(2)(d) specifies that "exploitation of the results" means the manufacture of the joint venture product or the licensing of the intellectual property rights to third parties. But joint marketing is not covered.

Among various conditions, the exemption applies if:

1. the work is carried out within the framework of a defined program;

2. all the parties have access to the results;

3. where there is no joint exploitation, each party is free to exploit the results independently;

4. the know-how and the patents which result from the research contribute substantially to technical and economic progress and are indispensable for the manufacture of the joint venture product.

By imposing conditions concerning the duration of the venture and market shares, the regulation also aims to prevent agreements that might result in the elimination of competition in the relevant market. If the joint venture is of the conglomerate type, i.e., if the participants do not compete on the relevant product market, the exemption applies for five years, regardless of market share. If the joint venture is of the horizontal type, the exemption also applies for five years, but only if the parties' combined share of the relevant product market does not exceed 20 percent.

A comprehensive list of permissible clauses (the so-called white list) and prohibited (the so-called black list) is also included.

The main aspect of the Regulation is that the European authorities, confronted with the dilemma mentioned above, consider that cooperation in R&D, in many cases, cannot be limited to the sole level of pure R&D, and that it will generally lead to joint exploitation of the results in order to stabilize the agreements and to solve the appropriability problem. Moreover, the Regulation gives priority to basic research and tends to secure an efficient sharing of information. Finally, it rejects arrangements able to monopolize the market.

However, several problems remain. From the businessman's point of view, the regulation is complex; it is necessary to overcome its opacity by issuing new guidelines. The 20 percent threshold market share for horizontal joint ventures is disputable, especially in high technology. The exclusion of joint selling and marketing is an important limitation, given the close interconnections between the various phases of the activities.[27] From the point of view of public interest, the regulation might have the unwanted side effect of exempting many production joint ventures from notification, especially given the broadness of some concepts and criteria used in the text. The drafters of joint venture contracts could indeed be tempted to include an R&D element in their agreements in order to fall within the scope of the block exemption. In this context, the Commission must be conscious of the dangers of any further relaxation of its antitrust policy, which until now has been a powerful instrument for the survival of a competitive common market.

Finally, one wonders whether modifications to the competition rules are the crucial tool needed to prod industry into forming new R&D joint ventures. As long as antitrust rules in the field of R&D cooperation reflect a form of industrial policy to foster innovations and improve international competitiveness, more positive incentives would seem appropriate. One of them could be specific tax deductions and/or subsidies like those provided by the Esprit program. A complementary one would be transnational legal structures, such as the recently adopted European Interest Grouping,[28] which provides firms with flexible instruments for pooling some business functions, while retaining their economic and legal independence.

CONCLUSION

The European Commission White Paper *Completing the Internal Market* (1985) underlines the role played by cooperation among firms, which is viewed as an important means of improving European competitiveness.

Our analysis has shown that contrary to the conventional wisdom, various factors facilitate the adoption and the stabilization of collusive behavior. But in some areas such as R&D, the effects of these factors can be more than compensated by the role of specific characteristics, mainly the difficulty of appropriating the results of the joint effort. It follows that too much collusion tends to occur in activities where noncooperative, non-collusive behavior would be more socially efficient. Inversely insufficient cooperation can occur in domains where such behavior could lead to socially desirable outcomes. An important case is R&D where cooperative agreements can internalize externalities created by R&D spillovers, limit wasteful duplication, and provide a more efficient sharing of information.

These considerations stress the importance of a pragmatic competition policy. Article 85 of the Treaty of Rome, its efficiency defense, and the regulation on R&D cooperation seem globally well adapted to this role, but more transparency and explicit precommitments could increase the credibility of such a policy.

Appendix

In a recent article, d'Aspremont and Jacquemin (1988) have considered an industry with two firms facing an inverse demand function $D^{-1}(Q)$, where $Q = q_1+q_2$ is the total quantity produced. Each firm has cost of production $C_i(q_i,x_i,x_j)$ which is a function of its own production, q_i, of the amount of research x_i that it undertakes and the amount of research x_j undertaken by its rival. Both D^{-1} and C are assumed linear, so that

$$D^{-1} = a - bQ, \quad \text{with } a,b > 0, \text{ and}$$

$$C_i(q_i,x_i,x_j) = \left[A - x_i - x_j\right]q_i, \quad i=1,2, \ j \neq i,$$

with $a > A > 0$, $1 > \beta > 0$, $x_i + \beta x_j \leq A$, $Q \leq \dfrac{a}{b}$.

The R&D externalities or spillovers imply that some benefits of each firm's R&D flow without payment to other firms. In our specification the external effect of firm j R&D is to lower firm i's unit production cost. The cost of R&D is assumed to be quadratic, reflecting the existence of diminishing returns to R&D expenditures

$$\phi(x_i) = \gamma \frac{x_i^2}{2}, \quad i=1,2.$$

Firms' strategies consist of a level of research and a subsequent production strategy based on their R&D choice. At the second stage in which R&D are treated as exogenous, firms choose, noncooperatively or cooperatively, their optimal production q_1 and q_2. The preceding stage in which firms choose, non-cooperatively or cooperatively, their R&D level is then solved.

Using this framework d'Aspremont and Jacquemin have computed and compared the corresponding subgame perfect equilibria. Defining x^{**}, x^*, $\hat{x}$, and $\tilde{x}$, as the equilibrium levels of R&D obtained in the case of, respectively, the maximization of social welfare (consumer surplus + producer surplus), the fully noncooperative game, the cooperation limited to R&D, and the cooperation occurring in both R&D and output, they obtain the following classification

$$x^{**} > \tilde{x} > \hat{x} > x^*,$$

for large spillovers. For the total quantity produced, Q, the classification is the following

$$Q^{**} > \hat{Q} > Q^* > \tilde{Q}.$$

One clear conclusion is that cooperation in R&D increases both R&D and quantities of production with respect to the noncooperative solution.

Notes

1. An overview of this literature is given in Stiglitz and Matthewson (1986).

2. For an extensive analysis, see Jacquemin (1987).

3. For a discussion of price-setting supergames (repeated Bertrand games), see Brock and Scheinkman (1985).

4. Shapiro (1986) remarks that this leads to the following paradox: any underlying market condition that makes very competitive behavior possible and credible can, by lowering $\pi_{\underline{i}}^c$, actually promote collusion!

5. Aumann and Sorin (1986) have recently provided a theoretical basis for the situation in which players start by playing friendly and continue with tit-for-tat thereafter. Their model shows that utility-maximizing behavior on the part of each separate individual necessarily leads to cooperation.

6. An individual rational outcome is what a firm can obtain by minimizing over the strategies of its opponents the maximum payoff it can achieve against them, i.e., its minimax value.

7. For example MacLeod, Norman, and Thisse (1986), using a solution concept based on models of spatial competition, have shown, in a two-stage game, that once market areas have been determined by the Bertrand-Nash competitive process, collusion in price becomes feasible and profitable even given free entry. Indeed, a switch to the appropriate Bertrand-Nash pricing is a credible threat.

8. For further results, see Rothschild (1984), Dosimol et al. (1986).

9. It is in the light of these "noneconomic values" that Mestmacker (1980) has characterized the attitude adopted by German authorities with respect to the cartels before World War II. "The Nazis," he wrote, "had shown how to transform highly concentrated and cartelized economy into a central planning system... Boycotts and collective discriminations were applied against outsiders in order to discipline them in the public interest. If the more traditional measures of economic coercion proved

insufficient for the purpose, even the formal transformation of
private cartels into compulsory cartels was provided for after
1933" (p. 388). Mestmacker adds that acceptance of cartels was
not limited to conservatives who cherished them as safeguards
against the anarchy of free competition. Marxists also looked
upon cartels (and concentration) as forerunners of rational socialist
planning. He quotes Hilferding, who interpreted this development
as tending towards "a universal cartel, that is a rationally regulated
society"! According to Fox (1986), the U.S. Clayton Act's sponsors
were motivated by "a belief that Hitler had attained power
through the support of the German cartels. They feared that high
industrial concentration would tip the country either into socialism
or Communism, on the one hand, or fascism on the other" (p. 565,
note 60).

10. According to the Paris Convention of 1883, unfair
competition is "any act of competition contrary to the honest
practices in industrial or commercial matters." The corresponding
laws are intended to ensure that the competitors fight in a fair
way and carry out their social functions according to an ethical
code of conduct. The standard of business ethics plays an
important role in developing such a code of honest trade practices,
but it is ultimately ascertained through the common sense of the
courts.

11. According to the Advocate-General, "The rule of
national law on the subject of unfair competition should not
be...used for purposes which conflict with the general objectives
of the common market, and this places a corresponding limit or
restriction on the exercise of the rights to which in this field,
national rules give rise" (Reports of Cases Before the Court, 1971,
Part II, p. 970). The distinction between antitrust law and laws
governing unfair competition has been strongly attacked,
especially in the Federal Republic of Germany. There is an
increasing tendency today to consider that the "unfairness" of the
individual competitor in his struggle with the other competitor(s)
is mainly determined by his impact on the functioning of the

market. Such a view has been defended in Germany by various
members of the Max Planck Institute. For a recent analysis, see
Kaufman (1986).

12. This has been the typical position of the so-called
"Chicago School."

13. For a general criticism of this measure, see Jacquemin
and Slade (1989).

14. A relatively general result in oligopoly models is that
opposite results are obtained as firms achieve equilibrium in
output (Cournot) or in price (Bertrand) levels. The basic
explanation is that a firm faces a very different firm-specific
demand in the two cases: when the price of the rival is taken as
given, the firm's perceived elasticity of demand is larger than
when the quantity of the rival is taken as given. Thus in Bertrand
equilibrium, firms quote lower prices than in Cournot equilibrium.
The case of information pooling is an application of this general
idea. When the goods are substitutes, in Cournot competition,
pooling of information has two effects. First, it reduces the
variance of the errors about the random intercept of the (linear)
demand function and increases expected profits. Second, it
correlates the strategies that the firms choose. This decreases the
firm's expected profits, given that in the case of substitutable
goods the optimal choice to do for one firm is to produce a high
output when the other firm is expected to produce a low one.
The second effect dominates. On the contrary, in Bertrand
competition with substitutes, correlation of strategies increases
expected profits.

15. See, for example, von Weizsacker (1980), Dasgupta and
Stiglitz (1980), Perry (1984).

16. According to the report of the Attorney-General's
National Committee to study the Antitrust Law (1955), the
standard adopted in the Standard Oil of New Jersey case (1911)

"makes obsolete once prevalent arguments, such as, whether
monopoly arrangements would be socially preferable to
competition in a particular industry, because, for example, of high
fixed costs, or the risk of cutthroat competition or other similar
unusual conditions." See also Procter & Gamble (1967). In the
1984 revisions of its merger guidelines, however, the Justice
Department chose to enact as administrative policy what the U.S.
Congress has refused to enact as law: mergers that are illegal
under section 7 of the Clayton Act would be found legal if they
bring about a sufficient increase in efficiency.

17. Williamson (1977) provides himself a stimulating
discussion of several qualifications of his model.

18. This was already proposed in the 1970s (Jacquemin,
1970). Recently, Forrester and Norall (1984) have defended the
same position arguing that in determining whether there was a
restriction of competition within the meaning of Article 85,
paragraph 1, the economic nature and consequences of the conduct
involved have to be examined.

19. There is no duty to notify, but the possibility of
exemption can be one important incentive; freedom from fines is
another. There are certain agreements listed in Article 4 of
regulation 17 that are exempted from notification. Furthermore,
notifications are not required where there is no appreciable effect
on trade between Member States. However, this "de minimis"
concept is not very reliable.

20. As noticed by Forrester and Norall (1984), businessmen
"wish to discern the path to sanctity or absolution without passing
through the burdensome process of confession" (p. 308, note 2).

21. Recently the European Commission elaborated a general
project proposing a definition and a typology of joint ventures
setting out a framework of competition policy within which
"constructive joint ventures can flourish." The Commission intends

to provide general practical guidance for enterprises in the form of a Notice, ultimately to be published in the Commission's official journal. This kind of "policy announcement" could reduce the difficulty of unpredictable enforcement of the competition rules in everyday business life.

22. The following arguments are partly based on empirical studies and interviews. For the United States see, for example, Berg, Duncan, and Friedman (1982), and for the EEC, Jacquemin, Lammerant, and Spinoit (1985).

23. The characteristics of the industry play also an important role in the propensity to cooperate. In a case such as biotechnology which is in an early and highly competitive stage, in which patentable processes and know-how are of great importance, even basic research can lead to commercial concepts that companies can quickly connect to final products. There is then a limited interest in cooperative activity, non cooperative strategies being often more rewarding. On the contrary, in a more mature sector like semiconductor industry, cooperative efforts are frequent.

24. This is an essential distinction between R&D and capital, suggesting the danger of modeling R&D expenditures like investment in capital.

25. Compared with the patent system, cooperative R&D leads to a large diffusion of knowledge. Industrywide cooperative research laboratories (especially important in Scandinavia) and industry-university cooperation are especially useful as they allow the results of individual development projects from firm to firm to be generalized and transferred, "thus providing a degree of economies of scope to innovator programs across an industry or activity as a whole", (Ergas, 1986). Relying on subsidies meets several limits: it does not solve the diffusion problem, it can introduce new distortions, and it is not easy to control.

26. A possible model is the following one. Let us assume a two-stage game played by two competing firms. At the second stage (say, the choice of output) in which R&D levels are treated as exogenous, firm 1 (respectively, firm 2) produces output q_1 at unit production cost $c_1(x_1,x_2)$ where x_1 and x_2 denote the R&D level of, respectively, firms 1 and 2. Profit π_1 of firm 1 is then

$$\pi_1(q_1,q_2,x_1,x_2) = R_i(q_1,q_2) - C_i(x_1,x_2)q_i - v_i(x_i) \, , \, i=1,2.$$

with $\dfrac{dv_i}{dx_i} > 0$, $\dfrac{\partial c_i}{\partial x_j} < 0$, $j=1,2$.

The solutions, q_1^* and q_2^*, at the cooperative or noncooperative equilibrium, can be written as

$$q_i^* = q_i(x_1,x_2)$$

The first stage in which firms choose R&D levels is then considered. Using the second stage solution, profits of each firm are written as a function of the pair of R&D levels

$$f_i(x_1,x_2) = R_i(q_1^*(x_1,x_2),q_2^*(x_1,x_2)) -$$

$$c_i(x_1,x_2)q_i^*(x_1,x_2) - v_i(x_i), \, i=1,2.$$

The cooperative or noncooperative solutions to this first stage can be obtained by maximizing profit with respect to x_i. This gives rise to a subgame perfect equilibrium in the two-stage game. For preliminary results, see the appendix.

27. But, an exemption could still be obtained on the basis of Article 85, paragraph 3, following a notification.

28. Unhappily, the European form does not provide fiscal incentives, contrary to the French system.

References

Abreu, D. "Infinitely Repeated Games with Discounting General Theory," Harvard Institute of Economic Research, Discussion Paper No. 1083, 1984.

Aumann, R., and Sorin, S. "Cooperation and Bounded Rationality," Mimeo, August, 1986.

Axelrod, R. *The Evolution of Cooperation*. New York: Basic Books, 1984.

Berg, S., Duncan, J., and Friedman, Ph. *Joint Venture, Strategies and Corporate Innovation*. Cambridge, Mass.: Oelgeschlager, Gunn & Hain, 1982.

Bork, R. "The Goals of Antitrust Policy," *American Economic Review*, May, 1976.

Brock, W., and Scheinkman, J. "Price Setting Supergames with Capacity Constraint," *Review of Economic Studies*, 1985, **52**.

Clarke, R. "Collusion and the Incentives for Information Sharing," *Bell Journal of Economics*, 1983, **14**.

Dasgupta, P., and Stiglitz, J. "Industrial Structure and the Nature Innovative Activity," *Economic Journal*, 1980, **90**.

d'Aspremont, Cl., and Jacquemin, A. (1988). "Cooperative and Noncooperative R&D in Duopoly with Spill," *American Economic Review*, December, 1988, No. 5.

5

d'Aspremont, Cl., Jacquemin A., Jaskold-Gabszwicz, J, and Weymark, J. "On the Stability of Collusive Price Leadership," *Canadian Journal of Economics*, 1983, **16**.

Donsimoni, M.P. "Stable Heterogeneous Cartels,"*International Journal of Industrial Organization*, 1985, **4**.

Donsimoni, M.P., Economides, N., and Polemarchakis, H.. "Stable Cartels," *International Economic Review*, 1986, **27**.

Ergas, H. "Does Technology Policy Matter?" CEPS Papers, No. 29, 1986.

Flaherty, N.T. "Business and Technology History of Silicon Wafers for Integrated Circuits." Mimeo, 1980.

Forrester, I., and Norrall, Ch. "The Laicization of Community Law - Self Help and the Rule of Reason: How Competition Law is and Could be Applied." *Common Market Law Review*, 1984.

Fox, E. "The Politics of Law and Economics in Judicial Decision Making: Antitrust as a Wisdom," *New York University Law Review*, 1986, No. 4.

Gilbert, F., and Newbery, D. "Pre-emptive Patenting and the Persistence of Monopoly," *American Economic Review*, June, 1982.

Hilferding. *Das Finanzkapital*. Vienne, 1910.

Katz, M. "An Analysis of Cooperative Research and Development," *Journal of Economics*, Winter, 1986.

Jacquemin, A. "The Criterion of Economic Performance in the Antitrust Policies of the United States and the EEC," *Common Market Law Review*, April, 1970.

Jacquemin, A.   *New Industrial Organization.* Cambridge, Mass., and London: MIT Press and Oxford University Press, 1987.

Jacquemin, A., Lammerant, M. and Spinoit, B.   "Compétition Européenne et Cooperation en Matière de Recherche - Développement. Commission des Communautés Européennes, Evolution de la Concentration et de la Concurrence. *Collection "Document de Travail,"* 1985, No. 80. IV/761/85.

Jacquemin, A., and Slade, M.   "Cartels, Collusion and Horizontal Mergers," in R. Schmalensee and R. Willig (eds.), *Handbook of Industrial Organization.* Amsterdam: North Holland, 1989.

Kaufman, P.   "Passing Off and Misappropriation, an Economic and Legal Analysis of the Law of Unfair Competition," Max Planck Institute, CVH, Munich, 1986.

MacLeod, B., Norman, G. and Thisse, J.   "Competition, Tacit Collusion and Free Entry," *The Economic Journal,* March, 1986, 97.

Mestmacker, E.   "Competition Policy and Antitrust. Some Comparative Observations," *Zeitschrift fur die gesamte Staatswissenschaft,* September, 1980, Heft 3.

Ordover, J., and Willig, R.   "Antitrust for High-Technology Industries. Assessing Research Joint Venture and Mergers," *Journal of Law and Economics,* May, 1985, 2.

Perry, M.   "Scale Economies, Imperfect Competition and Public Policy," *Journal of Industrial Economics,* 1984, 32.

Osborne, D.   "Cartel Problems," *American Economic Review,* 1976, 66.

Reinganum, J.   "Uncertain Innovation and the Persistence of Monopoly," *American Economic Review,* September, 1983.

Rothschild, R.   "Market Price and the Stability of Cartels," *Economics Letters*, 1984, **15**.

Selten, R.   "Are Cartel Laws Bad for Business?"   in H. Hauptmann, W. Krelle, and K.C. Mosler (eds.), *Operations Research and Economic Theory*. Berlin: Springer Verlag, 1984.

Shapiro, C.   "Theories of Oligopoly Behavior," in R. Schmalensee and R.Willig (eds.), *Handbook of Industrial Organization*. Amsterdam: North Holland, 1986.

Spence, M.   "Cost Reduction, Competition and Industry Performance," *Econometrica*, 1984, **52**.

Stiglitz, J. and Matthewson, F. (eds.).   *New Development in the Analysis of Market Structure*. Mass.: MIT Press, 1986.

Vives, X.   "Duopoly Information Equilibrium. Cournot and Bertrand," *Journal of Economic Theory*, 1984, **34**.

von Hippel. "Appropriability of Innovation Benefits as a Predictor of the Source of Innovation," *Research Policy*, No.2, April, 1982.

von Weizsacker, C.   *Barriers to Entry*. Berlin: Springer Verlag, 1980.

Waterson, M.   *Economic Theory of the Industry*. Cambridge: Cambridge University Press, 1984.

Williamson, O.   "Economies as an Antitrust Defense: the Welfare Tradeoffs," *American Economic Review*, 1968, **58**.

Williamson, O.   "Economies as an Antitrust Defense Revisited," in A. Jacquemin and H. de Jong (eds.), *Welfare Aspects of Industrial Markets*. Leiden: Nijhoff, 1977.

Chapter 11

Integration of Financial Services in the European Community: Lessons from the Experience in the United States

Almarin Phillips

University of Pennsylvania

The plans for European integration by 1992 are ambitious ones. They include the removal of remaining internal tariff and nontariff barriers to trade for commodities and services and the extension within the Community of the nondiscriminatory treatment of each nation's enterprises (Cecchini, 1988; Colchester, 1989; Bhatt, 1989; Pinder, 1986; Nicoll, 1985; Capotorti et al., 1986; Brewin and McAllister, 1987; Langeheine and Weinstock, 1985). Within the general plans are more specific ones for the integration and harmonization of financial services according to objectives announced at the June 1989 meeting of the heads of the EC states in Madrid. These plans relate to various aspects of securities markets -- the underwriting and marketing of new issues, the securities exchanges, markets for unlisted securities, securitization of the assets of financial intermediaries and venture capital markets (Colchester, 1989; Bhatt, 1989; *The Economist*, (1988a, 1988b); Lopez-Charos, 1987; Tully, 1988; Winder, 1986;

Gordon, 1987). The plans call as well for the harmonization of insurance regulations, including those governing ties between insurance and other financial services. And, of course, the plans relate to commercial banking or, more generally, to deposit-type financial intermediaries (Key, 1989; Padoa-Schioppa, 1988). Here the topics range from the possible creation of a European central bank (de Cecco et al., 1989) through the harmonizing of prudential and protective regulations, to deposit guarantees and other schemes for assuring the stability of credit.

Plan of the Chapter

Fundamental organizational and regulatory innovations are being proposed and gradually effected. In the United States, similar and less sweeping proposals have historically been accorded hostile political receptions. Indeed, it has proven all but impossible to implement orderly, omnibus financial reform. Major reforms have occurred only in the context of crises; other less comprehensive changes have failed to follow a deliberate path and are as notable for the problems they have caused as for those they have cured.

The United States and the EC are obviously not alike. The resistance to rational change that has characterized the U.S. financial system may not be as strong in Europe. Nonetheless, there are aspects of the U.S. political and legal structure that favor unity and harmonization. The discussion that follows looks almost exclusively at the regulation of banks and other deposit financial intermediaries. It is intended to recount U.S. experience in a way that may at least suggest more focused questions about the gainers and losers from the pending reforms in Europe.

A SUMMARY OF U.S. EXPERIENCE

The Constitutional Setting

The Constitution approved in Philadelphia in 1787 mandated the equivalent of a full customs union for the several states. The federal government -- and only the federal government -- has the power to regulate trade among the states and with other nations. The states are explicitly prohibited from levying tariffs and from otherwise unduly burdening interstate or foreign commerce. Thus, much of what was intended by the Treaty of Rome and is now sought by the refinements for 1992 were put in place in the United States two centuries ago.

Curiously, the United States Constitution made no express provisions for any role of the federal government in the area of banking and financial services. There is a section authorizing the Congress to coin money and determine the value (i.e., metallic content) thereof. There is another that expressly prohibits the states from coining money and from issuing paper currency redeemable in anything other than gold or silver. The Federal government did undertake brief and limited experiments in central banking with the First and Second Banks of the United States (1791-1811; 1816-1836). The constitutionality for these activities was hotly contested. After 1836, no true central bank existed until the formation of the Federal Reserve System in 1913.

Gradual Development of the Dual (Federal-State) Banking Systems

Bank chartering and, to the extent that it existed, bank regulation was in the province of the states until 1863. The nation lacked a common currency and, even worse, the diversity and laxity in regulations created great uncertainty about the value and redeemability of the notes issued by the state-chartered banks. After 1838, most states passed general legislation governing bank chartering. Banks were typically restricted from engaging in activities other than the "business of banking" and non-banks were prohibited from the banking business. State regulatory agencies were born in this period. In subsequent decades these agencies developed agenda of their own. Chief on these agenda was "sovereignty" in bank regulation -- the prevention of federal intrusion into the regulatory affairs of the states became a central goal.

In this period, businesses wishing to expand geographically found the banking situation to be a major drawback (compare Cecchini, 1989). In addition to the lack of a currency of common and recognized value, the banking structure was cumbersome. Most banks were small, local, "unit banks" -- banks with no branches. Interstate branching was generally prohibited. Branching within states was either prohibited or severely circumscribed by state laws and regulations. The economic burden these arrangements placed on developing businesses were inadequate to bring forth federal actions until after 1860, however. The states -- particularly the states in the southern and agrarian regions -- strongly resisted any changes that threatened their own control of their own financial institutions.

The crisis of the U.S. Civil War (1860-1865) changed this situation. Southern states seceded from the Union, removing the hitherto overwhelming political opposition to a greater federal role. At the same time, pressing needs to finance the Union war effort were partially met through the chartering of National banks that were required to hold reserves in the form of government obligations. The National Bank Act of 1863 was accompanied by other legislation placing a 10 percent tax on the note issue of state banks, with the express intent of forcing the latter to convert to federal charters (Phillips, 1975).

The shifting of bank chartering and bank regulation to the federal government in Washington did not work out as planned. Bankers soon discovered that the regulatory burdens of being a National bank could be avoided despite the 10 percent tax on the note issues of state banks. The escape lay in the use of checking (demand) deposits as a substitute for note issues. Checking deposits grew rapidly after 1870 and, with them, the popularity of state bank charters reappeared. In fact, "chartering rivalry" developed between the state and federal jurisdictions and the number of banks rose dramatically. Branching remained the exception rather than the rule.

Limits on the Business of Banking and the Development of Non-Bank Deposit Institutions

There has been a deep distrust of corporate banking in the "populist" political tradition of the United States since the founding of the nation (Phillips, 1987). Thus, early in its history mutual (depositor-owned) savings banks (MSBs) were chartered by the states. The MSBs often were promoted by well-to-do patrons who wished to instill habits of thrift (and other virtues!) among the poor, but these institutions nonetheless prospered by serving market sectors that the commercial banks would not or could not serve. Consumer and mortgage loans were their primary assets and savings deposits were their principal liability.

In the same way that the popularity of state banks was increased by the burdens associated with National bank chartering, other deposit institutions appeared after the Civil War because of the limits placed on the business of banking. Chief among these were mutual savings and loan associations (S&Ls), dedicated almost exclusively to residential mortgage lending. Less obviously and often without benefit of a charter, neighborhood and work-related credit unions were formed. Consumer finance companies were organized to make what are now known as consumer installment loans -- frequently at usurious interest rates. Trust companies that operated independently from the banks also were chartered. And, of course, the New York Stock Exchange was in operation, and securities underwriting and brokerage firms abounded. These firms were incorporated by the states but essentially unregulated by any bodies other than their own cartel-like associations until 1933.

In all of this, what a particular type of institution was permitted to do, the character of its regulation, and, hence, the nature of business opportunities varied widely from state to state. The differences were not accidental; several states sought to encourage (or discourage) particular forms of financial and nonfinancial businesses by their regulations. There was an element of regulatory rivalry in this, also. There were as well strong elements of protection, with the deposit financial institutions in one state being largely insulated from the potential of competition from the institutions chartered in another.

Some have described the result as one with "too many banks and too few bankers." Banking markets were certainly not efficiently organized.

The Federal Reserve System: Further Harmonization

The antipathy felt by many with respect to banks in general was doubly strong with respect to the creation of a central bank. In addition to concerns about the political power such an institution might offer to banking and commercial interest, there was the historically-based worry that the federal government would abuse the power of a central bank to create money. Periodic crises and the lack of responsiveness of the existing system to the credit requirements caused by economic growth eventually overcame these hurdles, however. The Federal Reserve System was established in 1913.

The power of the Federal Reserve System was heavily circumscribed. It was (and is) technically owned by the member banks, not by the federal government. Its seven-person board of governors each serves overlapping 14-year terms and, once appointed, may not be removed by the U.S. President. As originally set up, the extension of Federal Reserve credit was limited by gold and commercial paper reserve requirements. National banks -- those chartered by the Comptroller of the Currency, U.S. Department of the Treasury -- are required to be members of the System; membership by state banks is optional.

The twelve regional Federal Reserve Banks have tripartite boards of directors with equal representation for the banks, commerce and industry, and the general public. Monetary policy was at first carried out primarily through variations in reserve requirements and the discount rate but, over time, open market operations in U.S. government securities have become the most important quantitative tool.

Debate exists concerning the extent to which the Federal Reserve has been (or is) subject to political influences. Overall, however, its performance has been largely unblemished by scandal even if at times its actions may have appeared to some as ill-founded, shortsighted, or pedestrian. It is important to note as well that the Federal Reserve has generally maintained excellent relationships with state bank regulators. The fact that it is a rather decentralized central bank may be the most important reason for this.

Depression and the Crises of the 1930s

All was not well with the American banking structure after the Federal Reserve was established. Chartering and regulatory rivalry continued. The number of banks exceeded 25,000 by the mid-1920s. Most of these were small, local institutions, and a disproportionate number were located in agricultural areas where big banks and branching were disfavored. Effective regulation was impossible.

The industry was ripe for crisis and, indeed, one rapidly unfolded. The post-World War I agricultural depression combined with the inefficiencies inherent in the operations of most small banks gave rise to a rash of bank failures well prior to 1929. As the Great Depression came on, these failures spread to the urban areas and to larger banks. Subsequent investigations showed that some of the more glaring failures were associated with stock market speculation, loans collateralized by securities, bank security dealings, and outright fraud.

The basic federal regulatory framework under which America's banks now operate was erected in this chaotic environment. The Banking Act of 1933 prohibited banks from paying interest on demand deposits and permitted the regulation of other deposit rates of interest. Deposit insurance was required for all banks belonging to the Federal Reserve System. While ostensibly optional for nonmember banks, the record of bank failures meant that practically all of these banks had to be insured because of depositor preferences for insured accounts. Herein lay the means for the federal government to restrict state chartering activities, since it was the federal government that had to approve of the insurance for any newly chartered bank.

The Banking Act of 1933 contains the highly controversial Glass-Steagall provisions. These prevent any firm dealing in any way in securities from accepting deposits. They also prevent banks from dealing in securities other than on the express order of customers and from being affiliated with any organization principally engaged in the securities business (Phillips, 1979).

The federal law with respect to branching was not appreciably changed in 1933. The 1933 Act and earlier legislation permits National banks to branch within a state only to the extent that state laws allowed state chartered banks to branch. A requirement for federal registration state-chartered bank holding companies was included in the 1933 legislative revisions.

Growing Tensions: Resistance to Reform

It became clear shortly after World War II that the regulatory structure fashioned in the 1930s had notable shortcomings. Each period of threatened inflation brought restrictive Federal Reserve monetary policy, with market rates of interest above those the banks were allowed to pay on deposits. For most of the 14,000 banks, this was a great boon, since their depositors had few competitive alternatives. These banks paid less than money center market rates for funds and re-loaned a good deal of these funds at substantially higher market rates to money center institutions. This, in fact, was the reason for the development of the U.S. "federal funds" market, a market for interbank borrowing of bank reserves. For the money center banks, however, the interest rate ceilings were constraining. Their customers turned elsewhere for both the "selling" and "buying" of funds.

In the early postwar years, the MSBs and S&Ls prospered. Long rates (on mortgages) were well above short rates, and the MSBs and S&Ls (the "thrift institutions") could pay higher deposit rates than could the rate-regulated commercial banks. Funds flowed easily into residential construction. At the same time, advances in data processing permitted the marketing of mutual funds. To many bank customers, higher yielding mutual fund accounts became substitutes for insured, lower yielding bank accounts.

By the mid-1960s, an active commercial paper market had developed.   Businesses   whose   credit   needs   could   not   be accommodated by traditional bank loans issued commercial paper. On the other side, individuals and businesses that traditionally had held surplus funds in bank deposits purchased that paper to get the higher market yields. The Eurodollar market grew in popularity in the United States for much the same reasons -- to escape interest rate and other regulations. Money center banks resorted to the issuance of large ($100,000 and over) certificates of deposits bearing market rates of interest to slow the erosion of their deposit base. The effects of these events gradually -- but only gradually -- spread outside of the money center markets.

The situation of the thrift institutions changed drastically by the late 1960s. Every time inflation threatened and interest rates rose, the earnings they experienced on mortgages placed some years before became inadequate to cover the cost of current funds. The extension of rate ceilings to the thrifts in 1966 put them on a more-or-less equal footing with the banks - - but it caused all of

the regulated deposit institutions to suffer disintermediation to
other parts of the financial market

The early 1970s saw the limited introduction of NOW
accounts -- savings accounts subject to check-like payment orders
that avoided the regulatory prohibition of interest on demand
deposits.   These were gradually permitted to all deposit
institutions. For their part, the investment bankers (often with the
trust departments of cooperating banks) offered "money market
mutual funds." The assets of these funds are in short-term, liquid
instruments, and the shares are redeemable   through third party
drafts. While these drafts look like and act like checks, the courts
have held they do not violate the Glass-Steagall Act. They are not
deposits since they are not liabilities of the sponsoring investment
companies.

In other legal contests, the courts have denied permission to
banks to sell shares in commingled agency accounts; these, it was
held, were de facto securities issues. More recently, however,
courts have approved of Federal Reserve regulations permitting
non-bank subsidiaries of bank holding companies to offer discount
and regular brokerage services. Subsidiaries of National banks
have been permitted to do likewise. Another Federal Reserve
ruling that allows subsidiaries of bank holding companies to
underwrite and deal in commercial paper, state revenue bonds,
and selected other instruments has gained approval so long as these
activities are not so large that they become the "principal" ones in
which the subsidiary is engaged.

One of the more curious regulatory episodes arose because of
the way a bank was defined in the Bank Holding Company Act.
To be a bank subsidiary of a banking holding company, the
institution must offer both commercial loans and demand deposits.
Thus, avoiding the reach of the Act required only that an
institution be formed that offered commercial loans or demand
deposits. This was done on a substantial scale, with the resulting
firms being labeled *non-bank banks*.

States have acted to broaden the ability of bank holding companies to operate banks across state lines. Aborting the parallel state restrictions on interstate branching has been less common. In virtually all of these instances, the changes that have occurred are due to the appearance of new institutions, new organizational arrangements, and new instruments that somehow escape the old regulations through "loopholes" found by clever lawyers and, in part, sympathetic courts and regulators (Langevoort, 1987). The basic federal laws passed in the 1930s have changed little.

The failure of laws and regulations to reflect new technological and market conditions has resulted in continued geographic and product line specialization that increases risk. Looked at in another way, the nearsightedness of many bankers and others who favor continuation of outdated laws and regulations reflects a managerial and regulatory mentality that is out of keeping with the current market situation. There have been wholesale failures among the thrift institutions and a smaller number of dramatic failures among commercial banks. These have reached such proportions that, again, crisis-bred legislation providing for a massive thrift "bailout" has been required. The federal insuring agencies no longer have adequate reserves to meet the claims of depositors of failing institutions.

The resistance to change in the basic regulatory framework has been amazing. Successive privately and publicly sponsored commissions and study groups have been recommending legislative reform since the early 1960s. The recommended changes would have removed the restrictions on interest payments by the deposit institutions, broadened their assets and liability powers so that they could adapt to technological change and highly volatile money markets, and expand the geographic scope of their operations.

The reasons that no such omnibus legislation has been passed are easy to find (Jacobs and Phillips, 1983). The situation is one in which (not counting credit unions) there are still some 20,000 deposit institutions with extremely diverse interests. Many remain sheltered from day-to-day market pressures. There are as well the traditional customers of these institutions -- home builders, mortgage bankers, small businesses, farmers -- who see broader powers as threats to their traditional sources of credit. The investment banks and securities dealers have been opposed to relaxation of the Glass-Steagall restrictions on banks entering their markets, although this opposition may be waning. And the state regulators are opposed to further federal incursions into their historic regulatory domains. All in all, it has not been difficult to find a majority of legislators to vote against any particular bill, even though most of them may favor some sort of re-regulation.

IMPLICATIONS FOR EUROPE

Complexities of the European Situation

In some respects, the political and economic situation in Europe is far more complex than that of the United States, making harmonization and unifying re-regulation of European financial institutions arguably more difficult. In the first place, the Treaty of Rome was just that -- a treaty. It has created an amazing "European Union," but the union has fallen short of being a constitutionally based unity of government (Brewin, 1987). The 1987 Single European Act changed the tone and the rules of the European Parliament, the Council of Ministers, and the European Commission in governing the EC, but the 12 member nations retain substantial autonomy (*The Economist*, 1989a).

Further, while a European Monetary System (EMS) was established in 1979 and the ECU is used increasingly in new issues transactions, interbank accounting, and other purposes, the EMS is not yet an economic and a monetary union (EMU) (Feeny, 1987; Goodman and Pauly, 1986; Rivera-Batiz, 1985). Some of the EC nations have not participated in the EMS. There is no

truly common currency.   Each nation has its own central bank.
The framework of the EMS requires a degree of coordination
among the central banks, but each still operates subject to the laws
of its own host nation, has its own monetary policy goals, its own
variations of policy tools, and its own peculiar needs with respect
to the accommodation of its own nation's fiscal and exchange rate
policies (Bramson, 1990; Krugman, 1990; *The Economist*, 1990;
Demopoulos et al., 1985).

Plans have been made to create a full EMU by 1995.   A
three-stage evolution is foreseen (Giovazzi et al., 1988; Colchester,
1989; *The Economist*, 1989b).   The first stage is the present EMS,
with all members participating and with greater coordination of
national economic policies.   The second stage, which will require
an amendment to the Treaty of Rome, would create a system for
coordinating European central banking and the gradual emergence
of a European Central Bank akin to the early U.S. Federal Reserve
System.   Guidelines for the monetary policies of the individual
countries would be set and movements in their currencies would
be more closely controlled.   In the third stage, intra-EC exchange
rates would first be fixed and then a single currency would
appear.   The control of the European Central Bank over monetary
policies would then become binding.

This will not be easy to accomplish.   Strong opposition has
been expressed in Britain, and there are considerable but quieter
reservations elsewhere. The reluctance to "go all the way" is not
difficult to explain.   The European nations have more pronounced
differences among the roles of banks, other deposit institutions,
and non-bank financial institutions in the intermediation processes
than has ever been true within the United States Following the
general analyses of Tobin (1956) and Gurley and Shaw (1956), the
differences in intermediation processes appear statistically in
highly varying ratios of the money stock and GNP (Monti and
Porta, 1981), but it is apparent also in the differences in the
functions of the various classes of institutions (Wessels, 1981;
Courakis, 1981; Aftalion, 1981).   In addition, the institutions of

the several countries have varying legal and regulatory obligations to provide support for agriculture, exports, small businesses, other sectors, and they have varying needs to coordinate monetary, exchange rate, and fiscal policies (Bramson, 1990; Krugman, 1990; *The Economist*, 1990a, 1990b).

The differences among the member nations with respect to branching may be less varied than those in the United States Nationwide, if not EC-wide, branching is common. Vast differences remain, nonetheless, with respect to prudential regulations, reserves, capital requirements, deposit definitions, loan rules and practices, and the investment banking functions permitted to commercial banks. Of more importance for full harmonization, there are wide differences among the member states regarding foreign bank entry, restrictions on the activities of foreign banks, regulations distinguishing foreign from domestic banks, and the modes of supervising foreign banks (OECD, 1981-1, 1982-2; 1983). These differences ought not be trivialized since, judged on United States experience, they may become the basis for thwarting the intent of reforms.

Political and Economic Interests of Incumbent Institutions

Reform in the United States has been made difficult because of the "rent seeking" (really, "rent retention") behavior of incumbents. The world in general may be made "better off" by financial reform, but the welfare of most incumbents -- at least, in the near term -- is threatened. The resulting political decisions resemble Condorcet's "voting paradox." While a majority have definable alternatives that are preferable to the present situation, the lack of congruence in ranking the alternatives against the present situation results in repeated votes to turn down proposals for reform. Only in crises can action be taken.

Here the European condition appears more amenable to coordinated and planned reforms than is the case in the United States But this is not because the incumbent institutions are more public-spirited and less inclined to protect their own interests. It is rather because of profound differences in the economic and political situations in which these institutions find themselves. Thus, in Europe, the typical financial structure is one with a relatively small number of firms, no one of which is isolated from "money center" market forces. Moreover, the experiences of these institutions in recent years have been of increasing exposure to international influences over which their own governments have little control.

In Europe, too, while there are differences in the degree to which banks engage in securities activities, none of these goes as far as the separations required by the Glass-Steagall law in the United States Perhaps as important, it seems that in Europe the separation of the business of banking from securities activities and other businesses is not considered with the same near-religious intensity that is accorded to it in the United States It is easier to reach accord in a small committee, with all members having similar values, similar experiences, and perceiving similar external threats than it is in a large committee with diverse membership. The fact that the deliberations of the European Commission and European Parliament are -- or may be -- one step removed from the visible argumentations made for domestic political reasons also favors the European situation.

First Steps: Full Harmonization Versus Mutual Recognition

Most observers of the European scene rule out the practical possibility of full harmonization of banking regulations by 1992 or, indeed, by 1995. Important first steps toward that goal can be achieved, nonetheless. The guiding principle for the first steps would be that of "mutual recognition"; after general, Community-wide standards for safety and soundness have been established, each state would allow entry by institutions from the others. Institutions could sell in other nations whatever they are allowed to sell in home markets, and largely under home control (Key, 1989; Colchester, 1989; Jacquemin, 1990; Padoa-Schioppa, 1988).

Only in the later stages would strong efforts be made to harmonize fully the regulations of the several countries.

Regulatory changes of this sort have met great resistance in the United States. The 1927 McFadden Act and the Douglas Amendment to the 1956 Bank Holding Company Act prevent interstate branching and the interstate expansion of the banks of holding companies contrary to state laws. This has remained the case despite the growing number of states that have recognized the advantages of open interstate banking. As noted above, a proliferation of compacts among the states has recently occurred. The institutions of the states that did not liberalize their regulations -- those against reform -- were often left behind. The attractive "dancing partners" in other states were taken by the time the "foot-dragging" states woke up to what was going on!

Some of the individual member states of the EC may, of course, opt to behave as the recalcitrant states do in the United States If they do, however, they also run the danger of being left without partners -- and without things to do -- when the dancing ends. In Europe, as in the United States, mergers will become attractive as banking moves across political boundaries (*The Banker*, 1989). Consolidation is a phenomenon that provincial regulations may hinder, but that it cannot ultimately prevent. Institutional means will be found to go around parochial protective regulations, and those successful in the short-term in gaining protection may pay dearly.

The wiser course for the EC nations -- as it would have been for states in the United States -- is to give greater freedoms to their domestic institutions to join in one way or another in the technologically and competitively driven expansion of markets. Policies based on mutual recognition are important first steps -- but steps that may not be acceptable for domestic political reasons.

Some Questions Concerning the European Central Bank

The proposals for a European Central Bank are currently difficult to comprehend because of the high level of ambiguity attaching to them (de Cecco and Giovanni, 1989). The proposed Central Bank does not seem to be a traditional central bank, however. Suggestions that it would not have any direct quantitative monetary powers raise more questions than they answer. What is a central bank with no ability to alter the credit (base money) of the relevant economy? Ought this be done through 12 subsidiaries? How does such a bank operate? What are its assets? What are its liabilities? Is the proposal for no more than a coordinating agency? Is the main goal simply increased monetary discipline for the individual central banks that, lacking such an institution would otherwise find irresistibly strong domestic inflationary and devaluation biases (Giavazzi and Pagano, 1988)? How would such a bank influence, if at all, the various fiscal policies and practices of the member states and the freedom of their own central banks to accommodate fiscal affairs (Branson, 1990; Krugman, 1990)?

The Special Problem of Deposit Guarantees

The steps toward freer markets in Europe will accentuate the problems involved in safeguarding the stability -- the safety and soundness -- of the credit system (Padoa-Schioppa, 1988; Gordon, 1987). It has been argued that the pressures put on earnings by increased competition cause financial intermediaries to accept increased risks. With greater risks, the failures of individual institutions become more probable and, given the strong interrelationships among the institutions, the problem of systemic failure becomes more acute.

Harmonizing and increasing bank capital requirements and unifying accounting conventions are steps in this direction. They contain dangers of their own, however. Added capital requirements, without attention to the riskiness and liquidity of underlying assets, may do nothing to improve the institutions' abilities to meet unexpected disintermediation. Moreover, higher capital requirements may disadvantage the class of institutions to which they apply relative to other institutions offering near-substitute services. In the same vein, binding accounting practices for a particular type of institution add to the incentive to do the same kind of business through another, unaffected type of institution. That has surely been the consequence of such regulations in the United States

Deposit insurance was introduced in the United States by the 1933 legislation. It was aimed at preventing further bank failures, but it gained a considerable degree of political favor because it protected the remaining banks from failure. The growing pressure to permit mergers and branching that accompanied the failures was contained by the introduction of deposit insurance. Similar motives may exist in Europe.

From 1933 until recently, deposit insurance worked quite well in the United States   Put another way, there were few failures among the insured commercial banks and the thrifts   -- few failures until existing regulations, new technologies, and new market forces made disintermediation a lucrative practice for many depositors and competing institutions. Then, in the modern context, deposit insurance became dysfunctional in two fundamental respects. First, since the deposit insurance premiums are fixed per dollar of deposits, insured institutions have no incentives to reduce risks in order to lower premium payments. The incentives, in fact, run in just the opposite direction. There is evidence that insured institutions have increased the riskiness of their operations to match the risks implicit in the premiums.

Second, as it has become known that particular institutions are in danger of defaulting, the rates they must pay on even insured deposits increases. This has given rise to "brokered deposits" -- the placing of insured deposits in risky institutions through arrangements made by brokers. Thus, the failing banks or thrifts receive funds for further expansion into their risky ventures, increasing the exposure of the insuring agencies. Perhaps even more important, the safer institutions find that they must compete for funds against such insured, higher-yielding deposits, increasing their costs, tempting them to accept greater risks, and again increasing the exposure of the insuring agencies. These are hardly the results that one would seek from an ideal deposit insurance scheme (Kane, 1989).

It turns out, then, that neither higher capital requirements nor the U.S. type of deposit insurance will work well to satisfy the EC's desire for safeguarding the credit system. A better avenue to be pursued would be one that eschews insurance for the failing institution, as an institution. Institutions must be permitted to fail while at the same time the public interest in the ultimate redeemability (at par) of third-party payment transactions accounts is preserved.

A possible way of doing this is to establish regulations requiring all institutions offering third-party payment transactions account to hold short term, highly liquid assets with market value at least equal to the value of such accounts. These investments would constitute "secondary reserves." Insurance for the transaction accounts would also be required, but in these circumstances the insurance would operate differently from that in the United States By law, the secondary reserves could be used to meet no claims other than the third-party payment accounts. Further, as the institution appeared to be getting into trouble, the insuring agency would be empowered to force the institution to pay off the third-party payment liabilities, selling the secondary reserves instruments as the means for so doing. Alternatively, the insuring agency could require the institution to divest itself of both these liabilities and assets through their joint sale to another institution. The perverse tendencies for banks to accept greater risk and for increased exposure of insuring agency would thus be avoided.

Bank failures have adverse effects on customers other than depositors. Borrowers and other established customers are forced to seek new banking relationships when failures occur. Widening the set of possible merger candidates and encouraging consolidations prior to default help in reducing these costs and would be one of the beneficial side effects of the European proposals. In addition, while mandated safety measures such as those suggested above are less easy to justify for time deposits and other non-transaction accounts, there may be room for voluntary, market-mediated, private insurance arrangements for other types of deposits.

CONCLUSIONS

Perhaps the most important conclusion to be drawn from the United States experience is that full harmonization of the banking system is not necessary to get most of the benefits of European Union. After all, the U.S. system remains highly fractionated, diversely regulated, and inefficiently structured, yet few would suggest that it has been a major drag to the performance of the economy. While the development of particular states and regions has been hampered by antiquated and cumbersome regulations and banking practices, the nation as a whole has suffered little since a uniform currency was introduced in the 1860s. The primary need for integration in Europe seems to be in the "real" sectors of the economy, not in the financial sectors.

There are reasons, too, for a careful "phasing in" of financial reform. The protections afforded by national regulations have, over the years, permitted the continued operations of some inefficient institutions. Moreover, there are undoubtedly unrealized economies of scale and economies of scope in banking operations which, as operating freedoms are granted, will cause significant restructurings. Beyond this -- and even within financial markets -- there may be issues of comparative advantage that will expose some nations' institutions to new risks of survival. Finally, imperfectly competitive markets are conducive to the strategic use of forms of rivalry that may undo even basically efficient firms. So -- go easy.

The fundamental question that incumbent financial institutions must face in the light of European integration is not how to protect their markets, however. The fundamental questions related to how their own laws, regulation, and modes of operation ought be changed to permit them an opportunity to compete in the new, internationalized world of banking. If they do not adapt and, particularly, if they rely on existing laws and regulations to give continued protection, they surely cannot survive for long except in restricted market niches. Financial markets are now irrevocably international; financial institutions must adjust to that fact or perish.

References

Aftalion, F.   "Government Intervention in the French Financial System," in A. Verheirstraeten (ed.), *Competition and Regulation in Financial Markets*, London: Macmillan Publishing, 1981.

"Big Fish, Little Fish," *The Banker*, January, 1989, p. 38.

Basevi, G.   "Monetary Cooperation and Liberalization of Capital Movements in the European Monetary System," *European Economic Review*, March, 1988, pp. 372-381.

Batchelor, R.A., and Griffiths, B. "Monetary Restraint Through Credit Control in the United Kingdom -- The Lesson of Recent Practice," in A. Verheirstraeten (ed.), *Competition and Regulation in Financial Markets*, London: Macmillan Publishing, 1981.

Bhatt, G. "Europe 1992," *Finance & Development*, June, 1989, pp. 40-42.

Branson, W.H.   "Financial Market Integration, Macroeconomic Policy and the EMS," in C. Bliss and J. Braga de Lacado (eds.) *Unity with Diversity in the European Economy: The Community's Southern Frontier.*   Cambridge, England: Cambridge University Press, 1990.

Brewin, C.   "The European Community: A Union of States Without Unity of Government," *Journal of Common Market Studies*, September 26, 1987, pp. 1-23.

Brewin, C., and McAllister, R. "Annual Review of the European Communities in 1986," *Journal of Common Market Studies*, June 25, 1987, pp. 337-372.

Capotorti, F.,Hilf, M., Jacobs, F.G., and Jacque, J.P. *The European Union Treaty.* Oxford: Clarendon Press, 1986.

Cecchini, P.   *The European Challenge 1992:   The Benefits of a Single Market Aldershot: Gower, 1988.*

Colchester, N.   "1992 Under Construction: Europe's Internal Market," *The Economist*, July 8-14, 1989, p. 48ff.

Courakis, A.S.   "Banking Policy and Commercial Bank Behaviour in Greece," in A. Verheirstraeten (ed.), *Competition and Regulation in Financial Markets.*   London: Macmillan Publishing, 1981.

de Cecco, M., and Giovanni, A.   *A European Central Bank?* Cambridge: Cambridge University Press, 1989.

Demopoulos, G.D., Katsimbris, G.M. and Miller, S.M. "Monetary Policy and Central Bank Financing of Government Budget

Deficits," *European Economic Review*, 31 September, 1987, pp. 1023-1050.

"Eurofuture v. Europhoria," *The Economist.* May 14, 1988(a), pp. 14-15.

"Europe's Capital Achievement," *The Economist.* June 18, 1988(b), pp. 14-15.

"European Parliament: Credibility Before Democracy," *The Economist.* February 11, 1989(a), p. 48; "EEC Council of Ministers: The Powers That Be," February 25, p. 49; "European Commission: The Locomotive of 1992," March 25, p. 56; "European Court of Justice: Where the Buck Stops," May 6, p. 48.

"The ECU Nationalists," *The Economist.* February 18, p. 12; "EMU in Motion," April 22, p. 16; "How to Hatch an EMU," April 22, 1989b, pp. 45-46.

"Roman Road to EMU," *The Economist.* February 17, 1990(a), p. 4.

"View from a Room," *The Economist.* March 24, 1990(b), p.86.

Feeny, P. "Loan Securitization: Euronote and Eurocommercial Paper Markets," Research Monograph No. 1, Institute of European Finance, University College of North Wales, 1987.

Giavazzi, F. and Pagano, M. "The Advantage of Tying One's Hands: EMS Discipline and Central Bank Credibility," *European Economic Review*, June, 1988, pp. 1055-1074.

Giavazzi, F., Micossi, S., and Miller, M. *The European Monetary System*, Cambridge, England: Cambridge University Press, 1988.

Goodman, L., and Pauly, P. "Equilibrium Properties of the European Monetary System," December, 1986 (unpublished).

Gordon, K. "1992: Big Bang or Little Whimpers?" *The Banker*, October, 1987, pp. 18-23.

Gurley, J.G., and Shaw, E.B. "Financial Intermediaries and the Saving-Investment Process," *Journal of Finance*, 11 May, 1956, pp. 257-266.

Jacquemin, A. "Collusive Behavior, R&D, and European Competition Policy," (this book).

Jacobs, D.P., and Phillips, A. "Reflections on the Hunt Commission," in G.J. Benston (ed.), *Financial Services: The Changing Institutions and Government Policy*, American Assembly, Englewood Cliffs, NJ: Prentice-Hall, 1983.

Kane, E.J. *The Insurance Mess: How did it Happen?* Washington: The Urban Institute Press, 1989.

Key. S.J. "Mutual Recognition: Integration of the Financial Sector in the European Community," *Federal Reserve Bulletin*, September, 1989, pp. 591-609.

Krugman, P. "Macroeconomic Adjustment and Entry into the EC," in C. Bliss and J. Braga de Macedo (eds.), *Unity with Diversity in the European Economy: The Community's Southern Frontier.* Cambridge, England: Cambridge University Press, 1990.

Langeheine, B., and Weinstock, U. "Graduated Integration: A Modest Path Toward Progress," *Journal of Common Market Studies*, 23 March, 1985, pp. 185-198.

Langevoort, D.C. "Statutory Obsolescence and the Judicial Process: The Revisionist Role of Courts in Federal Banking

Regulation," *Michigan Law Review*, February, 1987, pp. 672-733.

Lodge, J. (ed.). *European Union: The European Community in Search of a Future.* London: Macmillan, 1986.

Lopez-Charos, A. "The European Community: On the Road to Integration," *Finance and Development*, September, 1987, pp. 35-38.

Monti, M., and Porta, A. "Bank Intermediation Under Flexible Deposit Rates and Controlled Credit Allocation: The Italian Experience," in A. Verheirstraeten (ed.), *Competition and Regulation in Financial Markets.* London: Macmillan Publishing, 1981.

Nicoll, W. "Paths to European Unity," *Journal of Common Market Studies*, 23 March, 1985, pp. 199-206.

OECD *Regulations Affecting International Banking Operations*, Paris, 1981-1, 1982-2.

OECD *The Internationalization of Banking: The Policy Issues*, Paris, 1983.

Padoa-Schioppa, T. "Toward a European Banking Regulatory Framework," *Economic Bulletin, Banca d'Italia*, February, 1988, pp. 49-53.

Phillips, A. "Competitive Policy for Depository Financial Institutions," in A. Phillips (ed.), *Promoting Competition in Regulated Markets*, Washington, DC: Brookings Institution, 1975.

Phillips, A. "The Metamorphosis of Markets: Commercial and Investment Banking," *Journal of Comparative Corporate Law and Securities Regulation*, 1979, 1, pp. 227-243.

Phillips, A. "The New Money and the Old Monopoly Problem," in
    E. Solomon (ed.), *The Payments Revolution: The Emerging
    Public Policy Issues.* Hingham, Mass: Kluwer-Nijhoff
    Publishing, 1987.

Pinder, J. "The Political Economy of Integration in Europe:
    Policies and Institutions in East and West," *Journal of
    Common Market Studies*, September 25, 1986, pp. 1-14.

Tobin, J. "Commercial Banks as Creators of Money," Deane
    Carson (ed.), *Banking and Monetary Studies.* Homewood, Ill:
    Richard D. Irwin, 1963.

Rivera-Batiz, F., and Rivera-Batiz, L. *International Finance and
    Open Economy Macroeconomics.* New York: Macmillan
    Publishing, 1985.

Tully, S. "Europe Gets Ready for 1992," *Fortune*, February 1,
    1988, pp. 81-84.

Wessels, R.E. "Monetary Policy and the Loan Rate in the
    Netherlands," in A. Verheirstraeten (ed.), *Competition and
    Regulation in Financial Markets.* London: Macmillan
    Publishing, 1981.

Winder, R. "The Capitalization of Europe," *Euromoney*, August,
    1986, pp. 109-119.

Chapter 12

Creating an Integrated EEC Market for Financial Services

Brian Hindley

London School of Economics and Political Science

The European Commission estimates that a very large gain will result from the integration of financial services (banking and credit, insurance, brokerage, and securities) in the European Community. Cecchini (1988, p. 42), gives a figure of ECU 21.7 billion as the potential gain in consumer surplus.

That figure should be interpreted cautiously. One reason for caution, of course, is that the figure is gross, not net. Part of the gains that the Commission forecasts for users of financial services are losses to providers of financial institutions, and these losses are not netted out of the Commission's figure. A more fundamental and interesting reason for caution, in the case of financial services, is that the performance of the financial service industries affects the performance of every other sector of the economy. It is therefore very difficult to estimate the overall impact of a major change affecting financial services, such as the 1992 proposals will bring about if and when they are put into effect.

Nevertheless, the basic data used by the Commission in arriving at its estimates have a certain intrinsic interest. The Cecchini Report (Table 6.1, pp. 38-39), provides these data, which are presented in a slightly recalculated form in table 12-1.

Table 12-1 gives the price of the service in the Member State with the lowest price as 1, and expresses all other prices as a multiple of that price. Thus, for example, line 1 of table 12-1 shows that Belgium has the lowest cost of consumer credit and that the German price is four times the Belgian price.

Many questions might be asked about these data. They range from the methods by which they were collected, through possible differences in the quality of the services compared, to underlying differences in the cost of supplying a service in different jurisdictions. For example, the number of motor car accidents may be greater in one country than another, so that, other things being equal, the cost of insuring against the risk of accident will be higher. Nevertheless, it is difficult to believe that the very large differences shown in the table can be entirely explained in such terms.[1]

If the differences revealed by the table cannot be explained in such terms, however, they imply that the interests of users of services are not well protected by the existing national regulatory systems. That suggestion is strengthened by the fact that within the EC there is a right of establishment for service providers from other Member States.

Establishment means that a service provider based in Member State A accepts the regulatory system of Member State B when it establishes there. That there is such an approximation of free entry to the national markets adds plausibility to the hypothesis that the regulatory systems of the Member States are responsible for much of the variance in the price of services across Member States. The Commission's figures indicate the possibility that the interests of users of financial services would be

better protected by competition between suppliers from different
Member States -- and by competition between national regulatory
systems -- than they are by the existing system of national
regulation.

PRODUCTS	Table 12-1. Prices of Standard Financial Products in EC Member States (Prices expressed as a multiple of the lowest member-state price)							
	COUNTRY							
	Bel.	Ger.	Spa.	Fra.	It.	Lux.	Neth	U.K.
Consumer Credit	1.0	4.0	2.4	n.a.	3.7	1.3	2.2	3.7
Credit Cards	2.6	2.3	1.8	1.0	2.7	1.3	2.0	1.6
Mortgages	1.6	2.0	2.7	2.2	1.2	n.a.	1.2	1.0
Letters of Credit	1.4	1.0	1.8	1.0	1.2	1.4	1.3	1.2
FX Drafts	2.0	2.4	5.5	2.9	2.3	2.5	1.0	2.1
Travellers Cheques	1.5	1.0	1.4	1.5	1.3	1.0	1.4	1.0
Commercial Loans	1.0	1.1	1.3	1.0	1.2	1.1	1.5	1.6
Life Insurance	2.7	1.5	2.0	1.9	2.6	2.4	1.3	1.0
Home Insurance	1.0	1.2	1.7	1.8	2.2	1.9	1.4	2.3
Motor Insurance	1.6	1.4	2.4	1.3	3.0	2.1	1.1	1.0
Commercial Fire and Theft	1.1	1.7	1.5	3.0	4.1	1.0	1.2	1.5
Public Liability	1.3	1.8	1.9	2.6	2.1	1.3	1.0	1.1
Private Equity Transactions	1.6	1.2	1.9	1.0	1.1	1.2	2.5	2.6
Private Gilts Transactions	3.1	5.1	8.6	3.3	1.0	3.4	7.0	3.7
Institutional Equity Trans.	2.4	3.2	4.8	1.8	2.8	3.2	2.4	1.0
Institutional Gilt Trans.	6.0	1.5	2.5	2.5	3.0	1.0	1.9	n.a.

Source: Cecchini (1988, Table 6.1).

Yet there is a problem. These gains were always available.
In the past, however, the Commission's proposals for approaching

them have largely been blocked in the Council. What has happened to change the situation? More pertinent, is the current movement toward the integration of markets for financial services within the Community soundly based and irreversible?

One thing that has changed is the institutional structure of the EC. The two important institutions that are essential to an understanding of the past blockages are the Council of Ministers, in which all of the member governments are represented, and the European Commission.

Essentially, the Commission administers the EEC Treaty. In some areas, such as competition policy, it can act without the approval of the Council. But in many areas, the Treaty is a statement of principles rather than a plan of application. When the Commission wants to apply the Treaty in a new area, which is to say virtually all of the areas in which progress might occur, it must publish a draft directive which states its proposals for the application.

For the Commission to actually proceed with its proposed application, however, the directive must be approved by the Council. The Council -- in effect the governments of the Member States -- can block proposals of the Commission. The Council, moreover, takes its decisions -- or non-decisions -- by vote.

Until recently, approval in the Council has usually required unanimity. That is not an easy condition to achieve in politics. As the EC expanded from its original 6 members to 9, then to 10, and finally to its present 12, and as its membership became less and less homogeneous, it became even harder to obtain. Hence, anything approaching the status of a radical change -- and a good deal that was not by any stretch of the imagination radical -- was likely to be blocked in the Council.

The Single European Act (SEA), which came into effect in the middle of 1987, changed this situation. The SEA has removed the requirement of unanimity from many Council decisions. In particular, almost all decisions regarding the internal market can now be taken on a majority vote -- with the very important exception of taxation.

The majority vote, of course, is not a simple majority. Nor are votes allocated on the basis of one state, one vote. The four largest members have 10 votes each, Spain 8, Denmark and Ireland 3, Luxembourg 2, and other members 5. A qualified majority is 54 votes out of a total of 76.

This system certainly creates more flexibility than a requirement of unanimity, but it is also true that there are on many issues natural blocking coalitions. Thus, for example, to block plans for increased spending, Britain and Germany need only one other small country (and can usually count on one of Denmark, Belgium, or the Netherlands to join them on such issues). On the other hand, in matters affecting the Mediterranean, Italy, Spain, and Greece together possess 23 votes -- just the minimum number required to block.

The Single European Act is a reflection of what might be called the bicycle theory of the EEC -- that if you don't move forward, the whole thing collapses. Whether that is so or not, the SEA certainly improves the Commission's bargaining power with respect to the changes it has proposed for the internal market. Nevertheless, I shall suggest that it is very far from eliminating the problems of the past.

PAST PROBLEMS

The Treaty of Rome (Article 3) calls for "the abolition, as between Member States, of obstacles to freedom of movement for persons, services and capital." Title III of the Treaty, "Free movement of persons, services and capital", elaborates Article 3(c). The Title is divided into four chapters: "Workers" (Article 48-51); "Rights of Establishment" (Article 52-58); "Services" (Article 59-66); and "Capital" (Article 67-73).

This structure and wording are significant. That freedom of movement for services is distinguished from freedom of movement of factors of production clearly implies that what is at issue in Articles 59-66 is trade in services: transborder flows of services without movements of factors of production. The provisions on factor movement would otherwise have been sufficient, and Articles 59-66 would have been unnecessary.

Nevertheless, until very recently, progress toward integrated European Community markets for services contrasts sharply with progress toward such markets for goods. Two years ago, it was possible to say that in some services, movement from the starting line defined by the signing of the Treaty of Rome was close to imperceptible. That was not true of any manufacturing industry.

This lack of progress was not merely due to a lack of political will. The problems entailed in liberalizing service markets are more difficult than those in goods markets. The abolition of tariffs and quotas made a vast step toward integration of goods markets in the EEC. Moreover, because tariffs and quotas are easy to detect, it was a relatively straightforward step from an administrative and legal standpoint, whatever its difficulty from a political standpoint.

Service industries, however, are not usually protected by tariffs or quotas (and because of their "invisible" properties, usually cannot be protected by those means). The service sector therefore offered no prospect of any achievement so major and so straightforward. "Grey-area measures," or nontariff barriers, are at the core of the remaining issues in integrating EEC markets for goods. They are the central issue in services trade.

In the EEC, the major problem has been that services are regulated within national jurisdictions but that the form and/or the level of regulation differ between jurisdictions. National regulation raises two primary problems. First, regulatory powers can be used to create barriers to competition and trade. To identify where legitimate action ends and protection begins is often difficult (as when health and safety regulations are used to impede trade in goods). The basic fact of the matter, however, is not widely disputed.

Such regulatory protection against service suppliers in other Member States may occur in the EEC. However, it is not necessary to invoke that possibility to explain the problems of liberalization in the service sector. Difficulties in the EEC service sector occur because regulation is likely to affect the costs of producers of the service. Hence, when producers established in Member State A are free to sell services in Member State B without establishment in B (or without otherwise being subject to the B regulatory system), there is not only competition between A and B producers but there is also competition between the national regulatory systems of A and B. Some Member States have been unwilling to permit such competition. That refusal is at the heart of the difficulties of achieving integration in the EEC service sector.

A first question to ask, therefore, is whether a rejection of competition between different regulatory systems can be defended on grounds of the general interest -- either that of the citizens of the Member State concerned or of those of the EEC as a whole. Having sketched the economics of such competition, I shall look at the way in which the institutions of the Community have in fact handled the problem.

THE ECONOMICS OF COMPETITION BETWEEN REGULATORY SYSTEMS[2]

The general interest basis for objections to trade in nationally regulated services is that suppliers subject to the heaviest regulatory requirement will be penalized in competition. Thus, suppliers subject to a system that requires larger reserves, more years of education, or higher minimum prices will be at a competitive disadvantage against suppliers who are subject to less stringent requirements.

But is this true? The argument assumes one of two things. Either it assumes that the more stringent requirements are not valuable to buyers of the service (or more precisely, that buyers do not value them at a level commensurate with their cost), or that buyers are ignorant of the advantages that will accrue to them from dealing with suppliers subject to these more stringent requirements.

Buyers may perceive the value to them of the more stringent regulation but not think it worth the extra cost (as they might prefer to buy a VW rather than a Mercedes). In that case, the argument for protecting the more demanding regulatory system from the effects of intra-Community competition "in the general interest" is very weak.[3]

More interest attaches to the proposition that buyers are not well informed enough to perceive the value to them of the more stringent regulations, but would find the extra cost worthwhile were they fully informed. This, of course, is very close to one of the classic rationales for regulation. But misinformation on the part of buyers leads directly to a case for informing buyers, not to one for regulating sellers. If it makes a case for an official agency, it is for one that acquires and processes information for buyers, not for one with powers to coerce producers.

To move to a satisfactory case for regulation -- that is, to a case that such an official agency should have powers to coerce sellers -- transmission of relevant information from the agency to buyers must be expensive. If potential buyers can obtain information quickly and cheaply (whether from an official agency or from other sources), there is no good case for regulating sellers.

A case for regulation starts to take shape, however, when information is expensive to transmit. In that event, an information-disseminating agency may possess knowledge that would cause any well-informed buyer to refuse to purchase from a particular supplier. The agency cannot pass that information to buyers, however, because the costs of transmitting it are too great. A solution is to provide the agency with the power to force the withdrawal of the supplier from the market. The agency then becomes a regulator rather than an information disseminator.

But even high costs of transmitting information are not sufficient to establish a secure case for regulation. A further problem is whether the agency can accurately judge what well-informed buyers would or would not do. There is a Mercedes-Volkswagen problem. Unless all buyers would react in the same way to a piece of information, to provide the agency with the power to force sellers to withdraw from the market is to create the risk that it will force the withdrawal of firms whose products would be chosen by well-informed buyers, and therefore to create the risk that regulation will deprive such buyers of their preferred options.

This case for regulation therefore depends upon the fulfillment of quite restrictive conditions. It requires that (i) buyers will be seriously misinformed in the absence of regulation; (ii) it is expensive to transmit information to buyers; and (iii) buyers will react in the same way to information.

These conditions are less easy to fulfill than the amount of regulation might lead one to suspect. But the immediate issue is that of competition between regulatory systems within the EEC. In that context, the relevant point is that an argument that such competition is against the public interest cannot obtain a sound foundation from these conditions.

Suppose that Member State A has a demanding regulatory system, and Member State B a less demanding one. Producers of services established in B therefore are able to offer a service which, at least on the service, is more attractive than that offered by producers established in A. (Were this not so, sales by A producers in B presumably would not be large, and the policy issue not major.) The problem is that if suppliers from B can freely sell in A, some buyers in A might buy the B service under the mistaken impression that it also offers the advantages, whatever they may be, of the A regulatory system.

But is this really a serious problem? To ensure that buyers are clearly informed that the service they propose to buy is accepted under the B regulatory system but does not meet the requirements of A does not seem difficult. Nor is there any obvious reason to suppose that basic information about the differences in the A and B regulatory systems and the consequences of those differences are difficult or expensive to transmit. But if it is easy to ensure that buyers are informed, the case for regulating B-based sellers out of the A market is weak and the case for informing potential A buyers of the relevant differences is strong.

As patriotism is the last refuge of scoundrels (according to Dr. Johnson), the welfare of widows, orphans, and the incompetent is the last refuge of supporters of regulation. Individuals free to make their own decisions will indeed make mistakes. Even if potential buyers are clearly informed of the regulatory regime, some will not understand its significance. Even if large amounts of information are available on that significance, some will not bother to obtain it.

A regulatory system that genuinely attempted to serve the public interest would take these facts into account. It would not, however, allow them to be decisive. The cost of regulating to protect the slothful and the incompetent is that other persons are prevented from making arrangements that in full knowledge they would prefer. Moreover, of course, the incompetent might be lucky: regulation prevents them from making a choice that is by accident the one they should have made.

An excessive willingness to suppress the freedom to contract of the competent in an effort to preserve the incompetent against error is difficult to understand on the view that regulation is aimed at protecting buyers from incompetent or rapacious suppliers. It is more easily understood on the alternative view that national regulation protects national <u>suppliers</u> of the service, who "capture" the powers of the regulatory agency and use them to suppress competition from other sources.[4] In that event, it should certainly be expected that there will be efforts to extend the scope of regulation. Protection of the foolish against error provides a rationale for almost infinite extension.

I conclude that:

1. The Treaty of Rome requires integration of national markets for services in the EEC, and that fulfillment of that requirement, in the absence of agreed harmonization of national regulations, calls for competition between the national regulatory systems.

2. There is a substantial theoretical case that the general interest will be furthered by allowing competition between national regulatory systems in the EEC, even if those systems are structured solely on the basis of improving the welfare of buyers of services; and

3. The evidence gathered by the Commission suggests that there are elements of "capture" in some national regulatory

systems, so that they do not serve well the welfare of buyers of services -- and that in any event, the Commission's figures indicate that such competition will give rise to considerable net gains.

I now turn to the way in which the Commission, the Council, and the Court have dealt with these issues in practice.

HARMONIZATION AND THE COMMISSION'S NEW APPROACH

For many years, the Commission tried to solve the problems raised by the specter of competition between national regulatory systems through harmonization -- the negotiation of Community-wide regulations. The Council, with equal persistence, largely blocked these attempts. As a result, the harmonization approach foundered.

It became clear that if acceptable Community-wide regulations could be negotiated at all, they were going to take a very long time to arrive. The point is illustrated by the Non-Life Insurance Draft Directive that first appeared in 1975, but until a recent decision by the European Court (to be discussed in more detail below) was blocked in the Council. Even now, this directive has been considerably compromised and attenuated.[5]

The Commission therefore struck out along new lines. The new approach was heralded in the 1985 White Paper Completing the Internal Market. Instead of aiming to for overall harmonization, the Commission decided to focus its efforts on the negotiation of minimum standards of regulation, to apply across the Community. Once such Community minima have been established, a service-selling organization established in one country of the EEC will be able to sell its products in any other EEC country without interference from the latter's regulatory authority.

This approach has already been applied to mutual funds, and that agreement went into effect on October 1, 1989. The Council is now debating its application to banks. The Second Banking Coordination Directive was published in February, 1988. When (and if) it is accepted, a bank set up and approved in one member country will be able to sell its products in any other EEC country without needing separate approval or capital from the host country. It will be regulated by the authorities in its base country, not by those in the host country,[6] and it will be able to offer the same products in all EEC countries. A British bank, for example, will be able to offer British-style mortgages in Spain without approval from the Spanish authorities.

In insurance, however, a somewhat different route is being followed. Open competition will apply only to large risks -- defined as any policyholder who can satisfy two of three criteria: (i) 250 or more employees; (ii) turnover of more than ECU 12.8 million; (iii) balance sheet assets of ECU 6.2 million. Buyers of insurance who cannot satisfy two of these criteria will essentially be left in their present position.[7]

What is the reason for this difference? After all, if holders of small deposits or borrowers of small loans are to have the benefits of competition, why not the purchasers of small insurance policies? Or, alternatively, if competition is not safe for for small customers of insurance companies, is it safe for small customers of banks?

A possible conjecture is that the hesitation in applying the new approach to small insurance contracts is implied by the legal foundation of the Commission's new approach. This foundation is in large part provided by the decision of the European Court in the case of Cassis de Dijon.

Cassis arose from a German requirement that fruit liqueurs must have a minimum alcohol content of 25 percent, a regulation that excluded from the German market some liqueurs from other Member States. The Court's view was that the fixing of a minimum alcohol content could not be seen as "an essential guarantee of the fairness of commercial transactions, since it is a simple matter to ensure that suitable information is conveyed to the purchaser by requiring the display of an indication of origin and of the alcohol content on the packaging of products."

On the basis of this proposition, the Court ruled that a product "lawfully produced and marketed in one Member State must, in principle, be admitted to the market of any other Member State." In so doing, the Court, rescued the Community from the worst excesses of the Commission's harmonization programs from goods by eliminating the need for harmonization where simple alternatives were available.[8]

Cassis is a case about the information available to buyers of products; and the rationale of much national regulatory activity in service industries lies in the notion that buyers of services are ill informed. To apply the reasoning of Cassis to services is therefore attractive, and it provides a major part of the legal foundation for the Commission's current activity in the services sector.

The Court, however, has never applied the Cassis reasoning to a service. It was given the opportunity to do so in the case involving Herr Schleicher, a German insurance broker who had been fined DM 18,000 by the Berlin District Court for placing insurance contracts covering risks situated in the Federal Republic with British-based insurance companies.[9] The German Insurance Supervisory Law requires that the risks of Herr Schleicher's clients should be placed only with insurers licensed and established in the Federal Republic (though interestingly enough, if the clients had gone to Britain to purchase the insurance, the law would not have been infringed -- an element of liberality that, in the opinion of the Advocate-General and the Court, substantially weakened the case for regulatory control of the type which led to Herr Schleicher's fine).

The Court was called upon to decide a number of insurance cases simultaneously with this one, and its decision is complex and in parts ambiguous. From the present standpoint, however, the relevant strand of the decision is the distinction between commercial and private purchasers of insurance. The Court argued that where the risks insured are of substantial value, the person (or corporation) seeking insurance can be expected to be capable of assessing for himself the reasonableness of the insurer's terms. In such cases, the Court argued, cross-border trade should be permitted (that is, that a Member State can impose a requirement of prior authorization only where it can be objectively justified in the public interest). This decision was the trigger for the opening to competition of large insurance contracts, which was touched upon earlier.

The relevant contrast is with a private person. The Court did not feel able to assume the competence of such a person to assess his own best interests in the matter of insurance. Such persons are therefore left to the protection of the national regulatory authorities.

Whatever the truth of that proposition, it represents an implicit refusal by the Court to apply the reasoning of Cassis to small insurance contracts. It follows that the Commission cannot rely on Cassis as a basis for its liberalizing efforts in that sector of the insurance market: hence the restricted scope of the Commission's proposals for insurance, as compared with banking.

Yet if the Court will not apply Cassis to small insurance contracts, is there any reason to suppose that it would apply it without major qualification to any other service industry? In this area, the bargaining power the Commission can bring to bear in argument with the Council largely depends on the decision of the

Court. It is therefore worthwhile to briefly review the past decisions of the Court on services.

THE COURT OF JUSTICE AND ARTICLES 59-66

The Court's decision in <u>Van Binsbergen</u>[10] established that Member States may impose restrictions upon suppliers of services based in other Member States provided that such restrictions were aimed at (and capable of achieving) "an objective of general interest." A succession of ensuing cases appear to imply that a restriction can be justified only if:

1. it does not discriminate, either overtly or covertly, between residents of the Member State imposing the restriction and residents of other Member States;

2. among measures capable of achieving the objective of general interest, it is the one with the least effect on the freedom to supply services; and

3. it is not disproportionate to the end to be achieved.[11]

The force of these principles obviously depends (among other things) on an interpretation of what is "an objective of general interest." The Court has found restrictions justified in two cases. These merit special attention for the light they shed on what has been acceptable to the Court in practice. They are <u>Debauve</u> and <u>Webb</u>.[12]

The case of Debauve arose from the presence of advertising on cable television programs received in Belgium but originating in other Member States. There is in Belgium a prohibition on advertising on television, but this is not true of some neighboring Member States. Hence, the issue arises as to whether the Belgian government has a right to prohibit advertising on programs received via cable in Belgium but originating in a Member State permitting such advertising.[13] In Debauve, the Court concluded that in the absence of Community action, each Member State retained the power "to regulate, restrict or even totally prohibit television advertising on its territory on grounds of general interest."

Yet what was the general interest served in this case? A typical argument for regulation is that it is in the interests of consumers or, in this case, viewers. That viewers in a country with a small numbers of channels are best served by a ban on advertising on those channels certainly is a defensible proposition. But that is not an argument that cuts very deeply here. So long as neither the existence nor the quality of the Belgian Channels is threatened by the possibility of receiving in Belgium programs originating elsewhere, the availability of the choice cannot have made any Belgian viewer worse off, whether the programs from abroad contained advertising or not.

To make an argument in terms of viewer well-being, therefore, seems to call upon one or both of two propositions. The first is that Belgian viewers of programs originating abroad would be even better off were the advertising contained in them to be eliminated. The second is that the existence or the quality of the Belgian channels would be threatened by the continued reception of foreign programs containing advertising.

The alternative to the reception of the advertising (which was aimed in part at Belgian viewers), apparently was to black out the advertising material. This is likely to have been expensive for the Belgian cable relays and therefore to have increased the cost of obtaining cable services (as well as presumably reducing their quality in the estimation of viewers: it is difficult to see that anyone would prefer blackouts to advertising). An argument that the welfare of those Belgians who wished to watch programs originating abroad was increased by the ban therefore seems untenable.

That the quality or the existence of the Belgian channels was threatened also seems implausible, however. Indeed, the siphoning off of viewers to programs that might have been of a different type than those broadcast in Belgium opens the possibility of shifting the mix of Belgian programs to better suit those Belgians who chose not to have cable reception of broadcasts originating elsewhere.

The only conceivable basis for a perception of threat seems to lie in a belief that in the absence of the enforced blackouts (and the costs of creating them) so many Belgians might watch broadcasts originating elsewhere that political support for public finance of the Belgian channels would diminish, and therefore their actual finance. That conjecture, however, presumably is based on an opinion as to the number of Belgian viewers who will perceive foreign broadcasts (advertising and all) as superior to Belgian ones. Once again, the basis for substituting blackouts for advertising in the interests of viewers is weak.

Indeed, it is so weak that there seems to be room for alternative explanations of the ban on television advertising. One plausible conjecture is that the ban was intended to support the advertising revenue of Belgian newspapers. Were that so, the Court's decision upholding the legality of the ban would amount to a decision to support the advertising revenue of Belgian newspapers against the competitive efforts of television stations based in other countries. That raises delicate issues. Whether it is an appropriate ground for an exception to the Treaty provisions on freedom of movement of services nevertheless seems very much open to question.[14]

Whatever the merits of the Debauve decision, the case clearly illustrates the issues underlying disputes about the meaning of the treaty. Freedom of trade in services threatens national regulatory systems in a way that freedom of establishment does not. Freedom of trade in the absence of harmonization implies competition between regulatory systems. Hence, regulations that

<u>are valueless to buyers</u> are likely to become less tenable or to fail to achieve their actual objective.   Freedom of establishment implies that suppliers from other Member States accept the regulatory system of the host state.   The regulatory system is not fundamentally threatened by that.

The case of <u>Webb</u> concerns the manager of a British company whose primary business was the supply of technical staff to businesses in the Netherlands (so that the workers supplied by Mr. Webb were paid by his company, while his company was paid by the user of the labor).

Mr. Webb was convicted and fined under Dutch law for supplying manpower in the Netherlands without possession of the license required of such suppliers in the Netherlands.   Although Mr. Webb possessed a United Kingdom license for supplying manpower, the Court upheld this action.

Part of the Court's decision states that:

...It is permissible for Member States, and amounts for them to a legitimate choice of policy pursued in the public interest, to subject the provision of manpower within their borders to a system of licensing in order to be able to refuse licenses where there is reason to suppose that such activities may harm good relations in the labor market or that the interests of the work force affected are not adequately safeguarded.   In view of the differences there may be in conditions in the labor market between one Member State and another, on the one hand, and the diversity of criteria which may be applied with regard to the pursuit of activities of that nature on the other hand, the Member State in which the services are to be supplied has unquestionably the right to require the possession of a license issued on the same conditions as in the case of its own nationals.[15]

The argument in Webb follows the form of the <u>Van Wesemael</u>[16] decision (in which the supply of entertainers from a

French employment agency to Belgium was found not to require a license issued in Belgium because French licenses were issued under conditions "comparable" to those pertaining in Belgium). In Webb, however, the steps of he argument between the premise of the public interest and the "unquestionable right" to require a license seem open to extensions that would cripple Articles 59-66. After all, any regulatory system has a rationale based on the public interest.

The European Court report of Webb, however, has a rather shadowy quality. Netherlands law provides that "a license shall be refused only when there is reasonable cause to fear that the provision of manpower by the applicant might harm good relations on the labor market or if for that reason the interests of the labor force affected are insufficiently safeguarded".[17] The cutting edge of the treaty might have been better displayed had the case appeared in reverse -- had Mr. Webb applied for a Netherlands license and been refused. In any case, the report is silent on the questions of why he did not apply for one; or of whether an application from him would have been refused by the Dutch authorities and, if so, on what grounds; or of what costs such an application would have imposed upon his company.

The Dutch law appears to allow a large amount of administrative discretion. Yet, (as the Commission pointed out in its submission), much of what the government of the Netherlands said it sought to protect by the licensing system (for example, a ban on temporary work in the building and metallurgical industries) could have been protected as effectively by the adoption of general provisions regarding the contracting out of labor in the Netherlands. Such provisions could be enforceable against those using the labor (who, of course, would be established in the Netherlands). That method would not have hindered the free supply of services. The point does not appear to have been taken up by the Court.

In its submission, the Government of the Netherlands argued that the result of a decision that a British license holder does not have to hold a Netherlands license to supply labor in the Netherlands would be that "...Netherlands license holders might endeavor to become established in the United Kingdom as well in order to evade the provisions of Netherlands law by obtaining a United Kingdom license".[18] This is a puzzling statement. No argument was made that Mr. Webb should be exempt from Dutch law in any respect other than the license. It therefore is not clear what advantage a Netherlands license holder would gain by possessing in addition a United Kingdom license. What is evident, however, is the concern about competition between regulatory systems.

The same concern is evident in the Coinsurance cases. There, "establishment" (and therefore the requirement to conform to the regulatory system of the country in which the transaction occurs) is defined so broadly as to threaten the existence of cross-border trade:

> ...it must be acknowledged that an insurance undertaking of another Member State which maintains a permanent presence in the Member State in question comes within the scope of the provisions of the Treaty on the right of establishment, even if that presence does not take the form of a branch or agency, but consists merely of an office managed by the undertakings own staff or by a person who is independent but authorized to work on a permanent basis for the undertaking, as would be the case with an agency[19] (emphasis added).

In addition, the Court went out of its way to note that:

> ...a Member State cannot be denied the right to take measures to prevent the the exercise by a person providing services whose activity is entirely or

principally directed toward its territory of the freedom
guaranteed by Article 59 for the purpose of avoiding
the professional rules of conduct that would be
applicable to him if he were established within that
State. Such a situation may be subject to judicial
control under the provisions relating to the right of
establishment and not of that on the provision of
services.[20]

The Court manifests a deep concern to protect national
regulatory systems from competition. But as argued above, that
concern is not warranted on grounds of the general interest of the
European Community as a whole. The Court accepts too
uncritically the judgments of national governments as to the
"general interest." The general interest served by a national
government is not necessarily that of the EEC, and the
conservative bias implied by the Court's reluctance to question
national interpretations necessarily limits the force of Articles
59-66. If the Court is similarly reluctant in future cases, the
thrust of the Commission's drive toward integration in the
Community services sector may be seriously blunted.

CONCLUDING REMARKS

If Articles 59-66 of the Treaty are to be given substance, it
is difficult to see that there is any alternative to the Commission's
new approach, based on the Cassis de Dijon principle of mutual
recognition of regulatory standards. That approach, moreover, has
a substantial underlying economic justification.

The Court, however, is acting as a brake on the process of
putting this approach into effect. In the past, the Court has
played a major role in clearing a route through the resistance and
obscurantism of the Member States to a more integrated
Community market for goods. The Cassis decision had a sharp
cutting edge. The Court's decisions on Articles 59-66 have not, so
far, displayed the same radical sharpness.

Yet the economic grounds for the Court's caution are weak. Perhaps, therefore, the Court's future rulings on Articles 59-66 will come closer to the standard it set for itself with the Cassis decision.

Notes

1. Cecchini reports figures only for the countries shown in table 12-1. Research by the Bureau of European Consumer Organizations (BEUC), however, apparently suggests that the differences are even larger in some of the remaining member states. According to BEUC, a 10-year term insurance policy will cost a 30-year-old male nonsmoker ten times the UK price in Portugal and four times the UK price in Greece (reported in The Financial Times of 9 March, 1988).

2. This section and the final half of the penultimate section of this chapter draw heavily on Hindley (1987).

3. A special case occurs when a person is buying a service to benefit not himself but some third person--compulsory third party motor insurance, for example. In that case, a person is likely to be interested primarily in fulfilling the needs of the law; the quality of the policy is likely to be a secondary consideration.

4. The basic references on the capture hypothesis are Stigler (1971) and Peltzman (1976). Rottenburg (1980) summarizes much of the available evidence.

5. See Poole (1984) for an excellent account of these problems in the insurance industry.

6. As proposed, however, the host country will be able to intervene on grounds of monetary policy, to monitor liquidity, or to regulate the securities activities of a bank.

7. Until 1992, the thresholds will be double these amounts. Greece, Ireland, Spain, and Portugal have special dispensations and will not have to conform fully until 1998 (1996 in the case of Spain).

8. See Gormley (1985, pp. 46-51) for a discussion of the impact of Cassis de Dijon.

9. In the White Paper, the Commission is quite guarded. In paragraph 102 (p. 27), it comments merely that: "Some comparison can be made between the approach followed by the Commission after the 'Cassis de Dijon' judgments with regard to industrial and agricultural products and what now has to be done for insurance policies, home-ownership savings contracts, consumer credit, participation in collective investment schemes, etc."

10. Case 33/74 Van Binsbergen v. Bedrijfsvereniging Metaalnijverheid, 1974, ECR, p. 1299.

11. Several similar lists appear in the work of legal writers, though there are discrepancies between them. See, for example, Watson (1983), Chappatte (1984), and Weirich (1985).

12. Procureur du Roi v. Debauve, 1981, ECR, p. 833 and Alfred John Webb, 1982, ECR, p. 3305.

13. This fact has given rise to several television cases with interesting implications for trade in services. Legal commentaries broaching some of these points are Bennett (1980) and especially Hunnings (1980).

14. The Court has recently (April 1988) found that a ban by the government of the Netherlands on Dutch-language advertising

on foreign television channels available in the Netherlands is contrary to Articles 59-66. A Draft Directive dealing with Community television was issued in 1986.

15. 1981, ECR, p.3325

16. Cases 110 and 111/78, <u>Ministere Public v. Van Wesemael</u>, 1979, ECR, p. 35.

17. 1982, ECR, p. 3311.

18. 1981, ECR, p. 3312.

19. Judgment in Case 205/84, point 21.

20. Case 205/85, point 22.

References

Bennet, Tim. "The Debauve and Coditel Cases," *ELRev*, 1980, pp. 224-232.

Chappatte, Phillippe. "Freedom to Provide Insurance Service in the European Community," *ELRev*, 1984, **9**, pp. 3-27.

Cecchini, Paolo. *1992: The European Challenge.* (London: Gower), 1988.

Gormley, Laurence. *Prohibiting Restrictions on Trade within the EEC* (Amsterdam: North Holland), 1985.

Hindley, Brian. "Trade in Services within the European Community," in Herbert Giersch (ed.): *Free Trade in the World Economy* (J.C.B. Mohr [Paul Siebeck] Tubingen), 1987.

Hunnings, Neville. *CMLRev*, 1980, 17, pp. 565-569.

Leenen, A.T.S. "Recent Case Law of the Court of Justice on the Freedom of Establishment and the Freedom to Supply Services," *CMLRev*, 1980, 17, p. 259.

Peltzman, Sam. "Toward a More General Theory of Regulation," *Journal of Law and Economics* (August), 1976, pp. 211-240.

Pool, William. "Moves toward a Common Market in Insurance," *CMLRev*, 1984, 21, pp. 123-147.

Rottenburg, Simon (Ed.): *Occupational Licensure and Regulation* (American Enterprise Institute for Public Policy Research), 1980.

Stigler, George J. "The Theory of Economic Regulation," *Bell Journal of Economics*, 1971, 3.

Watson, Phillipa. "Freedom of Establishment and Freedom to Supply Services: Some Recent Developments," *CMLRev*, 1983, 20, pp. 767-824.

Weirich, Malou. "Freedom to Provide Services," *ELRev*, 1885, 6, pp. 471-7.

Chapter 13

Telecommunications and the Scope of the Market in Services

Gerald R. Faulhaber

Wharton School, University of Pennsylvania

The promised liberalization within the European Economic Community in 1992 is likely to be the most significant economic event of the coming decade. Should this transformation actually occur, it will at last create a market, the world's largest, appropriate to the economic potential of the region. The free movement of goods, people, and information among 325 million consumers, workers, and stockholders promises to create enormous wealth for Europeans and enormous opportunities for the rest of us. I would like to focus on the role of telecommunications services in this transformation, which I believe is far more vital than is generally recognized. Note I use the word "services." Much has been written and said about the market for telecommunications <u>equipment</u>, including the "threat" of the Japanese and American manufacturers. I am going to ignore completely the trade in telecommunications equipment problem; I view this market as mature, in which transactions are few in number but large in value, very highly politicized, and well studied by others. What I find of far greater interest is the role of telecommunications services in defining the <u>scope of the market</u> of services, which, after, all is what 1992 is all about.

MARKET SCOPE IN SERVICES

The free movement of goods, people, services, and information has long been viewed as an important factor in creating wealth within a market. The United States, the world's largest market, is also its richest. Workers within the market can seek employment anywhere they are in demand; highly specialized firms have a very large pool of consumers from which to draw; firms that depend upon scale economies have a market whose scale matches their needs. And all this without trade barriers, without barriers to the movement of people.

And also with the world's largest, most reliable, and most ubiquitous and diverse telecommunications system. For a manufacturing or agriculture-based economy, the benefits from access to a large market depend upon the ability to move one's product to market quickly, reliably, and cheaply. For a services-based economy, these benefits depend upon the ability to move <u>information</u> to market quickly, reliably, and cheaply.

Traditionally, economists and others have seen trade restrictions against the goods of foreigners as the chauvinistically shortsighted barrier to achieving the efficiencies of large markets. The fact that goods moving from New York to New Jersey pay no duty, and goods moving from Germany to France pay duty, if they are permitted to move at all, is argued to be an important contributor to the relatively greater per capita wealth of the United States. Less well-recognized is the growing importance of moving people and information freely from New York to New Jersey. There has been some attention paid within the EEC to the free movement of people within the Community post-1992, so that British accountants can easily do business in France or Italy. However, there has been less attention paid to the problems and prospects of the unrestricted and inexpensive movement of information across borders.

Currently, European telecommunications remains in a traditional public monopoly mode: state-run or state-regulated, focused on its protected monopoly position, unresponsive to market needs. Even British Telecom, usually held up as a model to the rest of Europe, is still a regulated monopolist. How can this fragmented, insular industry hope to cope with the demands that service firms, anxious to expand into new markets, will place upon it for new, expanded service at low cost? Where are the competitors that will offer expanding service firms the diverse array of telecommunications they will need to capture new markets?

In order to concentrate our attention, I would like to consider two service industries which are apparently becoming more telecommunications-intensive at the same time that their geographic market scope has been increasing: financial services and retail trade. You will not be surprised to hear about the first, although I suspect you will be surprised to hear about the second. In each industry, I make three points: (1) the changing scope of the market; (2) the importance of telecommunications as an enabling technology for this change; and (3) the forces that have been or will be brought to bear from within and without the telecommunications industry to meet the needs of these industries.

The point of this exercise is to sketch how the market forces attendant to the liberalization within the EEC in 1992 may play out in the market for telecommunications during a period of long-run disequilibrium, both in the telecommunications market as well as in downstream markets.

TELECOMMUNICATIONS AND THE SCOPE OF FINANCIAL SERVICES

The fundamental changes taking place in the financial services industry have been well documented elsewhere. At base, these changes have been about increasing the geographic scope of the market, as well as a merging of markets; in fact, the term "financial service industry" is a very recent one, suggesting that the old industry distinctions of commercial banks, investment banks, insurance, and brokerage are irrelevant today.

Pre-1970, banking was almost exclusively a local industry; the local banker knew his credit risks as well as his deposit base and interactions with other banks and other parts of financial services was minimal. Apart from a few New York banks, so-called "money center" banks, U.S. banking was nearly a cottage industry. This tendency was reinforced by federal restrictions on interstate banking, rules which protected local banks from competition, but forced them to hold a relatively undiversified portfolio of assets.

Today U.S. banking is at least multistate and more likely global, tightly linked with other financial services firms, seeking to expand into related product and geographic markets.

The scope of the market, therefore, has gone from local to global in under two decades.

What were the causes of this transformation?

This transformation *could* not have happened without fundamental changes in technology; the two key technologies involved are information processing and telecommunications. Money, after all, is an electrical phenomenon.

This transformation *would* not have happened unless profits were to be earned in doing so. In fact, the economic agents primarily responsible for forcing this transformation were not banks, but customers of banks and non-bank institutions.

Financial regulations, far from inhibiting these changes were in fact the *cause* of the changes. During the 1960s, banks' large customers learned to function in overseas capital markets on their own and earn higher returns than they could with their bankers' help. An important necessary condition was the ability to transfer information quickly and cheaply. During the 1970's, U.S. banks learned that although they were prohibited from investment banking in the United States, they were not so constrained in other markets, so that much of their activity moved offshore. Again, an important necessary condition was the ability to maintain management control of global operations quickly and cheaply. Finally, in the 1980s, the London Exchange showed that deregulation and going totally electronic would attract business from around the world. Screen-based trading by brokers around the world 24 hours a day seems to be where this industry wants to go. Again, the information and telecommunications technology is the necessary condition.

One might wonder why banks and other financial institutions were so anxious to go global. What was it about foreign markets that made them so attractive? Financial services went offshore principally to avoid home-country regulation; if commercial banks could not engage in investment banking at home, they could (and did) in London. If nonfinancial firms were limited in their access to domestic markets by regulation, they would enter foreign markets to achieve higher returns. It was the new electronic technology which allowed this to happen (see Kane, 1981).

On the U.S. domestic front, similar things were happening. States that passed stringent laws regarding consumer credit found that banks established their credit card centers in Delaware and other "safe haven" states with less stringent laws. One of the more striking trends in U.S. banking has been the development of regional banking, the most profitable segment of the industry. Through aggressive acquisition strategies, these banks have brought together the knowledge of local bankers with a large bank's sophisticated products. However, this trend also depends upon the availability of high-speed data links to tie together local banks' processing needs into large computer centers. Nor is this need just for transactions processing; regional banks use this market information, such as customer financial profiles, to develop and market new products through its distribution network.

The hypothesis, then, is that the scope of the market in financial services vastly expanded with the advent of cheap telecommunications and information technology. That expansion is still going on, and is transforming this industry dramatically. Just as this revolution was fueled by the dizzying array of products and services available in the computer industry, so also has it thrived on (1) the uniformity and ubiquity of the basic U.S. telecommunications network, and (2) the wide availability of multiple telecommunications vendors, including internal, or self-supply. Big firms do not have to wait for the telecommunications utility; they can, and will, do it themselves.

Our hypothesis is that telecommunications has been an enabling technology for these market scope changes in financial services. Do the data support this hypothesis? As measured by assets, the growth in international banking by U.S. banks has grown both absolutely and as a fraction of domestic banking, as shown in figure 13-1. Although our data on the presence of foreign banks in the United States are more spotty, figure 13-2 suggests that the growth of offshore banks in our domestic market has been substantial as well. In figure 13-3, we show the growth of international telephone traffic over a similar period, and we again note a quite rapid increase.

Figure 13-1.   ASSETS OF FOREIGN BRANCHES
OF US BANKS

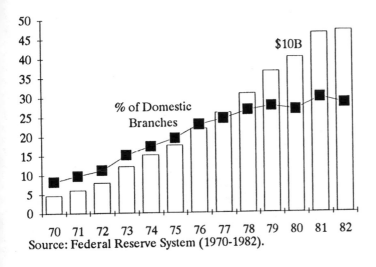

Source: Federal Reserve System (1970-1982).

Figure 13-2.   NUMBER OF BANKING
FAMILIES WITH US BRANCHES

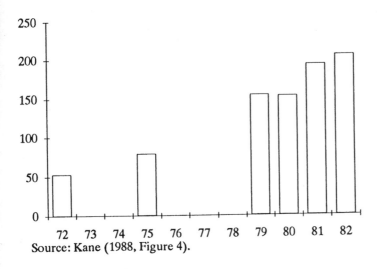

Source: Kane (1988, Figure 4).

We do not have industry-specific numbers for international telecommunications traffic, so our comparison here is suggestive rather than compelling. Yet the contemporaneous rapid growth of both international banking and international telecommunications is consistent with our hypothesis. The European community, which is faced with uncertainty of 1992, is especially needful of understanding this link between banking and telecommunications.

What are the potential consequences of liberalization of services trade within the EEC in 1992 on telecommunications services? There are two:

o   Germany and other countries will be pushed toward the most liberal standard in the EEC, which now appears to be Britain. Previously insular national systems will be opened up to competitive challenge by other firms; those most responsive to markets will be the most successful. The process of transforming European telecommunications into a more competitive industry will be quite long, difficult, and subject to much political debate. The damage to both the capital and the employees of the traditional PTTs could be most serious, as the American experience has shown us.

o   Large financial service firms, and consortia of such firms, will energetically turn to self-supply. This will lead to the development of private networks to carry commercial traffic. This solution may be inefficient from an economic point of view, but clearly necessary for such firms to avoid the anticompetitive local telephone monopolies. It will also lead to entry by others into this market, especially American financial service firms which possess a high level of competence in information and telecommunication technologies.

TELECOMMUNICATIONS AND THE SCOPE OF RETAILING

Retailing is in many ways the quintessential low-technology industry: highly labor-intensive, and dependent upon face-to-face transactions that resist technical change. Of course, various innovations such as point-of-sale terminals and their attendant communication nets and optical scanners have brought electronic technology to this market in the recent past. But a quite dramatic change in retailing has been wrought in the last decade by the twin innovations of credit cards and "800 Service," a telecommunications service in which a firm can purchase an incoming line over which their customers may call them free of charge. Since 800 Service became nationwide in 1977, a whole retail sub-industry has grown up, dependent upon their customers reaching them by telephone to place orders.

Of course, the so-called mail order business is not new. It was pioneered by Sears Roebuck in the United States, aimed at a market segment that was unable to visit ordinary retail outlets because of their rural remoteness. The business depended upon the ubiquity and reliability of the U.S. mail service, a paper technology. In recent years, such firms have generally been in decline.

By contrast, today's mail order business depends on the speed of electronic communication. Its market segment is not those with too much space (rural America) but those with too little time (upwardly mobile, two-income America). It is a very rapidly expanding sector, whose growth seems to parallel that of the growth of 800 Service revenues. Anyone who has lived in the United States and found their mailbox stuffed daily with such catalogs will need little convincing of this trend.

Figure 13-3.   INTERNATIONAL MESSAGES
                                    TO EUROPE & ASIA
                                        (millions)

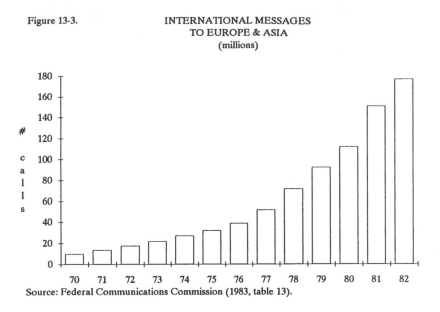

Source: Federal Communications Commission (1983, table 13).

Figure 13-4.   MAIL ORDER SALES AS
                              % OF GENERAL MERCHANDISE
                              AND 800 SERVICE REVENUES

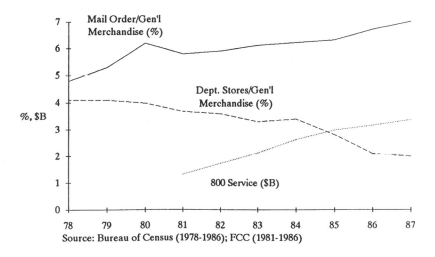

Source: Bureau of Census (1978-1986); FCC (1981-1986).

In figure 13-4, we show the growth of mail order sales as a fraction of total general merchandise. By comparison, we also show the evolution of sales for mail order department stores, of the more traditional variety. Against the backdrop of the decline of traditional mail order, the growth of the new mail order is most impressive. Included in this chart is the growth of 800 Service revenues over the same period of time. Again, we have no industry-specific numbers regarding 800 Service, but the contemporaneous growth of the two is suggestive, to say the least.

The United States telecommunications industry, with its larger market and more competitive market structure, has moved far in front of its European colleagues with this service, and has done much more to help the U.S. domestic retail industry. Even with the United States experience as a model, European PTT's have not aggressively pursued this market, and European retailing as well as telecommunications and ultimately the consuming public have been the worse for it.

What are the prospects for the EEC in 1992? If more competition comes to the telecommunications market, we can expect that retailers will demand this type of service to be available throughout Europe. If the national PTT monopolies drag their heels, we can expect that the retailers themselves will adopt private systems which access consumers through the PTT's distribution network, and bring political pressure to bear should the PTTs resist. Again, the process will most likely be a long and difficult one.

The opening up of the Common Market to this type of retail trade will be even more dramatic than in the United States. For example, Britons spend twice as much on mail order (of the traditional variety) than do Americans. What might we expect when they can shop by phone around Europe? As the market opens up, we should expect that the firms that will do best, at least initially, will be American. It is the L.L. Beans and the Lands Ends that have the human capital in this business, and they will have an initial advantage over the Ikeas and the Carrefours. In fact, the date that L.L Bean establishes its first 800 Service number in Europe will mark the real dawn of pan-European retailing.

References

Bell System (to 1983) and AT&T Communications (from 1984) Monthly Revenue Report 0004 (MR-4), Federal Communications Commission.

Federal Reserve Bulletin, 1970 - 1982.

Kane, Edward J. "Accelerating Inflation, Technological Innovation, and the Decreasing Effectiveness of Banking Regulation," *Journal of Finance*, **36**(2) May, 1981, pp. 355-367.

Kane, Edward J. "How Market Forces Influence the Structure of Financial Regulation," mimeo, AEI Financial Markets Project and Ohio State University, 1988.

Monthly Retail Trade Survey, 1978 - 1986. Bureau of the Census.

Statistics of Communications Common Carriers Table 13. Federal Communications Commission, 1983.

Chapter 14

Implications of 1992 for European Telecommunications

Jürgen Müller

DIW, Berlin and INSEAD, Fontainebleau

When analyzing the effect of the unified single market of 1992 of the "Europe of the 12", we must recognize:

o   1992 is essentially a public relations target that has had a considerable influence on national as well as EEC-wide policy making. It is a point in time at which the degree of integration can be assessed.

o   The term "European telecommunications" presumably refers to all of Europe and not just the European Community. While this chapter will mainly focus on the EC, we must also remember not only the role of the EFTA countries, which are equally affected, but also the countries of Eastern Europe, and look at what is happening to them as a result of the accelerated integration of the EEC.

o   Telecommunications policy is still mainly national policy.
    The decision making is therefore very much the result of
    national policies, EC policies, and other international
    tendencies.

The Myth of 1992

The real significance of 1992 lies much more in the effect of
the PR campaign than in the program itself. The campaign of
marketing 1992 has been enormously successful in alerting the
public and especially the entrepreneurs to the potential of a
unified European market and the opportunities for European
ventures. It has restored self-confidence in the European ideal,
which was fast slipping in butter and wheat mountains and lakes
of olive oil.   To quote Lord Weinstock, "Nothing new has
happened except that this time these joint projects work. 1992
has changed things. People have woken up" (<u>Financial Times</u>,
December 30, 1988).   Thus, even if objective reality has not
changed very much, the manner in which it is perceived has, and
the spirit in which program implementations are carried out has
also. In a way, it is already apparent that some opportunities will
be seized which were not before, not because there were official
obstacles to them, but because business horizons were too national
in outlook. Furthermore, the spirit with which past directives are
now being implemented indicates a much greater sense of sincerity
than in the past: for example, in the case of public procurement
policy or financial market liberalization. How far the process will
actually go is difficult to say.   The idea of creating a single
market of 320 million people is certainly misleading as a guide to
the real degree of economic integration to be achieved. Europe is
much too heterogeneous in its cultures, its institutions, and its
demand patterns.   What is likely, therefore, is that trade
liberalization will primarily affect supply, through integration, but
differences in demand will continue to persist. From an economic
perspective, 1992 is, therefore, more about the creation of greater
product diversity within more competitive national markets. The

major effects will therefore derive from wider product variety as a result of integration, and the greater degree of competition through the liberalization of the traditional national regulatory structures. Telecommunications equipment and services is, of course, an area in which market entry has in the past been inhibited, either by domestic regulation or public procurement policy.

The policies that form the basis of the 1992 program were first put forward in the 1985 White Paper of the Commission (Completing the Internal Market COM (85) 310). Most of the proposals aim to reduce obstacles to the integration of the markets for goods, such as the abolition of fiscal frontiers, the reduction or elimination of border controls, and the movement of goods and people. Emphasis is also given to the elimination of nontariff barriers through different national standardization and regulation and the opening up of national procurement policies to EEC-wide tenders. Altogether there was a list of 300 measures, a number of which have since been implemented. These measures were taken further by the Single European Act, which became effective in 1987. In it, the completion of the internal market by the end of 1992 was stated as the main objective, and except for proposals relating to fiscal policies or the movement of individuals between countries, the unanimity of proposals adopted by the Council of Ministers, which become binding on individual Member States, is no longer necessary.

Major Policy Aspects of the Green Paper

Since the formation of the Community by its six original Member Countries - Netherlands, Belgium, Luxembourg, West Germany, France and Italy - in 1957, several initiatives (reducing import tariffs, removing intra-Community technical barriers, and so on), helped to keep the dream of a united Europe alive. But the double recession related to the oil crises and the enlargement of the Community to a 12-nation market in 1986 (by which time Spain, Portugal, Denmark, the UK, the Irish Republic, and Greece had joined), brought many new problems, and the de facto integration was slowed down. Together with the recession, increased protectionist policies emerged. In information technology in particular, preferential procurement policies, which relied to some extent on disparate technology standards, led to only a limited amount of integration, especially in the more sensitive areas of public sector procurement for telecommunications equipment. The closed market has been further underlined with stringent testing and certification requirements. Even in the areas outside of the telecommunication monopolies, integration was slow.

It is against this background that the commitment toward a progressive completion of a single market by 1992 arose with the agreement of the EEC's heads of government in 1985. Lord Cockfield, vice president of the European Commission and one of the driving forces behind the attempts for a single united European market, initiated a White Paper (COM (85) 310) that outlines 300 reforms that are to form the basis for the current effort.

Of course, the White Paper covers many industries and market regimes, from buildings and automobiles to such service sectors as banking, insurance, and telecommunications. The EEC's Green Paper on The Development of the Common Market for Telecommunication Services and Equipment (COM (87) 290 final), focuses only on one specific subsector of Community activities. Its purpose is to initiate a wide-ranging discussion on the issues of a common market and to help in the establishment of a coherent Communitywide framework in the ongoing changes of the present system of telecommunications regulation. It followed the spirit of the 1985 White Paper of the Commission (COM (85) 310), where the cost of physical and technical frontiers are identified as basic obstacles to completing the internal market. The main advantage of reducing these technical and administrative frontiers was seen in the greater integration of markets, in other words, making them more competitive while at the same time allowing increasing specialization and utilization of economies of scale.

This latter point seems to apply particularly to telecommunications equipment, while in telecommunication service provision, economies of scale are now more or less realized at a national level. Except for the UK, we have usually only one operator and one physical network if one ignores the sizable networks of public utilities and the military. (There are several network operators in Italy, Denmark and Portugal, but their responsibilities are strictly delineated according to geographical or functional lines). Increased integration in telecommunication services could therefore only arise on a limited scale, but the harmonization of the different regulatory procedures and an increased availability for competitive offerings could have important economic effects.

Effects in the Equipment Market

Telecommunications equipment is used to construct the network infrastructure for telecommunication services. It usually consists of transmission and switching equipment and customer premises equipment (CPE) which is needed for access to such networks. These three product categories make up the most important market segments, in addition to a small set of miscellaneous products. Table 14-1 gives an overview over these four markets, which shows the dominance of central office equipment with almost half the market volume, depending on the definitions used. Other market studies have a slightly different delineation, but all come to similar size magnitudes. The interesting point in connection with the Green Paper is that the majority of products fall under public procurement rules, while only part of CPE equipment and some switching and wiring in private networks is really sold more or less in an open market. Three influences are likely to be felt:

Table 14-1. Telecommunications Equipment Markets in the
Principal OECD Countries, 1984 (in US $M)

	public switching	private switching	public transmission	CPE
World Market	10000	9420	14590	6495
France	730	251	650	448
West Germany	457	492	690	400
U.K.	687	361	460	250
Italy	710	129	400	131
USA	2850	5400	5220	2830
Japan	627	808	1520	316
Canada	327	210	210	72

Source: Rausch (1987, p. 20)

Table 14-2. The Presence of Major Central Office Equipment
Suppliers in Different European Countries (EEC
and EFTA) 1986

	EEC										EFTA			
	Be	Dk	Sp	Fr	UK	Ir	It	Nl	Pr	Ger	Au	Ch	Sw	No
Ericsson	x	x	x	x	x	x	x					x	x	
GTE							x							
ALcatel	x	x	x	x			x	x	x	x	x	x		x
ATT-Philips								x						
GEC-Plessey					x									
Siemens	x									x	x	x	x	
Italtel							x							
Northern/STC				x							x	x		
Teli														x

1) refers to actual plant sites; excludes Greece

o   the first relates to increased Communitywide standardization,

o   the second to an increasingly open public procurement policy (extending the earlier EEC Directive 77-62 and its more recent Recommendation 84-550), and

o   the third to the liberalization of the CPE market.

Concerning the first effect, standardization, the greatest influence will be felt in central office equipment, where at the moment a number of different non-compatible European systems exist. In assessing the likely effect of the EEC's policy, one has to compare the EEC's role in standardization efforts compared to those activities already carried out by other internal standard-setting bodies. The setting up of a European standards institute and the move toward more open interfaces (also the support of OSI standards in public sector procurement) will lead both to rationalization and competitive effects. Rationalization effects are here mainly due to increasing lot sizes, while competitive effects arise because more competitors can now compete in markets that were previously separated. The EEC's recent estimate indicates that savings in the neighborhood of 5 to 10 percent of the current European Centrl Office switching market of about 5 billion ECU may be possible, thus saving the PTTs eventually 0.25 to 0.50 bn ECU per annum. The competitive effects could increase this number in the long run.

The other two product groups, transmission and CPE equipment, are already more standardized, so the effects of the Green Paper's standardization efforts are likely to be smaller. Nevertheless, there might still be dynamic competitive effects.

More important is the effect expected from more open public procurement policies in line with the EEC Recommendation 84-550. This recommendation foresees that 40 to 50 percent of public contracts are to be opened by 1992 (compared with 10 percent of all tenders today). If this policy is used in a strategic way, applied mainly to the non-standardized, semi-closed markets, sizable savings might be possible. The EEC's estimates are as high as 15 percent, or 3 billion out of a total of 17.5 billion ECU, using 1985 market volumes.

Already there is a great deal of restructuring in the European central office equipment industry as we mentioned above: Alcatel has taken over all the ITT facilities in Europe; Siemens has acquired the European operations of GTE and formed a joint company concerning its U.S. activities, and together with GEC, it is taking over Plessy; LM Ericsson has taken over CGCT in France; and AT&T has made cooperation agreements with Philips and STET (the Italian holding company for Italtel and SIP). Nevertheless, in order to achieve savings of this kind we would expect considerable political opposition to the rationalization policies that would have to follow. If public telephone operators (PTOs) nevertheless were able to adapt the aggressive procurement rule envisaged under EEC Recommendation 84-550, recourse would probably be taken to extra government funding from other public sources to maintain some of the activity employment in the industry on the regional basis still prevailing. As a consequence, the 3 billion ECU savings mentioned above represent perhaps only the maximum price reduction possible.

But such rationalization effects are probably not realistic because of the political opposition to the necessary restructuring to achieve the kind of price levels currently being achieved in the United States. The reason is that economies of scale take place in software production (spreading roughly 1 billion U.S.$ development cost over a certain market and 0.1 billion annual updating and modernization efforts), but also in the actual hardware production and assembly. Even if plants also produce large private branch exchanges, for which some components, software, and testing tools of CO equipment can be used, the European production scale is by comparison still small, suffering from a cost disadvantage that is equivalent to 20 to 30 percent, when comparing a plant of 7 million lines per annum capacity to one of 1 million lines per annum.

That even scales of this size (i.e., 1 million lines per annum), are not always possible is indicated in table 14-2 (1.4), which shows the distribution of CO manufacturers. Some of them have often more than one plant per country, with the smaller countries actually accounting for only very small market demand.

The economies of scale in the production of transmission equipment is significantly less, especially as the off-the-shelf components can be used for part of the transmission applications. Significant scale effects exist, however, in the production of cables (both copper and optical fibers) and standardized microwave components. Satellite receiving dishes, traditionally part of transmission technology, are now becoming actually part of CPE, as they are more and more proper in the cable television homeowners' market.

Despite these high benefits in specialization, we currently find, at least in the public procurement area of transmission and switching and to some extent also in CPE, highly protected national markets within each EEC Member Country. There is little intra-EEC trade, but a fair amount of export to countries outside the EEC. Total imports account for much less than 10 percent of final demand, a further confirmation of the national orientation of these markets. (Of these imports, more than 50 percent come from the United States and Japan.)

The reasons for this peculiar "closed" market structure are threefold: selective procurement and certification policy, incompatible standards, and "input specificity" (goods and services specifically customized to the user's specification: for example, to allow compatibility with previous investment in a complex network system).

Selective procurement policy is related to assistance of national governments - for industrial policy reasons - on maintaining a technology base in such an advanced manufacturing sector as telecommunications equipment.

Restrictive certification policy and incompatible international standards are sometimes also used as instruments of such a "technology base" policy. But often they are related to a specific technology orientation of an administration, often in close accordance with domestic manufacturers for influence in certification and standard setting to raise entry barriers to outsiders.

"Buyer or input specificity" is especially relevant for CO equipment. Given the high adjustment cost of moving from one type of system or standard to another, it is, of course, difficult to open national markets quickly. The degree of buyer specificity is less strong for transmission equipment and CPE because the interfaces between different types of equipment have already been more or less internationally standardized, allowing smaller specialist suppliers to survive in different national markets.

As a consequence, while we believe that the restructuring in the CO area and partly in transmission will move rather slowly, and also because the Community at the moment does not have strong enough policy tools for implementation (the 40 to 50 percent rule is only contemplated by 1992), stronger adjustments in the private markets, including CPE, are expected. The likely dynamic implications of such a move are illustrated by the recent growth in the liberalized U.S. and UK CPE markets. As a consequence of private purchasing, depreciation rates dropped considerably, simple handsets were replaced much more frequently than before, leading to a significantly larger turnover. Similar tendencies, perhaps less dramatic, occurred in the market for private branch exchanges (PABX). Nevertheless, it is here where AT&T has recently filed an antidumping petition with the Department of Commerce, against manufacturers from Japan,

Korea and Taiwan. Instead of the projected import penetration for CPE equipment of 20 to 23 percent which was predicted by the International Trade Association in 1984, total annual import penetration has in some markets risen above 50 percent. A similar picture emerges from an analysis of the UK, where imports in the CPE sector, and especially that for mobile handsets, have increased dramatically after opening these markets, with many of the imports coming from either the United States or the Far East.

These observations suggest that if the Green Paper recommendations were implemented fully, considerable structural rearrangements would result, with significant long-term benefits to users. These positive results must be seen against the adjustment cost of producers and the fear of the loss of regional or national technology bases. It therefore seems likely that national industry objectives and differentiated standards will continue to play a role in this adjustment process. The full fruits of integrating the telecommunications equipment market can only take place if some common agreement between the governments concerned can accompany this restructuring: for example, about where centers of R&D and the relevant national technology bases ought to be located (as in the case of the Airbus Consortium).

To summarize the effects on the equipment side, we find significant savings as a result of moving toward a single European market in telecommunications equipment. The reasons are insufficient exploitation of scale and and specialization economies as a result of limited national markets and the insufficient competitive pressure because of protective procurement and certification policies. These implication must not be seen as a threat, but rather as a potential. The threat has already been outlined above. The potential, on the other hand, is often forgotten. It lies not only in increasing the available market area which would make certain marginal applications profitable, which would otherwise have to be foregone, but also in stimulating the competitive pressure at each of the different submarkets for equipment, production, and utilization. Increased competitiveness means a painful restructuring for some, but it also means lower prices and an increase in application potential for others with important demand expanding effects.

Completing the Internal Market for Telecommunication Services

Improving the performance of the market for telecommunications equipment would already result in lower telecommunications cost. Performance on the service side can be increased further through more effective service provision, fewer restrictions on network utilization, and the availability of additional, Communitywide standardized services. These effects may be due to

1.   lower cost per given output and

2.   better network utilization through more rational pricing.

The recommendations of the Green Paper (points A-G of the Green Paper) may produce these two effects. The main recommendations, which concern us here, are

o   the provision of competitive "non-reserved" services by private firms (proposition C),

o   open network provision on the basis of nondiscriminatory terms (proposition E), and

o   a more liberalized market for CPE (including receive-only earth stations) in combination with

o   more Communitywide standard setting (proposition F).

Important are also the insistence on stronger antitrust rules (propositions H and I) and the recommended separation of regulation from operation (proposition G). While the scenario of full network service competition, as practiced in the United States and eventually envisaged in the UK, seems unlikely, the threat of competition through non-reserved services and marginal network services (such as mobile and satellite services) might be enough to increase productivity levels of the PTOs.

Productivity comparisons are difficult to carry out but we are currently undertaking such an exercise in an elaborate comparative study at the DIW. Initial results suggest that significant productivity differences between the PTOs exist, perhaps as a consequence of differences in the production technology used and the degree of X-inefficiency within the organization, but also as a consequence of important outside (political) constraints on the PTOs that prevent a movement important over time, i.e., if some administrations are able to achieve continuously higher productivity records. If this is combined with scale effects of the network, the more efficient networks will be able to pass on these savings at lower average costs than slowly growing less efficient networks.

The second effect that we mentioned above relates to the effect of a more rational tariff policy, when the recommendations of the Green Paper to move tariffs close to due costs take place. Greater network efficiency is not only achieved through lower cost per given output but also through better network utilization as a consequence of a more rational pricing structure, since current EEC telecommunication tariffs diverge significantly from cost (see table 14-3). As a consequence, the price signals to the users of the telecommunication networks are distorted, causing the users to make allocatively inefficient decisions and preventing the dynamic productivity effects of entrants, whose service is prohibited because of the danger of creamskimming through arbitrage. (This refers to the incentive that any potential service supplier would want to enter mainly in the lucrative long-distance market, thereby "skimming" the cream needed to subsidize the deficit services - rentals and local calls.) Innovative services that may have been developed in-house by larger enterprises either in-house or between their subsidiaries or cooperating partners (for example, in the case of airlines and banks) can be sold to third parties only under certain restrictions and sometimes not at all. This implies significant barriers to entry for the so called value-added network services (VAN services) that are based on telephone networks, but also discriminates against small and medium sized users who cannot develop or utilize these in-house because of their small scale. While the dynamic benefits lost as a consequence of current tariff policy are difficult to estimate, static losses, measured on the basis of consumer surplus foregone are already quite sizable. (The consumer surplus is how much buyers would have been willing to pay over and above what they actually pay for a service.) A move toward cost-oriented tariffs would probably result in welfare gains of 10 percent of current call revenue, i.e., 4 to 5 billion ECU. If productivity could be increased by a further .5 percent per annum, and this differential be maintained thereafter, further actual savings of 2 to 3 billion ECU may be possible.

What is interesting to the outside observer is that these two effects, i.e., increased productivity and a move toward cost oriented tariffs, are really only a goal of the Green Paper without the proper implementation tools. As long as PTOs retain their more-or-less public structure and service competition across the Community does not arise, these effects are unlikely to take place. The number of potential losers (mainly the workers of the PTOs) are even more concentrated than those in the equipment firms and often organized better, so that the political resistance to such moves will be very high. It is interesting to see how cautious the Germans, the Italians, and the French are moving in this connection despite their lip services to fully embracing the Green Paper. Only if the regulatory framework of the Commission can be strengthened to increase performance and if the PTOs are released of infrastructure policy tasks by pursuing them through more direct policy tools (taxes, subsidies, personnel retraining) will the kind of rational tariff and operating policies result, which will yield the benefits we outlined above. In other words, the likely effects of the Green Paper for telecommunication services could be of a sizable magnitude, but the policy problems involved in getting there are such that the full technology potential of the information technology cannot be realized within the current institutional framework.

National Policies

When analyzing the benefits of European integration, an "anti-monde" to the completion of the internal market by 1992 must be constructed as a reference point. Such an anti-monde is based on what would happen if current industry trends were to continue without the extra stimulus of the policies associated with 1992. When thinking of such an anti-monde, we must already note that significant structural changes are taking place in the various national markets, both on the equipment side and on the service side.

o   On the equipment side there is already a fair amount of rationalization taking place and more apparently to come in view of the emerging integration.

o   On the service side, we note the high degree of service integration already achieved between the national telecommunication operators: for example, through the Conference of European Post and Telecommunication Administrations (CEPT) and the activities of the ITU. The CEPT standardization activities have now been taken over by the ETSI, but in a way it is only a continuation of the policies of the past. This mood in national policies will influence to what extent the concept of 1992 can be realized.

Table 14-3.   MAJOR TARIFF VARIABLES IN THE EC (1986)
               (in ECU; includes VA charges where applied)

Country	Connection	Monthly Rentals		Local Call Tariffs(LC) (3 min)	Call Area Size[1]
		Residence	Business		
Great Britain	150	9.00	14.02	0.21	221
Italy	151	4.48	11.54	0.20	9
Belgium	116	10.50	10.50	0.14	78
Ireland	235	11.20	15.10	0.14	78
Luxembourg	58	5.78	5.78	0.12	n.a.
France	36	5.67	13.82	0.11	120
West Ger.	31	10.80	10.80	0.11	135
Denmark	189	9.88	9.88	0.10	n.a.
Netherlands	97	9.81	9.81	0.06	5
Portugal	66	7.98	7.89	0.05	1
Greece	199	2.23	2.23	0.03	5
Spain	83	6.66	7.03	0.03	n.a.

	Tariff for a 3 min call				Int'l. Leased Lines [3]	TC1 LC	TC2 LC
	Trunk Calls		Int'l Calls [2]				
	<100km (TC1)	max km (TC2)	From	To			
Great Britain	0.56	0.56	1.94	2.12	1162	2.7	2.7
Italy	1.62	1.72	2.92	2.16	3500	8.1	8.6
Belgium	0.69	0.69	2.22	2.10	1625	4.9	4.9
Ireland	1.26	1.26	2.88	2.30	1878	9.0	9.0
Luxembourg	n.a.	n.a.	1.41	2.10	1702	n.a.	n.a.
France	0.85	1.59	1.85	2.10	1541	7.7	14.5
West Ger.	1.00	1.66	1.67	2.13	2352	9.1	15.1
Denmark	0.36	n.a.	1.37	2.31	1312	3.6	3.6
Nether.	0.26	n.a.	1.75	2.09	1743	4.3	4.3
Portugal	1.19	n.a.	2.88	2.40	2889	23.8	23.8
Greece	0.97	1.15	2.73	2.33	2582	32.3	38.3
Spain	0.60	1.07	3.15	3.15	2481	20.0	35.6

[1] measured in thousands of exchange lines
[2] average peak charges from a country to EC members and vice versa
[3] monthly rental and connection charge in $ for eight private circuits to
    adjacent country and two transatlantic.

Source: Telefonica. Revista T., No 16 , Oct. 1987; DIW for International Leased Lines,
        IBM 1987; for International Calls: European Comission, XIII 1178 (1988)

As far as overall liberalization is concerned, the UK still tends to be in the forefront, but with close cooperation from the Netherlands and Denmark. Germany, which in the past was very much a typical PTT monopoly, has now joined this coalition of pro-liberalization administrations. It was interesting to note that in a recent meeting of telecommunication ministers in Antibes, only the British and the German ministers supported the EEC's Service Directive (which is to allow private operators to provide value-added services in competition with PTOs and to provide basic data communication services from 1993 on), while France led the coalition of the five Member States which took the European Commission to court for allegedly overstepping its powers, both on the equipment liberalization scheme and the Service Directive. In France the recent report of Prevot (which was commissioned to look at the French deregulation path, after the previous policies of Gerard Longuet of the previous Chirac government had to be abandoned) suggests a very modest liberalization, moving France Telecom from a government department to a wholly owned state-run enterprise, such as Air France or the French railways, and the separation from post and telecoms. Pragmatic liberalization is therefore the order of the day, with few radical changes to be expected, except in the continuation of some industrial policy aspects which would tend to favor France Telecom's activities abroad.

In Italy, the long-awaited rearrangement of the equipment market will accelerate after the linkup between AT&T and Italtel, the major equipment company which is a subsidiary of the state-held STET company. On the service side, the government is once again intending to create a Super STET in which the three main carriers, ASST, SIP, and Italcabel (and Telefspacio), will be combined to create one monopoly carrier. Again, little prospect for liberalization exists, except for the notorious inability of the Italian legal system to stand in the way of market forces.

A similar policy might take place in Portugal, where three operators are currently in place (two domestic, one international).

On the other hand, a political coalition for a "super telephone company" is not as strong, and an alliance with an international network carrier might be possible, in which one or two carriers maintain the option of independence.

There is likely to be little change in Belgium, where concern has always been more on the equipment side, and in Denmark, where four separate telephone companies seem to be doing remarkably well. The Greek telephone sector may eventually move out of the political shadow which it occupied under Pappandreou, given the forthcoming Olympics and the need to catch up in telephone penetration with European standards.

In the Southern countries (Portugal, Spain, Italy, Greece) there is therefore much more interest in increasing national penetration and keeping an eye on industrial policy considerations (maintaining control of a certain segment of the domestic equipment market) than enthusiasm for the policies advocated in the Green Paper, while the coalition of UK, Denmark, Netherlands, and Germany will probably be leading the drive toward greater service integration.

How far industrial politics situations can take a carrier have been most vividly shown in Spain, where Telefonica, through purchasing powers, also reorganized the domestic equipment sector by bringing in L.M. Ericsson and AT&T, and now also had its own linkup with British Telecom on the mobile side. It has also been active in the privatization attempts in Argentina and Chile.

An assessment of 1992 requires, therefore, a focus on the national activities which are in the spirit of 1992 and the tendency to imitate certain policy leads, i.e., Japan and the United States, rather than a focus on the Community's policy implementation which is much slower and riddled with compromise than the rapid policy changes that are possible at the national level.

Chapter 15

New Technology, Physical Distribution, and a Single EC Market

Brian Bayliss

Center for European Industrial Studies,
University of Bath

The most important new technologies in relation to the transport sector in the 1990s are developments in high-speed trains, combined transport, the Channel Tunnel, and telecommunications. However, the development and extension of these technologies as well as the development of a common market in freight transport within the European Community depends perhaps more upon political forces than upon economic rates of return.

State intervention has historically been so extensive in the transport sector that governments, even if they have the will to do so, find themselves having to formulate current policy with respect to those historic parameters. Developments in the transport sector, both of a technical and a market functioning type, can only be assessed in relation to historic and political practices.

In 1986 in its Medium Term Programme for Transport Infrastructure the Commission detailed a network for road, rail and inland shipping which was of "Community Interest," and identified projects of Community interest in relation to that network with a total investment of over 20 billion ECUs for the 10- to 15-year period under consideration. Among the priority projects identified were:

o   the removal of bottlenecks on sections of axes with high transit traffics, e.g., the access route to the Mont Blanc tunnel on the axis Benelux-France-Italy, and the Aachen-Koeln section on the axis Benelux-Germany-Switzerland-Austria.

o   the strengthening of rail axes which relieve bottlenecks or for combined transport in overloaded road corridors, e.g., the Alps, the axis of Amsterdam-Brussels, Luxembourg-Metz-Strasbourg-Basle-Milan-Rome, and so on.

o   road and rail access to a fixed Channel link.

o   the completion of high-speed passenger networks between capitals and major urban areas.

In 1988 the Commission formulated an Action Program in the Field of Transport Infrastructure with a View to the Completion of an Integrated Transport Market in 1992. Among its priority points were:

o   construction of a combined transport network.

o   development of new telecommunication and information technologies to improve the management of road traffic and information to car and commercial vehicle drivers.

o   construction of a high-speed rail line between Paris, London, Brussels, Amsterdam, and Koeln.

As argued earlier, the development of new technologies, support for Community interest projects, and the development of a common market in freight transport can only be considered within their historical and political context. There are, of course, risks in attempting to summarize history in a few paragraphs, but failure to take such a risk would render a discussion of the above factors meaningless.

HISTORICAL PERSPECTIVE

Before the development of road transport, policy in most Member States had been directed at controlling a railway monopoly, and subsequently at the use of the railway as an instrument of State economic and social policy. There was a natural progression from one policy to the other. In order to prevent monopoly practices, governments controlled rates. It was, therefore, a relatively easy step to the position where governments manipulated rates to advance their economic and social needs.

Broadly speaking, the rate manipulation was of three forms. Standard rates were: reduced for export goods (export subsidy); increased for imported goods (external tariff); reduced to aid certain regions, industries, and groups of travelers. The railway was also sometimes regarded as a reserve employer of labor.

In the case of passenger transport, special groups of traveler, such as workmen, forces, pensioners, disabled, and school children, were carried at reduced rates. In the case of freight, for example before the creation of the European Communities, home-produced coal in Germany was carried at rates, according to distance, up to 23 percent lower than imported coal. Rock and sea salt in France, intended for export, was transported according to distance, at a rate up to 38 percent lower than that for internal movements. In Italy machinery and materials destined for Southern Italy, Sardinia, and the other islands was subject to reductions of up to 50 percent in the normal tariff. And in Germany the special seaport tariffs provided for lower rates when merchandise was carried to the German seaports so as to prevent traffic going to the cheaper Dutch ports.

The policy of requiring the railway companies to undertake social service obligations was one which was very favorable to government budgets, for the system was in the main internally financed within the railways and based upon extensive cross-subsidization. The railways were well suited to this purpose. They were very large undertakings, operating over large areas, and they ran scheduled services with published tariffs.

The system worked without substantial operational problems until the appearance of motorized road transport on a rapidly increasing scale in the years following the Great War. Road operators, under no social service obligations, began to exploit the most remunerative markets, thus depriving the railways of the surpluses necessary to cover their unremunerative operations. Governments had to choose between three possible courses of action: to abandon previous policies and allow the railways commercial freedom; to grant financial aid to the railways; or to control road transport, either with a view to preventing its competing with the railways or with a view to making it also an instrument of policy.

Governments exhibited no desire to discontinue their previous policies toward the railways; and it was generally decided that road passenger transport could serve as an instrument of state economic and social policy but that road haulage could not.

Many road passenger undertakings were relatively large and operated scheduled services with published tariffs over relatively large areas. It was therefore possible for governments to consider them in the same light as the railways. The road haulage industry, on the other hand, composed of numerous small units operating tramping services, was entirely unsuited to a policy which required central control, regulation of prices, scheduled services, and cross-subsidization.

Except in Italy, there was general reluctance to grant financial aid to the railways in the early days of road competition. The policy which was more generally favored was that of protecting the railways from competition from the road haulage industry and aligning the road passenger industry with the railways as an instrument of policy.

It is indeed interesting to consider the views of at least one of the railway companies on such a policy: "It would be possible for Parliament to remove a large number of statutory disabilities to which reference has been made, but such action would probably create confusion and be strongly opposed by the trading interests. From the railway companies' point of view many of their disabilities could be best dealt with by regulation of road transport" (see Royal Commission on Transport 1928-29, 1929).

However, despite restrictions on road transport, rail deficits continued to grow and governments had also to provide substantial support for them - support which, in some countries, has continued to take an increasing share of public expenditure. By the mid-1980s total rail subsidies had reached about DM 14 billion in Germany, about FF 35 billion in France, and about Lira 11,500 billion in Italy.

The degrees of protection and financial aid varied from country to country; and indeed in the Netherlands, where, because of the short distances and extensive network of inland waterways, the railway had never been in a monopoly position, no legislation to control road haulage was introduced until 1954. Legislation has, therefore, played a very important role in determining the relative importance of the different carriers. In Germany and France, where legislation is the most restrictive, only about two-fifths of the total tons per kilometer performed by the transport industry are by road, whereas in the United Kingdom, with a liberal system, the figure is about four-fifths. Clearly factors other than legislation have played important roles in determining the present modal split; but legislation has been an extremely important and, in the examples quoted above, certainly the overriding factor.

Any attempt to control and restrict national operators would be of limited value if foreign haulers had freedom of operation. International operation can, therefore, usually only be carried out by haulers in possession of the requisite license. In the past the number of licenses has been fixed under bilateral agreements, but more recently multinational agreements have been reached within the European Community and between the member states of the European Conference of Ministers of Transport. The huge bulk of international freight movement by road is, however, still determined by bilateral agreements, and these have varied according to the liberality of national legislation in negotiating countries. However, no agreement allows the right of "cabotage", i.e. the right of a foreign hauler to undertake purely national carriage within the territory of another country.

Many observers might want to argue that the primary reason for the introduction of controls in the road haulage industry was to prevent cut-throat competition. Indeed the EC Commission in a draft Regulation of June 1967 argued that regulations on access to the market are necessary on account of the "characteristics of the road haulage market, particularly those of a structural nature which are likely to cause imbalance between the supply of and demand for transport."

However, an analysis of the legislation shows this not to be the case. Thus, although it was argued that the small operator was the cause of instability, short-distance haulage where the small operator predominates was usually excluded from stringent control because it was not seen as competing with rail, although this market was significantly larger than the long-distance one. In Germany, for example, in the short-distance market (up to 50 kms.) seven or eight times more tonnage[1] is moved by road than in the market over 50 kilometers. Increases in the permitted capacity bore no relationship to increased demand; thus in France in 1934 all operators were required to register the carrying capacity of their fleets, and the quota was fixed at the tonnage level. Not until a quarter of a century later, in 1959, was any increase in the registered tonnage allowed. Also the resale value of licenses was extremely high - over DM 100,000 in Germany at the end of the 1960s.

Transport systems have thus been developed in Member States that have been dominated by state control and subsidies. In recent years problems of congestion, energy, and the environment have come to the fore, and these have tended to favor the movement of traffic from road to rail so that control and subsidy have been supported on these grounds.

New technologies and a common market are considered in the light of this historical background.

NEW TECHNOLOGIES

High-Speed Trains

The French philosophy of high-speed trains is to provide long-distance services without intermediate stops. This applies to daytime trains, e.g., Paris-Bordeaux (581 kms.), Paris-Valence (533 kms.), and Paris-Avignon (658 kms.) and eventually to the nonstop journey Paris-St Raphael (900 kms.), and even more to night trains, e.g., Paris-Figueres (996 kms.).

Forecasts of future demand for such services involve assumptions about government control and price setting for other modes of transport. Particularly important here is air transport which is highly regulated in Europe.

In a recent EC Commission study forecasts were made on the basis of a number of scenarios. On the basis of a medium scenario, in the absence of a high-speed network, international trips by rail were forecast to increase from 6.7 percent of the total in the base year 1982 to 7.1 percent by the year 2010. On the assumption of a limited high-speed network, this share rose to 8.6 percent, and on the assumption of a large high-speed network to 10.5 percent. Important here, however, were the forecasts of changes in the average distance traveled on international rail trips. This was forecast to rise from 770 kilometers in the base year 1982 to 795 kilometers by 2010 with a limited high-speed network, and to 841 kilometers by 2010 for the large network.

There is a strong political backing for a high-speed rail network on environmental, congestion, and Community linking criteria, and with favorable economic forecasts the development of this network during the 1990s appears very certain, particularly in France and Germany.

Combined Transport

Combined transport is perceived as combining the best attributes of road and rail, and of being of particular importance in relation to congestion, environmental, and energy factors. Two basic forms of inland combined transport exist: container and piggyback transport.

Containers are made in a variety of sizes, but are generally categorized as large, medium, and small. In relation to combined transport with specialist trains it is a question of large containers. The outer dimensions of the large container are 40 feet, 30 feet, and 20 feet, and they have respective gross laden weights of 25 tons, 20 tons, and 10 tons.

Containers are adapted for specialist use and fall into seven categories:

1. General purpose: closed containers with one or more openings.

2. Insulated or controlled-temperature containers.

3.   Gas or liquid containers.

4.   Bulk powder containers.

5.   Flats without superstructure.

6.   Flats with limited superstructure.

7.   Air transport containers.

In the case of inland transport road/rail containers, as opposed to maritime containers, side doors are fitted for loading and unloading when on a wagon.

Full containers are lifted with overhead gantry or mobile cranes, while empty containers are moved either with forklift trucks or ancillary cranes.

A wide range of piggyback techniques is in use: these involve three basic forms, namely, the carriage of complete road vehicles on rail wagons, the carriage of semitrailers, and the carriage of swap-bodies.

The first necessitates placing the complete vehicle (tractor unit plus semitrailer) on a rail wagon, the second means separating the semitrailer from the tractor unit and carrying the semitrailer, and the third form involves separating the body of the semitrailer from its wheels and carrying just the body.

Each form (as listed above) becomes progressively cheaper in terms of pure carrying costs by rail, but loading costs vary as do collection and delivery costs. Thus the lower rail haul costs have to be set off against higher costs elsewhere, and the advantages of each form will depend upon the circumstances of a particular situation.

A 1979 EC study[2] made an estimate of the potential combined transport traffic in terms of units for 1985;it is shown in 15 15-1.

Table 15-1. ESTIMATES OF POTENTIAL INTERNATIONAL COMBINED TRANSPORT IN 1985

	Assumption	Combined Transport unit loads (000s)	Combined Transport as % of total road unit loads over 22.5 tons
(1)	Piggyback forecast charge and total C & D* = 100 kms	1355	21%
(2)	Piggyback forecast charge and total C & D = 50 kms	1787	28%
(3)	Piggyback forecast charge and total C & D = 150 kms	982	15%
(4)	Assumption (1) + 10% increase in charge	1068	17%
(5)	Assumption (1) - 10% decrease in charge	1742	27%
(6)	Container forecast charge and total C & D = 100 kms	117	2%

*Collection and Delivery.

The estimates in table 15-1 of the potential market for combined transport in 1985 were made under ideal assumptions. In particular it was assumed that combined transport would in no way be considered inferior in quality of service terms to long-distance road haulage by shippers; that there would be no infrastructure or equipment constraints on combined transport; and that current policies (both of governments and transport undertakings) would continue.

It is very clear from the results that piggyback transport demand is very sensitive both to the rail-haul tariff and the collection and delivery distances. An increase in the rail-haul part of the piggyback tariff of one-tenth reduces the number of unit loads by over one-fifth; and likewise, an increase in the total collection and delivery distance of only 50 kilometers reduces demand by well over one-quarter.

These findings demonstrate how sensitive the forecasts of potential markets are to the assumptions mentioned above. It is quite clear that a very extensive network of terminals is required if combined transport is to capture substantial amounts of traffic from long-distance road haulage - thus the assumption of no infrastructure and equipment constraints is very pertinent to the results. It is also clear that if there were to be a change on the part of the railway companies toward their charges policies for combined transport, demand could be substantially less than that predicted on the basis of present charging practices.

The significance of charging policies and the role of government policy can be highlighted in the case of container and swap-body tariffs from Lyon to Koeln and Nuernberg. There is no difference in the operating costs of moving containers and swap-bodies, yet on the Lyon-Nuernberg route the container charge was some 80 percent greater than the swap-body charge, and was also some 50 percent greater than the container charge for Lyon-Koeln, even though the distance was shorter. An important factor here is that swap-bodies count legally as road traffic and containers as rail traffic, and that the German railway in particular offers very favorable rates for swap-bodies as haulers have to surrender their licenses for the period of the movement, i.e., they cannot use their vehicles to move other traffic. The low charge policy is thus aimed at reducing competition.

Telecommunications

There are two broad types of interaction between telecommunications and travel: substitution and complementary.

A number of investigators have argued that facilities such as teleconferencing will substantially reduce the number of business trips and, insofar as more people will work from home, the number of commuting trips. One U.S. study estimates that on certain assumptions up to 19 million work trips made in the United States in 1970 could be eliminated. Also shopping trips could be reduced through facilities such as electronic funds transfer. However, on the complementary demand side other investigators have suggested that increased communications will lead to increased travel.

More clearly on the complementary side, advances in automatic monitoring and communications will increase efficiency. Thus airline ticket booking is being extended through direct links with corporations; road pricing as shown in Hong Kong is feasible; and on-line magnetic loops are allowing continuous monitoring of road traffic.

The most advanced magnetic loops allow up to 22 different road vehicle types to be differentiated so that traffic forecasting and identification of potential bottlenecks are facilitated as well as traffic control. All countries are extending their number of Automatic Traffic Counters: Germany and France have each over 700, and the Netherlands has one at about every 10 kilometers on its principal networks. This network of counters will greatly facilitate the identification of potential bottlenecks on the main EC axes.

Channel Fixed Link

In a 1963 report British and French officials concluded that a rail tunnel would provide a better economic return than a bridge, and that, depending upon the assumptions made about traffic levels, the rate of return would lie between 7.4 percent and 14.4 percent. Ten years later another report estimated an internal rate of return of 17.6 percent, and sensitivity tests found the rate to be relatively robust to market changes in the basic forecasting assumptions. In an EC Commission report (1980) it was concluded that in relation to profitability the return on a road bridge plus single rail, the double-track tunnel and the single-track tunnel would be 6.8 percent, 12.6 percent and 14.3 percent respectively. The single and double-track tunnels passed the stringent tests of promising profitability by the year 2000, while it was predicted that neither of the bridge schemes was likely to be profitable in the same period.

The French and UK governments subsequently agreed to the building of a fixed link across the Channel on the basis of private funding, and tenders for the project were requested. The project accepted provided for a rail link capable of carrying both passengers and vehicles with a high frequency of service. Work on the link has now commenced and completion is anticipated in 1993.

The final decision to construct the Channel Tunnel was thus made on political and financial grounds. The French and UK governments agreed that it was in the material interests of both countries to have a fixed link, and the private sector considered it to be commercially viable.

The political will was extremely important. In the case of the United Kingdom, for example, the government avoided years of planning procedural delay by authorizing the building of a tunnel through an Act of Parliament.

A COMMON MARKET

On May 22, 1985, the European Court ruled in favor of a complaint from the European Parliament against the Commission in relation to the failure of the latter to have brought about a common market in transport. The Court held that such a market should be introduced by 1992.

As previously outlined, state intervention in the transport sector had been extensive, and Member States and particularly Germany and France had acted to prevent any moves that would have resulted in any liberalizing of their *dirigiste* regimes.

National and international movements need to be differentiated. A non-common market in international freight transport would clearly handicap the realization of an overall common market, and efforts to reach agreement have been directed at the international market. For a long period the Germans in particular argued that there could be no liberalization without harmonization. But it was not just a question of harmonization of the conditions of operation but the enforcement of those conditions. A recent study by Philips (1988) on the social regulations for road transport concluded, "It is all too easy for Member States to adopt such legislation and then deliberately to give it a low enforcement profile with minimal sanctions for non-observance."

However, in June 1988 the Council of Ministers agreed on the liberalization of all international road haulage by 1993, whereby any hauler holding a national license could participate in international operations. Such liberalization does not, however, necessarily allow the operator to pursue an optimum operation. First, he has no right of cabotage which means that operating costs could be increased. Second, the ability to locate in another Member State and so set up an optimum network of depots throughout the EC is subject to obtaining national licenses with all the problems involved. Third, professional and own account transport are differentiated; thus own account operators participating in international carriage cannot reduce their net costs by carrying in part for others. In the case of the United Kingdom the removal of this differential has resulted in improved overall efficiency.

Although the decision of the Council of Ministers of June 1988 will greatly assist in the development of a single market, the making of entry into international operations subject to restrictive national legislation will mean that such operations will not be conducted optimally.

CONCLUSIONS

The foregoing suggests, therefore, that new developments in technology, particularly in relation to high-speed rail services, the Channel Tunnel, and telecommunications, will have important influences on both passenger and freight transport, but that in relation to freight the difficulties of creating a single European transport market could inhibit their exploitation.

Notes

1. In European and domestic markets, tonnage, rather than ton-mileage, generally reflects more accurately net output: see Bayliss (1988, "Inputs and Outputs in Freight Transport").

2. Conducted by the author. The main models and findings can be found in Bayliss (1988).

References

Bayliss, B.T. *The Measurement of Supply and Demand in Freight Transport*, Aldershot, England: Gower Press, 1988.

Bayliss, B.T. *Planning and Control in the Transport Sector*, Chapter 6, Aldershot, England: Gower Press, 1981.

The Channel Tunnel: A United Kingdom transport cost benefit study, London: HMSO, 1973.

EC Commission. *Study of the Community Benefit of a Fixed Channel Crossing*, Brussels, 1980.

Philip, A.B. *Implementing the European Internal Market: Problems and Prospects*, London: Royal Institute of International Affairs, 1988.

Proposals for a Fixed Channel Link, London: HMSO, 1963.

Royal Commission on Transport 1928-29: *Evidence of Sir Josiah Stamp on behalf of the Four Amalgamated Railway Companies and the Metropolitan Railway Company*, para. 53. London: HMSO, 1929.

Stanford Research Institute. *Technology Assessment of Telecommunications/Transportation Interactions*, Vols 1-3, 1977.

Index

Z
Zanussi 150, 159,
        161, 166